Century Sentence
The Untold Story of China

A diary written to God, accusing all of the world

Xu Xue Chun
徐雪春

Library of Congress Control Number: 2019910499
Paperback: 978-1-950771-71-4
eBook: 978-1-950771-73-8
Hardcover: 978-1-950771-72-1

Revised Date: 07/2018

BOOK-ART
PRESS SOLUTIONS

30 Wall Street, 8th Floor
New York City, NY 10005
www.bookartpress.us
+1-800-351-3529

Note

The reason why I have an impact on the world political situation is not that I have something special, but the truth I revealed, just like a small boy who says the emperor is not wearing anything in the fairy tale 'The Emperor's New Clothes'.

In order to better your understanding, part of the articles is translated from Chinese to English as you will see, but I have not fact-checked the translated works because of my limited level of English. The English version may not correctly express the original meaning of the author, so it is just for your reference. For the original meaning of the article, the Chinese version shall prevail.

The Chinese version is in my website: http://www.aaamary9.com.

Contents

2015.5.13	108. Psychoanalysis of the troublemaking from some people wearing masks in the streets in Hong Kong	301
2015.8.5	109. The Kuomintang should promote a referendum on reconciliation	303
2015.8.6	110. The cross-strait status quo is maintained on the basis of reconciliation	305
2015.8.7	111. The Taiwan issue must be solved	307
2015.8.10	112. Taiwan's democracy is the world's dirtiest democracy	309
2015.9.8	113. Chinese government should make clear the attitude to dogs	311
2016.2.4	114. The government shall audit the authenticity of P2P project	313
2016.4.3	115. In economic crimes, if the victim commits suicide, the main mastermind should be executed	314
2016.4.7	116. There should be legislation on compensation of dogs hurting people	316
2016.4.14	117. Taiwan has sent one hundred thousand spies to destroy the economy of Chinese mainland; this is a war	318
2016.4.19	118. Taiwan issue and South China Sea dispute	320
2016.5.13	119. Arresting prostitutes indicates that the social system is in favour of the rich and against the poor	321
2016.6.6	120. Fighting-to-death lawyers are cults	322
2016.8.18	121. Marriage for the purpose of beauty is a kind of whoring, while marriage aimed at benefit is like prostitution and financial fraud	324
2016.9.7	122. If telecommunication frauds make victims commit suicide, swindlers should be executed.	328
2016.9.7	123. Nail households should be settled by demolition	329
2016.12.29	124. It is mandatory for pet keepers to pay to charitable foundations	331
2017.1.1	125. Citizen information should be publicised in default, and the fraud should be heavily convict	334
2017.1.8	126. Housing price in China is higher than that in America, is determined by Chinese culture	337

1. About the author

I am Xu Xue Chun, a leader and scholar of Chinese civil opinion. In April 2004, when China's new prime minister and chairman just took office, soon I saw Chinese news about the event of the Tieben Steel Company.

I was suddenly inspired by God that I needed to accuse the wrongness, absurdity, and injustice of this world.

Then, I wrote five articles on the reform of state-owned enterprises and reported and gave publicity to the situations to the Chinese government at all levels for many times through network and mails, which are called petitions in China.

Accidentally, they were accepted and emphasised by Chinese government. At the stage when China's state-owned capital was about to collapse, the direction of state-owned enterprise reform was completely reversed, and they became the basic policy of state-owned enterprises and have been used until today.

From this matter later, I feel that I am a responsible person, although I'm just an ordinary netizen.

I have been making comments and exchanging about hot events happening in China, on the network as an ordinary netizen. My suggestions were basically adopted and emphasised by the government. It can be said that I played a key role in the success of China's economic reform.

Since then, China has gradually escaped from the dispute and turmoil, unified thinking, embarked on success, and now China's society is stable, economy is developed, people become rich, and social order is good.

I think I can give the Chinese government some suggestions to make China successful. I can also give other countries some suggestions to allow them to change and succeed.

I set up a website in 2013 to put the translated articles of mine on it and promote the Chinese model to other countries in the world. From the news at that time, other countries were in exchange with China and learning the Chinese model.

In August 2014, when I saw the atrocities of the Islamic State from the news, I was furious and decided to accuse the world to God.

I developed my own website, and my suggestions were demonstrated in my diary for God, to complain about this world to God. So God will reply to me, and he will have an impact on the world political situation. Reasonably, they will listen to me carefully and take my advice.

The success of Chinese reform, the election of US president Donald Trump, the reversion of the Middle East war situation, support of the Syrian government forces, the Taiwan issue, the Hong Kong issue, the defeat of the Islamic State, the objection to Islam—all of these can be seen in my diary to complain to God. Finally, all of these have come into reality, which I think are the replies from God and his determination.

You all can verify what I said according to my diary dates and the violent change of world political situation.

The reason why I have an impact on the world political situation is not that I have something special, but the truth I revealed, just like a small boy who says the emperor is not wearing anything in the fairy tale 'The Emperor's New Clothes'.

What persuaded and changed them are reality, truth, and justice. What I have done is tell the reality, truth, and justice.

The only things I have in mind are true things and putting forward my solution as a reference. People who choose the truth, justice, and reality categorise themselves progressively to God.

2. Brief introduction of the book

This book uses humorous, witty, sharp, exaggerated, and miraculous writing style, which is so interesting and makes people belly laugh. Someone even laughed to tears. As an ironic book with strong logic and knowledge, this book enables readers to experience the happy life value and brings you endless wealth.

Don't you believe that it can bring you wealth? Now Chinese tourists are the most popular around the world because of their strong purchasing power. Why is Chinese purchasing power so strong? Do you want to be as rich as Chinese? Just read this book, and you will find the secret and be enlightened.

As I can ensure social stability, economic development, well-off family, good social order, and absence of terrorist attack in China, I will make your countries see the same effect. Just follow my advice.

You might think that I am arrogant. Actually you are wrong; I am qualified to say so. I am the most influential civic opinion leader and strategic scholar in China.

I tried to put my judgments online, but only those who were more brilliant than geniuses agreed with me and took my advice. However, it really disappointed me that what the ordinary people accepted when they were confronted with truth and reality was authority; obviously, they gave up the former.

The only thing I can do is tell you what I have done and what contributions I have accomplished as well as how I verify my accomplishments, to make you trust me as a successful person, to believe in me and listen to me cautiously.

This book collected my comments and suggestions on all-important events which occurred in China and around the world from 2004 until now, which are also my appeals to God against the injustice and unfairness of the world.

Every article in the table of contents has its writing time marked so that you can verify my influence on the political situation of China and the world, according to the writing time of each article, my opinions, my suggestions, and dramatic change of the world political situation.

You can also verify how God has responded to my appeals and requests, according to the writing time of each article, my opinions, my suggestions, and dramatic change of the world political situation.

The Commentary on China

The commentary on China proceeded from the analysis of the Chinese political phenomena on the basis of the creation of human consciousness, subconscious, culture, and the origin of Chinese culture in order to provide opinions on China's reform from the perspective of an ordinary worker and to try to change the political environment in China with the strength of a netizen.

Though most of my remarks had been deleted for being too extreme, in my point of view, my remarks posted on the internet did make a difference on public opinion, thus affecting the political direction of China.

People's opinion on Chinese people and government is also changing constantly. With the majority of netizens being on the side of downright negation in the very beginning, they denied socialism and hankered for wholesale Westernisation when seeing the welfare and advancement of the system in Western countries. I had a fierce debate with them on the internet putting forward my opinion of socialism and specific measures of the reform; therefore, it is safe to say that I influenced the direction of China's public opinion and reform.

China now is not Westernised; on the contrary, she goes on its merry way of socialism whose experience is worthy to be learnt by the whole world. I consider it necessary to write what happened in China to provide people in other countries a reference and a new way of thinking.

3. Preface of truth

About 2007

According to the self-perception of people and understanding of the society, people can be divided into many types and grades of ideology. Different people will have different attitudes towards the myriads of things in the world according to their different understanding of the world so that they will take different actions in dealing with them; finally, the different actions will trigger different results.

Some people start from scratch and become billionaires. Some people are so wealthy that they speak louder than others but finally end up on the street. Some people have tremendous property but are anxious every day. Some people are not wealthy, but they feel satisfied, with no regret in life at all. Some people are in poverty, desperate, and anxious. Some people are full of ambition in life and confident all the time.

We are in this era, and our fate is elusive, with much mystery and fanatics. What are the basic factors that can determine the fate of people? The answer is the human concept, which is the understanding of the world and society of humans, the understanding of the direction of social development, and the understanding of the value and fate of humans.

Understanding determines the concept, the concept determines the behaviour, and the behaviour determines the fate.

You are endowed with something since you were born, and it is very difficult to make a change or it is impossible to make a change at all, such as a person's height, appearance, intelligence, family conditions, etc. All of them can determine one's destiny, but they are not the final conditions. The final conditions that can determine the fate are the concepts of society and the world.

But because the intelligence of people is different, people's understanding of the world is also diversified. Different people will have different views on the concept of things mentioned in this book.

If you feel surprised, ridiculous, absurd, indignant, resented, sad, please don't feel strange. You can throw this book away or burn it, because that's your human right. The author of this book does not mind at all. This book is for someone who is destined to read and digest it. He is able to get some inspiration from this book so as to change his concept and fate in life. If some people abandon what has been told in the book and slump into difficulties and setbacks, please do not resent society and do not be hostile to society, because the responsibility lies on you but not others. Your behaviour is what you have chosen by yourself. If your actions affect the operation of the earth, you will be abandoned by it. I do not want to see it and I do not want to see anyone slumping into bad outcomes, but this day will definitely come. If human society is to move forward, the earth is to move forward, the human civilisation is to move forward, the social relations, political relations, and economic relations between people have to move forward as well.

I know that changing the political and economic relations between people, for ordinary people, is a painful and hard choice. Maybe it's an advanced math problem for some people, and they never elaborate the answer. But today, as the development of human society has been kept for such a long time, something must be changed. As some people say, the Bible is the agreement between God and man. Thousands of years have passed, and the human perception of the universe and themselves has undergone fundamental transformation. There must be a new agreement between God and man. The relationship between people, the relationship between man and society, the relationship between man and nature, the political relations and economic relations between people themselves must be radically changed. The concepts of democracy, freedom, human rights, sovereignty, the political power and the property right, the state and individuals, systematic culture and individual culture, justice, evil, and so on need to be redefined and perceived.

The idea of man is the simplest and most complex, most trivial, and most fierce. A smile will replace conflicts if the obstacle of thought is replaced by a good solution. Whether it is a faint smile or blood in conflict, that is your choice and that is your own destiny. I just say the truth and the other things are not what I should care. What is going to happen will happen sooner or later and the earth will not stop for anyone. The universe will never stop either. Be fully prepared by yourself and face the new day.

4. What is human?

About 2007

We come into contact with a lot of people every day; we are human, but do you know what is human? Do humans themselves know?

I am someone who believes in science and research science. I am an electronic technician and try to study all equipment and electrical appliances I have touched. And basically I can repair all of them. I am not a theologian.

I think humans themselves do not know exactly what they are. The knowledge about humans that people have mastered is just some superficial knowledge. If the total amount of knowledge about humans is expressed as 100, I think the most advanced technology now cannot reach 1 per cent.

A lot of people may be unconvinced of what I say.

You can go ask the top scientists, whether in the field of biology, nuclear power, physics, or chemistry. Humans need how many years, how much scientific knowledge to use sunshine, air, water, stone, and these natural inorganic substances as raw materials to create true, complete, living, and conscious people? Don't say people, a pig, a frog, a caterpillar, even the most primitive life, protozoa and virus, can they create?

We still need how many years, how much knowledge to use inorganic substances to create the simplest life like God.

Don't believe Darwin's biological theory of evolution. It is true that biology is an evolutionary phenomenon, but it is just a basic function of organisms, like a bird will preen its feathers, no one to teach, nothing strange. It is just an inborn function of a bird.

Not to mention humans, who have a lot of amazing powers, they just don't know, let alone using them, such as qigong, etc. This can't be explained by natural science theory.

In my estimation, if humans want to reach the level of using natural inorganic substance to create people, they still need at least five hundred years, even thousands of years of scientific knowledge and development of the science and technology, then they can achieve this level.

Maybe many people don't believe—human scientists have created cattle and sheep with asexual reproduction. Humans are very great.

In my opinion, this is a joke. Cloning is to use one living organism or several

18

organisms to create organisms. It is to use one living material to create another living material. Cloning is like a car assembly, or assembled is more appropriate.

But one point must be cleared: an assembled car is a completely different concept from using iron ore in iron-making and steel-making, then design, process, and production of parts finally taking shape with assembly. To assemble a car needs a few workers and a small amount of technology to complete. But to design and produce a car needs almost all of the science and technology and industries in the whole society. Requiring a series of science and technology knowledge, if compared with the amount of knowledge, it will be different at myriad times, and they are completely separate concepts.

Now the top science and the most advanced technology still need five hundred to a thousand years, even tens of thousands of years to create the simplest life. So in ancient times, with wind, sunlight, water, and soil buried in natural conditions, to create life more complex than computers is not logical and not scientific.

The change of things is from quantitative to qualitative; all have cause and effect. It is the same as the origin of life; the earth can't be in the case of natural force to naturally complete a work that needs a senior intelligence—life development from nothing.

Even the simplest life is more complex than the computer used now. Life development from nothing is not as simple as 0 to 1, but the sudden change from 0 to 10,000—even 1,000,000. This sudden change is absolutely not completed by the natural force as wind, sunlight, rain, soil buried.

I remember my biology teacher told me, 'Nature, thunder and lightning may produce proteins, and some scientists have made similar experiments. The natural combination of protein can create life.' I think this is nonsense.

If they exist, the materials can constitute life such as proteins or amino acid in nature, and these materials cannot become life by the simple stack.

But in the case of natural force, assuming there are bicycle parts everywhere in nature, if we just rely on the wind, sunlight, rain, soil buried, these parts will always be parts (if not rot). It will absolutely be impossible for them to become a bicycle under the condition of natural force, because life is not a simple stack by various elements, the ingenious combination with super-advanced knowledge and strength, even the same to the simplest life.

Natural force can only simply stack, but without wise combination function, it is absolutely impossible to create a life.

So I think life on earth is created by foreign intelligent life rather than natural force. Natural force is not intelligent and without the ability to create a wise creature.

As for what's the purpose of intelligent life creating the universe and human life, where they are now, I don't know. But they have created all things is the most scientific explanation. Our ancient legends also prove this point. All sorts of different cultures are the support of creationism. God is intelligent life, and science and technology and knowledge is at least ten thousand years more advanced than the modern top technology.

Even I think some of the human knowledge and cultures are from intelligent life. Because human knowledge and intelligence is a process from quantitative change to qualitative change, but I think there are a lot of civilisation that are not to be created in the society at that kind of civilised degree. Because of many ancient cultures, humans can't be able to fully absorb now. In today's science and technology and knowledge, it can't fully explain. So where did the human knowledge come from at that time?

Such knowledge and culture as China's Inner Classic of the Yellow Emperor, the philosophy of yin and yang, the Book of Changes can never be formed in ancient times and spread on oracle and bamboo slips. Just to record this knowledge will need to spend a lot of time and effort, not to mention study, thinking, and forming such profound ideas and cultures. This is not the kind of knowledge that can be obtained on hunting and fishing. And the modern human cannot fully understand this kind of knowledge, but there are many phenomena that show they are right. One of the explanations is that they obtain help and hints from intelligent life.

Human society is scientific and material; God in ancient legend is the intelligent life. So there is no need to debate idealism and materialism. God gives all things in life, but also the intelligent life gives humans life. Intelligent life has strong ability, limitless wisdom, and indeed omnipotent to everything. Humans compared with them are tiny and funny; self-righteousness is arrogance.

But there is also another kind of people on earth, too frightened by God's power, who even do not believe their own eyes and hands and completely do not have self-awareness.

From these two kinds of people, the human is really pathetic and ridiculous.

From all indications, the human society has always obtained help and hints from a supernatural power. And this power always guides people towards the light and wisdom.

So the human essence is the intelligent machine and creation made up of cells.

Creatures, even the simplest organisms, viruses, are also countless times more complicated and advanced than our computer.

So far, and for a long period in the future, humans cannot use stones, water, air, and other inorganic substances to create a simple life.

It is precisely because life is so complex, so the life creation of Darwinian theory is purely nonsense. Evolution is just a function of life, just like your computer to automatically update the system. But it does not mean that nature can naturally produce computer.

So creationism is the most reasonable theory to explain the origin of life.

God created man. God loves everyone.

If even the human themselves are not sure what they are, how can they change the destiny? How can they dominate the destiny?

Life, including humans, is the machine created by intelligent life.

Consciousness, emotion, reproduction, politics, economics, philosophy, war, killing, torture, extermination, survival, lechery, greed, lazy, and intelligence are all functions of the machine.

For these functions, humans should not fear, not escape, not hate, and not complain, to not be proud and not be arrogant.

In a sense, each of us is in the show. We are all actors, chess pieces, soldiers, and slaves.

5. Human nature

About 2007

Human nature is the root of social system. Social system serves for human nature as well as humans.

There goes an old Chinese saying that men at their birth are naturally good. Their natures are much the same; their habits become widely different. These words are nearly known by all Chinese people, drawing the greatest influence on them. The concepts of returning good for evil, treating others as you want to be treated, doing things for the good of others, and one good turn deserving another indicate the ancient wise men's understanding of human nature and the influence that Buddhist doctrines have on the Chinese people's nature. The Western concept about human nature advocates that men at their birth are naturally bad; men are born to do bad things. Children who do not listen to the adults' words and eat forbidden fruits furtively are bad kids and should be punished. The words in the Bible are all about punishment, killing, and God's punishment towards the heretics for his adoptionists. Therefore, the human nature of the Western people is evil.

The human nature includes fear of death and pursuit of safety. The common primitive instinct in a human's ego does not differ with the colours of skin. The reasonable superego is formed by the accumulation in the postnatal life and aggregation of experience.

Due to the different environment and cultures, superego varies quite a lot between Western people and Eastern people and between different races. Superego refers to humans' experience of society and the world, including their understanding of social system and the whole universe.

When it comes to human nature, the common characteristics are shared by all mankind. These distinct characteristics are ideas, desires, and impulses born with humans rather than postnatally accumulated. This is human nature, i.e. the ego.

What is a human's ego? Need for safety, fear for death and danger, various desires including eating, dressing, reacting to external stimulation, sexual intercourse, instinct of death in Freud's theory, impulse, and instinct to eradicate people who threaten your life and destroy your interests are all human nature. Humans are good when you think they are good; humans are evil when you think they are evil.

22

6. Why does a man do things for the good of others?

About 2007

Where does the phrase 'treat others as you want to be treated' come from?

It is the unique Chinese culture. The Western people who believe the Darwinist law of the jungle and theory of evolution will not believe in this phrase, which is completely against the law of the jungle. Sheep are eaten by tigers because they run slower than tigers and are too weak to fight against tigers. This is the law of the jungle. However, according to the Chinese law of treating others as you want to be treated, if tigers hope not to be eaten by lions, they should not eat sheep. Though sheep are weak and tigers are strong, weak and strong are relative rather than invariable. Sheep are weaker than tigers, and tigers are weaker than lions. If tigers hope not to be eaten by lions in the future, they should not eat sheep today, because sheep might have paid protection fees to lions. If a tiger eats a sheep today, the sheep's son will ask a lion for revenge on the tiger tomorrow. When will revenge come to an end? It's better to get along with each other well and not to eat some others, which is the Chinese logic.

A sheep knows that it is too weak to fight against a tiger, but it can ask a lion for protection. When in trouble, the sheep asks the lion to fight for it. This is the Chinese logic.

Therefore, the Chinese sheep put forward the idea of treating others as you want to be treated. Lion is the king of animals, but a dragon is larger than a lion. Dragon is the son of heaven, the emperor. Sheep are often chased and bit by tigers and lions, so sheep often ask the dragon for help, which is the application for an audience with the higher authorities to appeal for help.

Actually, treating others as you want to be treated, as well as application for an audience with the higher authorities to appeal for help, is not human nature but the reason in humans. This idea is not thought by everyone. It is summarised by the ancient wise men, celebrities, great men, and ideologists after reflection and experiences and taught by personal example as well as verbal instruction. This idea or the thinking mode is not merely disseminated through textbooks, but also through daily life, like the basic necessities of life, dramas, arts, entertainment, which are so-called culture, expressed in the words of famous people or works of art and literature.

However, culture is not humans' inborn nature. Thus, doing things for the good of others is not human nature but the reason of Chinese culture. Whether there is such theory in the culture of other countries, to be honest, the author has never studied profoundly. But one thing to be certain is that nations that regard the Darwinist law of the jungle as their national culture will not do things for the good of others and treat others as they want to be treated.

Are there any elements of doing things for the good of others in human nature? Let's first of all analyse the word good. What is good? Good is the opposite of evil. Then what is good? What is evil?

Who set the criteria of good and evil? There is no good when there is no evil. It goes the other way around.

Lewdness is the worst of all sins, while filial piety is the best of all good. This is a famous old saying in China. Lewdness and filial piety are the criteria of judging what is good and what is evil. In ancient times, are they human nature? What is lewdness? What is filial piety?

Lewdness is the behaviour of having sex with others besides one's spouse.

In the ancient matriarchal society, the age of knowing one's mother rather than one's father, is there a concept of lewdness? At that time, even the mothers themselves did not know how many men they had slept with, so they would not know who made them pregnant. Therefore, people at that time did not have fathers but only mothers. There was no concept of lewdness, which developed in the patriarchal society, where men dominated the society. To protect their properties, men forbade their spouses to have sex with other men to prevent bastards from splitting up their family properties. In fact, such behaviour was logical in the society at that time. Lewdness was not allowed by customs and even laws.

But is it human nature?

The author does not think it is human nature or the natural instinct but regards it as reason. Though men who dominated the patriarchal society strongly were against their spouses having sex with other men, they themselves would have sex with more than two women reasonably and lawfully. Polygyny had been popular for a long time in ancient China and all over the world. The Chinese emperors had a number of wives and concubines in the imperial harem. From the perspective of polygyny and the Chinese emperors, who had so many wives and concubines, two lovers always keeping each other company and living to old age in conjugal bliss are not the nature of men.

Similarly, the fact that women in the matriarchal society would sleep with dozens of men and their children did not know who their fathers were. It showed that monogamy and living to old age in conjugal bliss are also not the nature of women.

Monogamy and living to old age in conjugal bliss are ideas and concepts that the ruling class and social administration imposed on men or women in order to better rule the society which are not human nature but humans' reason.

Similarly, filial piety is not human nature but a concept and awareness that the ruling class and social administration imposed on people.

Therefore, to distinguish well from evil by lewdness, humans' nature is lewd and evil.

Humans' nature is their social behaviour conducted by their instinct. Nature is humans' social behaviour driven by their innate impulses and desires.

7. Filial piety

About 2007

What is filial piety? In the Chinese ancient culture, respect for parents is called filial piety, and fraternity with brothers is called fraternal duty. Is filial piety born with human nature? Obviously, it does not exist in human nature. If filial piety is human nature, it should be a common characteristic shared by all mankind of any nation or country. However, there is only the Chinese nation regarding filial piety as the criterion to distinguish right from wrong and good from evil. The Western countries that advocate freedom, democracy, and human rights take judging a man if he has filial piety or not as infringing his rights. Parents who interfere with their children's behaviour in the name of filial piety are reckoned to infringe the children's rights of personal freedom.

However, in Chinese feudal society, filial piety played a great irreplaceable role in maintaining the stability of the society and country. Filial piety is also taken as a tool to rule the feudal society, a favourable tool for the country, society, and families. On the condition of productivity at that time, Chinese ancient civilisation was superior to other countries over a thousand years, thanks to the doctrine of Confucius and Mencius and filial piety.

We are talking about the relationship between filial piety and human nature here, so let's talk about the contributions of filial piety later. Though filial piety has made undeniable contributions, it is not human nature but the ethical culture concluded by the Chinese ancient wise men which had been advocated by the ruling classes of the past dynasties. Otherwise, there would not be the miracle of leading the ancient civilisation for over a thousand years.

Since the basic grounds of the theory of original goodness of human nature is proved to be human reason, human nature can only be supported by the theory of original evil of human nature.

In fact, good and evil are relative. Since good does not exist in human nature, neither does evil.

The concept of good and evil is used to describe a man's behaviour from the social perspective, commented by a third person. To do things for the good of others is good, and to do things for the bad of others is evil.

Human nature is inherently used to cope with the external world and society and meet one's own needs. What is the external world? It's society, nature, and other people.

Human nature is the attribute and instinct of animals. It is born to serve oneself rather than society or other people. Society is not the service object of human nature, but the opponent to cope with.

When it comes to human nature, it is a natural attribute rather than a social attribute. Social attribute or reason is the accumulation of the analysis of experience in humans' brains, which is not human instinct or a natural attribute, but concepts or ideas formed in the postnatal life. A man's living environment and experience decides what his reason would be. Different people in different living environments and with different living experiences will have totally different reasons.

In terms of human nature, i.e., the ego in Freud's theory, from the perspective of observation of social events, humans' ego is decided by genes. Different races of people share similar original impulses, but men and women have a quite large difference in original impulses. Actually, though the author has never studied the difference between the original impulses of people of different races, the author thinks that there is no big difference or they are almost the same. In the world, men are the same with men, and women are the same with women. However, men are completely different from women. These are the results of the author's observation as well as the prediction and statement of Chinese ancient prehistoric civilisation.

8. Kindness of humanity

About 2007

Is there kindness of humanity? I consider it exists. What are people's demand and impulsion for? Being satisfied both sexually and mentally. Actually, all impulsions aim for that simple and also complex thing.

People will live and die by instinct.

To satisfy spiritual and material demands is for the sake of living, while the instinct of death is to eradicate all the factors and units that impede living. Thus, the instinct of death is to live.

Human fights with the nature for living or living better, i.e. immortality. However, kindness of humanity is the combination of life instinct and proper methods, i.e. the principles. Then, it generates the desire of being kind.

Such rational thinking is unique to humans. Interpersonal relationship in human society evolves continuously. There have been kinds of social relations from slave society to feudal society, capitalist society to socialist society. Every time the human society evolves, its main material factor is the increase of productivity, and another immaterial factor is kindness, which refers to anti-oppression and seeks the idea of liberty, equality, and human rights. That's it—kindness of humans. It is not only the nature of humans, but also the instinctive integration of rationality and nature. If one fails the substance of human rationality and civilisation, that one will be an idiot or psychotic, or an absolute animal. He does not have the concept of kindness, just like the goat or the lion who doesn't know the boundary of kindness and wickedness.

Humans' rationality, mentality, and trade-off are exactly the source of kindness.

What is kindness? It is the pursuit of liberty, safety, and the wish of living in riches and of being pleasant. It also means that all the demands can be satisfied in society and be recognised truly and permanently but not temporarily and hypocritically.

The ideas above about kindness, I swear, are a condition expected by all human beings, no matter what nation or colour they are. It is the instinct of living, and it is the fundamental desire and ideal state created by the instinct. People will strive for that ideal condition, without hesitation, even if they have to risk and pay for it, which also includes approaches, efforts, and behaviour obtained through brain analysing and experience summarising. That is the kindness of humanity.

9. Removal of the evil in human nature in a civilised way

About 2007

But in the nature and natural tendencies of humanity are lots of evil natures essential for survival.

Those natures enable man to survive in a natural state, but they must be limited and even cleared away in a civilised society.

If man cannot control the evil in his nature, the whole human society will shake off civilisation and recover barbarism, and this is what God hates to see. By that time, wars will befall the world to change the development direction of human society.

Most of the wars among humans are caused by social contradictions.

People are poor, pathetic animals. People, in particular the majority of people, have a very narrow dimension of consciousness. They only care about their own interests and their family's benefits but don't care for others.

When a serious conflict of interest arises between two types of people or the people of two regions after society develops and reaches a certain level, a war will come to change the status quo.

The human society developed from barbarism to civilisation and from slavery to feudalism and to capitalism, and Marx interpreted the development of society as the development of productivity. In my opinion, the development of productivity changed the level of the social civilisation. What is civilisation? Civilisation means making people's life more comfortable and better in the long run, with all things considered.

Productivity cannot directly change society, but the development of productivity has led to a change in civilisation.

Civilisation refers to the common transmission of an advanced culture.

The common people, the ignorant people, the social management, and the social elites, in particular the social management and the social elites—their acceptance of the advanced culture may directly lead to a radical change in the human social system. But productivity is just an inducement and a prerequisite. It is the civilisation of mankind, or the degree of the mastery of an advanced ideology or culture by the social elites, management, and common people that directly decides the social transformation.

The civilisation of mankind aims simply to overcome the evil in human nature, using reason and wisdom; overcome the evil in human nature with the help of reasonable, wise people and their social relations; and restrict the evil in humans by means of a rational system, so as to create a better living environment for the great majority of people.

Owing to the innate savageness, ignorance, and evil desire in human nature, the whole human society is still in utter confusion at present even though it has a civilised history of several thousand years. Savageness, hatred, contradiction, and pain exist throughout the world. Human beings fancy themselves civilised, but if the so-called civilisation is measured with an ideal interpersonal political and economic connection, you will see that the civilisation of mankind is just a little better than that in the primitive society, and there is not even an essential difference between the two.

Material prosperity does not mean great progress in people's way of thinking, as an upstart's wealth does not mean he is learned. Furthermore, a highly educated person may not definitely bring a big influence to the whole society, and this just means that he has more knowledge of a certain field.

By civilisation, I mean a civilisation based on an ideal interpersonal relationship, and a social management civilisation rather than material civilisation based on an understanding of the social order and a capacity for acts.

Correct management of the entire society was called the kingly way, or benevolent governance, in ancient China.

What Lao Tzu wrote in the Tao Te Ching is the way of social management and the requirements for management.

Of course, the Tao Te Ching is just a record of a way in which social management was understood more than two thousand years ago. Many concrete practices recorded in it are not worth holding in esteem, but the mode of thinking is very correct. The same mode of thinking or basic principle might lead to different and even completely opposite concrete practices in different specific circumstances. This is because as a specific event and condition changed, the specific problem-solving method was sure to change.

10. Use appropriate method to eliminate the evil in human nature

About 2007

In fact, evil and good are neither in heaven nor earth, but in people's hearts.

It is in everyone's heart and subconscious; there is desire of good and power of evil in our subconscious since we have consciousness. And there is no boundary between the good and evil; a human is good, but also a human is evil. A good man conversion with the devil is the doctrine; a demon may turn into an angel with the doctrine, but without the doctrine, the angel may turn into a demon.

Doctrine refers to the way which is correct, comprehensive, and tolerant of all people, in line with human nature; it is a perfect way to make humans coexist, with common prosperity.

This approach is changing with changing technology, which is mastered by people. That is, it is changing with people's productivity changing.

Therefore, the first sentence of the Tao Te Ching explains the method to get rid of all suffering, and contradictory to human coexistence, common prosperity is changing and transforming. It is conversion with conditions conversion, and nothing can be following decades of teaching of words and deeds. That specific wisdom method is gradually established combined with present situation.

Frankly, in my experience, almost everything tells me human nature is ugly, ignorant, and hopeless. So when I want to change the people around me, I find that I can change nothing. In the secular world, only money and power can change others.

But there are some things that change my ideas and views and also show the goodness of human nature. I really feel the power of rational good from humans. The senior leaders and academics who are the elites of society can struggle in the right direction, trying to change the fate of the country and the world. This is the charitable thought and good desire of humans in this world.

The performance of charitable thought and good desire of humans is not necessary to have lower people, for surface phenomena and posturing do good deeds, but for determining national interests as well as human destiny, which is really good deeds.

In fact, with common people, the range of consciousness is narrow. It is not easy for them to manage their affairs. Only the elite and people with superior ability can understand doctrines, follow doctrines, comprehend doctrines, and then improve the doctrines, developing and extending doctrines.

Common people have their own doctrines; they will be lucky if they can follow their own doctrine. This book is for the people who are obeying a big doctrine and those in high positions as well as the social elites, instead of the common people. I would like to explore the future of human society and the country's direction with the elite through this book. It is purely academic papers; if someone feels too far away from the point of view in this book and cannot accept it, please make sure your knowledge is more profound than mine and then comment on this book, or it does not make sense.

Of course, I have a little knowledge about all aspects. With the development of technology, people will have more explicit and clear understanding of the human world; meanwhile, the doctrine will continue to evolve and improve.

Human life is limited, the knowledge mastered is limited, but the development of science and technology and history are unlimited.

I wish that people in this world truly understand others' human nature and, understanding the foundation of variety of people happening in the world, therefore find a more suitable way for human development.

Do not be driven by the devil in your heart; do not be confused by the barbarism and ignorance. We should be real masters of our own destiny, to grasp our own happiness and future, meanwhile control the future of humanity.

However, only the perspective of good and evil to understand human nature is not enough and is superficial. We need more scientific and rational perspectives to analyse humanity.

11. What is consciousness?

About 2007

Consciousness is the quality or state of being aware of something within oneself or an external object and the reflection in people's brains.

Consciousness is the response not only to the existing stimulation, but also to the imagination. Even though you close your eyes and ears, lying on a bed, you can still remember or imagine the memories and replay, process, and imagine past feelings. Usually people's reflection on objects is a process of remembering, analysing, and processing them in a simple form of images.

For example, we may remember things that happened long ago. Though they were far back, we still have vague memories of them, maybe blurry images, sounds, or smells.

There is no clear boundary between consciousness and the subconscious, just like the bottom of the iceberg and the part above the water are integral parts of the whole. As time goes by, some things sink into the water or may be forgotten. Even so, their influence on us is permanent and remains in our brains. Hence, the author believes that humans' brains and consciousness mainly depend on their impression and affection for the external objects so as to memorise them, while images, sounds, and smells are the auxiliary means for memorisation. Sometimes or on most occasions, people would forget these auxiliary means. However, the impression and emotions in the brains are permanent, unless they are changed by some other objects.

The author thinks it is the basic mode of the generation of consciousness.

Humans are merely advanced computers, from their birth to death, memorising the effects that every experience has on the individual so that when similar things occur, the human brain will alert the body to react, which is zoologically called unconditioned reflex. People have made countless experiments, and the author merely explains this phenomenon by consciousness and the subconscious.

The innumerable events during one's life, whether small or big, will exert effects on him. From a technical perspective, the brain needs to memorise the process and result of everything that has happened, and the sense organs like eyes, nose, ears, and mouth are collecting information all the time. How to record information and pick up the records to do reaction are problems to be solved; the solutions are that our brains record and permanently save things and the effects and emotional impression that these things exert on us. The scenes of the happenings, which are simply recorded, will get vague

33

or be forgotten as time goes by, but emotions and impression will never be forgotten and can be picked up at any time. Why?

From the perspective of Chinese medicine's Inner Classic of the Yellow Emperor, a man has seven emotions and six sensory pleasures, which are the reflex and impression of the things that he is linked with. For example, one is delighted and joyful when one smells the fragrance of the osmanthus. However, one will feel sick and disagreeable when one smells the stink of excrement.

The Inner Classic of the Yellow Emperor states that the seven emotions and six sensory pleasures, respectively, control a certain visceral organ. The author has not deeply studied it to make sure if it is true, but he only knows a little about it.

A computer spares quite a lot of space to store a movie but little to store data.

If each of the seven emotions and six sensory pleasures represents a variable, there are thirteen variables. The first time I felt pleased to smell the fragrance of the osmanthus, I set the pleasure to a score of 60 and provided no other variables; the score of the other twelve variables is 0.

Similarly, I set the sick for the stink of excrement to a score of 50 because there are more disgusting objects than excrement. My first disagreeable impression on excrement is a score of 50, and the others are 0.

When we think of the osmanthus next time, though we do not see the osmanthus or smell its fragrance, our subconscious will immediately tell us that the pleasure score is 60 and other scores are 0, and we will naturally have a pleasant mood and impression. As time goes by, we may forget when or where we have smelt the fragrance of the osmanthus, but our pleasure scores of 60 will actually never be forgotten, unless we encounter other things and generate other emotions when we get to smell the osmanthus again. For example, you go to play in a park once again and feel delighted to see the osmanthus. This time, you get your nose close to the osmanthus to smell it, and you get bitten by a bug. Then your impression of the osmanthus may add a fear score of 30 and decrease the pleasure score to 50.

With a time lapse, you may gradually forget the displeasure, but the fear will never be forgotten, unless another one or more things occur and change your impression and feeling of the osmanthus again.

Freud has confirmed the generation mode of such consciousness again and again with countless cases.

The mode is of great significance to knowing a person or society. It helps us to know a person and his thoughts and awareness by quantitative and scientific analysis. Besides, I firmly believe that robots with real emotions rather than simple machine programs can be generated.

Human ideologies are quite complicated and scientific.

From the above-mentioned, a man has a pleasure score of 50, fear score of 30, and no other emotions on the osmanthus. If he forgets the cause of the emotions, these emotions will sink into the ocean of consciousness and become subconscious.

To summarise, the subconscious refers to consciousness that people know what to do and what they want to do, but do not know why they want to do it.

It sounds like the stories and plots in romantic novels. You like someone but cannot tell why you like him or her.

As Freud said, the subconscious is like an iceberg, and consciousness is the tip of the iceberg above the water.

People open their eyes and see the whole world and all kinds of things. Some people like these objects while others like those objects. Some objects are what you like and others are what you dislike. It's not everything that you can entirely tell why you like it or why you dislike it.

Actually, you are not able to make it clear. Why? Your attitude towards a certain object is the total emotions you have linked with this object and its associated objects.

The subconscious can be classified into two categories. One is ego and the other one is superego, defined by Freud. As far as the author is concerned, one is the inherent primitive drives and instincts, i.e. the attributes of animals. The other one is the accumulation of the impressions on the happenings in the brain, i.e. the accumulation of reason and intellect.

Experience subconscious and animal subconscious are the two sources of the human subconscious. The inherent fear of death, pleasure from sexual intercourse, desires for the opposite sex, desires for food and water are animal subconscious; so is the curiosity for the things to come.

The emotions for all kinds of things constitute a real human. If humans are not clear about it, they will ever be ignorant and they cannot explain or make sense of everything that happens in the human society. If we cannot understand humans or truly understand humans in a scientific way, we will not able to ascertain the objects of observation, but only subjectively assume about humans or borrow words of famous people to explain humans. That is like milking a bull.

Then we will not be able to figure out our work. The working approaches and performance will be no more than castle in the air.

Buddhism requires humans with great wisdom to have supernatural eyes, unsurpassed enlightenment, and wisdom. However, first of all, humans should be able to see through the appearance to perceive the essence. The author does not entirely agree on Freud's pansexualism nor has deeply studied sex. Freud's theoretical framework is based on innumerable cases, which is absolute truth.

The influential celebrity Lu Xun in China has ever flayed Freud's theory. Therefore, up to now, research on Freud's theory in the Chinese mainland is regarded as heterodoxy, which is the biggest mistake that the Chinese have ever made. Since Chinese and Chinese leadership cannot discern people and see their nature, the author thinks Freud's theory, at least his basic theories, should be included in the required courses in high school. Research on the subconscious and impulses helps us explain many human phenomena which cannot be explained by any other courses.

12. Dimension of consciousness

About 2007

Almost every nation and every country has the war in which feudal society replaced slave society. Various human wars against aggression and even certain wars brought by human aggression are the actions taken by humans in order to achieve the reasonable and perfect world order that they think. This is the good of human nature, or the good that some people take advantage of, and the good that is easy to be taken advantage of by some people, because many aggressive wars take good thoughts as their slogan or the initiators think they are doing good. For example, the propaganda or idea for Japanese war of aggression against China is to 'build greater East Asia co-prosperity sphere, implement benevolent governance, and establish benevolent land'. The Japanese militarists also thought they did the good thing, and the good thoughts were just one goal. If our direction is A, the principle of good thoughts or the ideal is B, the way from A to B is the process of doing the good humans think. For example, 'life for a life, a debt paid in full' is China's most classic justice and the most basic method of doing good.

In the Chinese classical philosophy, the best, the most ideal, and the most appropriate way of A–B is referred to as Tao. Lao-Tzu's Tao Te Ching is about the description of 'Tao', and 'Buddhist texts' takes 'Tao' as 'Du', which means crossing the river. There is a little description about it in Hinayana, and there are a few people that can achieve the perfect state. And Mahayana refers to the world beings, to achieve the perfect state of relief.

Actually, for people, many profound truths are seemingly out of reach and illusory, because our thinking pattern is very narrow.

A family, an enterprise, a city, a country, and a planet are actually systems. The relationship between people, humans and society, humans and nature seems independent but is actually mutually connected with mutual influence.

People, as individuals, bustle about every day in order to satisfy their own desires. The consciousness of others that vast majority of people can understand, only including a few loved ones, and even he himself, we call the ability to understand other people and surrounding people as a dimension of consciousness.

Reading, especially reading literature books, is to communicate with different people. Even watching movies and TV, listening to stories are a good way to get into the dimension of consciousness of others and understand others' structure. Most people just go over the story plot or see the handsome boy and the beauty when watching movies, watching TV, reading a novel. Actually, most movie directors and novel authors want to use this way to express an intrinsic way of thinking, which is the real intention of the author.

In real life, the dimension of consciousness determines a person's success and social status. In a certain sense, the dimension of consciousness is the psychology research object and is the psychological activity of others. But I hate to use the concept of psychology, because it is brain rather than heart that conducts thinking to produce feeling. Strictly speaking, it has no direct relationship with the heart. So I hate to use this word. Reason is the rationality or the truth. Within a certain time and scope, reason is relatively stable and constant, but the consciousness and ideas of people always change, so I also hate to use the word reason to express the concept of consciousness.

The consciousness I understand is in constant change, with uncertainty. But in spite of uncertainty, it also changes within a certain scope and is not beyond this scope.

Everyone's consciousness is like the light of a flashlight, which can only brighten the nearby place of a few square metres. What people can think of are the things within a few square metres, not beyond this scope. The things that people can realise are those within a few square metres. When a person responds to a thing, he will only find the answer and the way out in the small circle.

Actually, the language, expressions, clothes, words, and actions we are exposed to every day are used as a kind of method to express thoughts and feelings of people. They are ways, means, representations, but not purpose. The reason why I promote psychoanalysis is that it can tell people the real driving force behind the behaviour of people, or the real intention or purpose of people's behaviour. Buddhism says people should have supreme wisdom and sammasambuddha.

I think that it is the Buddha that tells people to understand the real purpose behind the behaviour of people but not to be confused by appearances. Because the real aim of people may be buried in the subconscious, and the party himself does not know the real aim for him to do that. But he is controlled by the real purpose all the time.

Maybe there are a lot of people that don't agree with me. They don't know their purpose. Do you really know what you want to do?

According to the basic theory of psychoanalysis, the consciousness of people is the thing that is able to enter the man's consciousness, which is just the tip of the iceberg, but the real iceberg is buried under the sea. It is unfathomable and unattainable. That is the real purpose of human behaviour.

What is the main body of the iceberg? It is composed of two parts.

1. Human animal's impulse is ego, and this force is the dominant force. It is the most fundamental factor for all behaviour, which means the indivisible consciousness at the bottom, and it is the most fundamental human consciousness, which means the person's true intention. I think people often can't perceive the consciousness at the bottom. That is the animal unconsciousness.

2. The rational part can be regarded as superego. Where does superego come from? It is the deposition of all things that a person has experienced in his whole life in the brain, the deposition in the subconscious. That is to say, it is experience subconscious.

13. Psychoanalysis is a tool to study humanity and the human soul

About 2007

Through psychoanalysis, humans can learn what humanity is or what true humanity is.

The contradictory understanding of humanity by Oriental and Western philosophers suggests that one side or possibly both sides are deceiving the public.

Why is it necessary to learn humanity?

The reason is that social systems serve humans and are also implemented and maintained by the latter. If the essence of humans is left unknown, all social systems, ideas, and cultures are just built on palaces in the desert. They are castles in the air, illusions, and lies.

Humanity is a theoretical simulation and nature determination of humans by theorists. In this way, the ethereal humanity can be studied and simulated according to certain logic and be derived theoretically. In other words, something invisible finds a concrete model for itself.

The reason for the failure of Marxist theories worldwide and huge losses of humans caused by it is that Marx was a pure theorist or a dreamer without any practical experiences. He did not serve as a worker or a capitalist, so he did not know the worker or the capitalist. It was apt to say that he did not have a thorough understanding of humans and humanity. Without extensive contacts and in-depth understanding, the failure of Marxist theories was the failure of Marx's understanding of humans. His understanding of the relationship between humans and the attributes of humans and his simulation of humanity were totally wrong.

Psychoanalysis is a full simulation of consciousness generation, structure, and layer by Freud based on his psychotherapy of mental patients all his life. Contributions of Freud towards humans were based on numerous practices, forming a sharp contrast to Marx, a sheer theorist and dreamer. Only understanding and research findings of Freud were fully in line with dialectical materialism methodology.

If a human is likened to a computer, psychoanalysis is the tool to analyse the fixed programs of the computer. How consciousness of humans comes into being is the research object of psychoanalysis.

Freud is a psychiatrist. Through research and analysis of a series of mental disorders, he summarised the generation process and operation model of human consciousness. Thanks to his efforts, human consciousness—something invisible, impalpable, immeasurable, and unquantifiable—has a scientific research method and a reasonable operation model.

Scientific research of human consciousness and soul can help quantise and position all issues related to the human society. Only in this way all these issues can be correctly understood and judged. Only in this way can humans see the essence of the bizarre, complex, and ridiculous phenomena in the human world, correctly judge them, and cope with them. For example, we can conduct psychoanalysis of Islam so as to root it out. We can conduct psychoanalysis of Democrats so as to reveal secrets deep in their heart. We can conduct psychoanalysis of people both accepting and refusing to accept refugees and refugees themselves so as to point out the essence of refugee phenomena in Europe.

We need truth and facts. Let's say no to deception. We are masters of our destiny. To the end, psychoanalysis is indispensable.

14. What is culture?

About 2007

This is to understand culture from the perspective of psychoanalysis.

Culture is a kind of subconscious mind from the perspective of psychoanalysis. It is not detectable and influences people's behaviour all the time. Only when compared with other cultures can it be obviously found out, and people will not pay attention to it without comparison.

As there are differences between men and women of the subconscious mind, all the people believe that their own behaviour is normal and correct. Instead, if a woman shows the male-specific behaviour or a man shows the female-specific behaviour, they will be regarded as abnormal, weird, and even perverted.

These common behaviour characteristics of men or women are in fact fully controlled by the subconscious mind, because all the wills of decision and the directions of thinking are the result of the driving of the subconscious mind.

What is a subconscious mind like? Just like vehicles. For example, one friend owns a car while another one doesn't have one and he can only travel by bus when he wants to go out. If both of them want to go somewhere far away, the ways of thinking of the car-driving friend and the bus-taking friend are totally different.

What the car-driving friend considers is which road is the shortest and the best one, while what the bus-taking friend considers is which bus line to choose to reach the destination and how he should transfer.

Although they are both able to reach the destinations, their ways of thinking and behaviour modes are totally different. The basic reason of the difference is about what vehicles they use: cars and buses.

Cars and buses can be equal to the subconscious mind, while their action lines are awareness. The specific actions for reaching the destination are exactly the behaviour.

It is commonly considered that cars and buses are hierarchical. However, there are no distinctions of high or low for the subconscious mind, between men and women. Humans are born with the subconscious mind, which has a close relationship with the sexual organs and the hormone secretion. The gender is determined by birth, which decides the sexual impulse to be active or passive, and the ways of sexual impulse determine the ways of thinking and the subconscious.

For example, there is a phenomenon in psychology as follows:

Compared with beautiful girls, the general-looking girls can easily be introverted and extreme. In life, especially after sexual maturity, they feel the differences from the boys, compared with beautiful girls. That is to say, they can feel their sexual satisfaction (spouse) is relatively more difficult than beautiful girls'. The dilemma and the difference that they face make the introverted girl have low self-esteem and lead the outgoing girls to be more extreme. Actually, their appearance decides the different ways of their spouse and sexual gratification. The difference of the spouse and sexual gratification determines the difference of their subconscious mind. The confidence, low self-esteem, and the extreme are just a manifestation of character, while internal factors—the difference of sexual satisfaction—lead to the difference of the rational part of the unconscious mind.

Above is my simple presentation about change of the subconscious mind and human behaviour, but there is a huge impact of the subconscious mind on countries and areas in the aspect of culture.

Cultural differences can be said to be national and regional differences in people's subconscious. The differences between Chinese culture and Western culture can be said as the differences between men and women, which are the differences in the subconscious rather than only one issue or one thing.

The culture we usually talk about may be referring to our understanding of culture of heritage, the ancient architecture, customs, ethics, morality, novels, literature, etc. However, these things are just manifestations of culture.

The essence of culture is a kind of idea and a comprehensive set of understanding, universal recognition, and basic philosophy of the relationship between people in society. In a country or a region, these widely recognised concepts in people's subconscious have been treated as an inherent condition and default, which is deposited in people's subconscious and affects people's every movement all the time. However, people never doubt that these things are the default behaviour model, and those who break these models are considered abnormal and will get sanctions of ethics, morality, and law.

The subconscious formed in people's concept of the relationship between humans, humans and society, and humans and nature in a certain country and society, which is recognised by the majority of people, is the culture.

Since it is present in people's subconscious and manifested and spread by people's language, behaviour, artwork, ethics, morality, and law, it has several features:

43

1. Because the subconscious of culture is precisely spread through daily behaviour, only the people outside of this culture come to this culture environment and can feel it through comparison. Usually it is in a default state that people cannot perceive its presence.

2. Because culture is spread through daily behaviour, it is everywhere and omnipresent and has subtle influence on people. Through daily behaviour, it is spread all the time by people, thus it can be handed down from generation to generation.

3. Only when the environment has been changed and the subconscious is proved to be wrong could the culture be changed gradually by people. Such a thing as culture only can be changed by external promotion for culture has its inertness and inertia.

4. The time for a change in culture is the time for social contradictions, and the change in culture can lead to the social contradictions. To change a culture is bound to have the conservatives and reformers, and the two factions are inevitably to have conflicts in the change of culture. However, this conflict is actually the distribution of benefits dispute. Because the social rule change will inevitably bring about the change in the way of the distribution of social benefits, during this, some people feel a loss while others get benefit; those who get loss will inevitably rise to resist, and the beneficiaries will have to protect their interests, thus the social conflicts and disputes are generated. But after the social rules are reformulated, people will find a new balance and build a new culture.

15. The culture of the feudal society of China

About 2007

China's feudal society was dependent on political power, moral religion, and economic feudal lords owning the land, which was the biggest means of production in the feudal society. The cultural feudalism forcibly repressed human nature, to maintain the feudal society.

Three aspects of politics, economy, and thought forcibly adjusted the social order.

Everyone in society cycles is stable running according to certain rules, to make the society steady, to minimise social contradictions. It was this pattern that made China's feudal society extremely stable and highly developed.

Social development needs social stability. Everyone has their own orbit, like the moon and stars travelling in orbit. Even if there would be change, it also should have certain laws and rules.

It seems that the monarch and his subjects, father and son, husband and wife, were in shackles; in fact, it also represented the responsibilities, which were the shackles and also were the umbrella. It also can be said that the monarchy protected the official in feudal times and that the monarchy was the umbrella of the official in feudal times, and the official in feudal times was governed by the monarchy. It can be said that the official's survival in feudal times depended on the monarch.

The wife must submit to her husband. The husband, to his wife, was an administrator, also could be said to be the ruler or the protector. The husband was the organiser of the family; the wife was oppressed by husband in a certain sense, and the wife was also protected by the husband. The rights and obligations difference was in pairs presenting. It cannot be just talk about oppression without talking about protection and obligation and responsibility.

The son must submit to his father in the same way. The father, to his son, was an administrator, oppressing person, also the protector of the son, the dependent person.

The husband and wife in China's feudal consciousness and the concept was the way of running the state, integrating extreme yin and the softest of Lao Tzu.

Lao Tzu had deep-rooted influence on China. But after the eight-power Allied forces broke the gateway of China, it was a shackle, the shackles to restrain Chinese people. So the Cultural Revolution had to break it. But after this kind of social culture was disillusioned, it must be filled out by another more rational culture. Otherwise, people still use the most practical traditional theory.

According to the Cultural Revolution after the liberation, the new ideas are on the equality between men and women, men and women each having half the sky. So how are they truly equal? How does each account for half the sky? Real and complete equality is the concept of relationship between men and women in Western counties. Men and women first are economically independent, and they should control their own money, and with political independence, men and women are self-safeguarding their legitimate rights and interests, including the right to privacy, human rights, the discretion of property, the right to education, action liberty right, and so on. This power must be mutually respected and so on, with zero tolerance for infringement of rights.

With independent thought, men and women, both parties have their own beliefs, must have mutual respect, mutual non-aggression.

All the content about human rights must be observed, and both should strictly observe it. Infringing on each other means provoking and insulting each other.

However, the Communist Party, in opposition to feudal ideas at the same time and against the capitalist ideology, praised highly the so-called co-production of communal-pot thought and the average thought, which now are considered obsolete ideas. Then, the communal pot was proved wrong; Chinese people became a group of no thought and no faith.

In the aspects of marriage and family relations, the feudal family values were overthrown. The West's human rights cannot be accepted by the Chinese people at all at one time. Communism did not propose any new family values.

Whatever the thought of men in the family is wrong, which either is a feudal decadent ideas or is the Western corruption, the reactionary thought; anyway, all the thought of men in the family is wrong, but it is only that the fear of the wife is right which causes the unique henpecked culture with Chinese characteristics. Through culture, art, film, and television works, it was passed down through generations; it is stunning and amazing.

The Chinese feudal culture is reasonable, and the Western liberal human rights culture is also reasonable, but only it is not that the culture of fear of the wife is unreasonable; it belongs to the cultural freak.

46

16. All ancient thoughts in China are philosophical culture of yin and yang

About 2007

As a matter of fact, so many thoughts in ancient China have a common feature that they study each unit, either big or small, such as universe, area, country, city, family, and so on, as a system. This is the biggest difference between Chinese and Western cultures. Western culture is based on individuals as the research object and explores the ideological and behavioural emancipation of individuals and the protection of human rights, etc. Everything is centred on individuals, with individuals as a starting point.

To interpret from the Buddhist scriptures, Western culture is like Theravada, while Chinese culture or Eastern culture is like Mahayana. Of course, the systematic culture in China started much earlier than Indian Buddhist culture and is more extensive than Buddhism. But the dominant idea is almost the same.

The philosophy of yin and yang is the most fundamental philosophical culture in China. Other classic cultures in China are based on yin and yang. They even crystallise and actualise the philosophy of yin and yang. However, there seems to be no record which philosopher was the first to present the philosophy of yin and yang. I think this is God's revelation to ancient Chinese.

1. The philosophy of yin and yang believes that everything in the world is divided into yin and yang.

2. The sun is yang and the earth is yin. Active is yang and passive is yin. Attack is yang and defence is yin. The back is yang and the belly is yin. Growth is yang and constriction is yin. Hot is yang and cold is yin. Bright is yang and dark is yin, etc.

3. Yin and yang must cooperate with each other so that everything can get on smoothly. If either of them is ignored, disasters will happen.

Things, from the large universe to small molecules and atoms, from tangible to intangible, contain yin and yang. All of them conform to the theory of yin and yang.

The philosophy of yin and yang is consistent with Mao Zedong's thought of unity of opposites, as well as Confucius's Doctrine of the Mean in China. Or rather, both Mao Zedong and Confucius borrowed the basic idea of the philosophy of yin and yang.

From a holistic view of human society, proletariat belongs to yang and bourgeoisie to yin. National interests belong to yang and personal interests belong to yin. Fairness and justice are masculine, and economic development is feminine. Obedience to social order is masculine, and pursuit of individual freedom is feminine.

Feminine submits to masculine and masculine cares for feminine, just like women submit to men and men care for women. This is a way of the universe and a heavenly principle. Those who submit to God will prosper, and those who resist shall perish. If yin and yang can be reconciled in harmony and unity, things will coexist with heaven and earth, the sun and moon. Otherwise, calamities will come one after another.

Both ancient history and modern history in China illustrate this point.

The theory of yin and yang is arguably one of the most fundamental characteristics of the system. A society is a system. A universe is a system. The earth is a system. A country is a system. An enterprise is a system. A family is a system. An individual is a system. A car is a system. A computer is especially a system.

The earth's climate also contains yin and yang. Yang represents sunlight and yin represents rainfall. It is with the presence of sunshine, rain, and dew that all things on the earth can grow. Moreover, sunshine, rain, and dew need a balance of yin and yang. Too much sunshine without rain, there will be drought. If rain and dew don't stop, flood will inundate. For human beings, this means great catastrophes.

The philosophy of yin and yang is a systematic philosophy and a fundamental thought in the ideological system in China. It has a very long history. I don't even think this kind of philosophy can be invented by people at that time with their own intelligence and culture. It might be a prehistoric civilisation, a civilisation existing before Chinese civilisation. At that time, people hardly had any characters. How could they possibly spread such profound knowledge?

17. The Book of Changes and the Inner Classic of the Yellow Emperor are books that specify the philosophy of yin and yang

About 2007

The Book of Changes is an embodiment of the philosophy of yin and yang, and it seems to tell about yin-yang change of matters and a general development rule of representative matters. However, according to the present technology and knowledge, it is hard to match the change process of all things to yin and yang.

But many persons with special talent can predict future change of matters by the Book of Changes, and what they do is also called fortune telling or forecasting.

However, judging from the text form of the Book of Changes, this book determines current and future status of matters according to yin-yang change of the matters. Therefore, it can be considered as a book studying a system. Although Chinese cannot fully understand the information of this book, the idea regarding yin and yang and systematic change in this book has deep influence on Chinese culture.

In the opinion of the author of this paper, this is a book studying systematic change.

The Inner Classic of the Yellow Emperor is a medical book, origination, and theoretical basis of traditional Chinese medicine, as well as a book completely related to system research. This book takes the human body as a full-size system to explain various internal organs, between which are parts of mutual relation and mutual function in the system.

Same as the Book of Changes, it fully applies the philosophy of yin and yang as a method and thinking way to study the human body system, and it is a book discussing the human body system. In addition, its theories are still in use today and help the Chinese to keep in good health and treat illness for thousands of years.

To be perfectly honest, till today, Chinese are unable to fully understand or agree with the description in the book. Therefore, to the thinking of the author of this paper, according to living and cultural conditions and intellectual development level at that time, the book cannot be an achievement that is developed by the ancient people individually. It is hard to believe that the ancient people and current technology are capable of studying such profound theories and culture that has been applied for thousands of years and is not fully understood even today.

In the meantime, as a successful application of the philosophy of yin and yang on the human body system, it influences China in some way and makes Chinese culture a systematic culture.

The Book of Changes and the Inner Classic of the Yellow Emperor are specific applications of the philosophy of yin and yang on prediction, fortune telling, and medicine. They should be words from God to ancient Chinese.

18. China's systematic culture

About 2007

Since the time of Confucius, systematic culture has influenced Chinese, who are profoundly affected because Chinese grow up in the system, are restricted by the system, and benefit from the system their whole lives.

The influence of systematic culture on people is the same as the effect of other cultures. Culture has strong impact on people.

The influence of culture on people is involved in every matter, every product, every eye contact, and every movement. The way that culture influences people is through changing or remodelling people's subconscious, thus influencing people's behaviour. The culture would not intervene in people's actions on specific things, but it can change people's dimension of consciousness and the subconscious. It transforms people's inner attitude to change their behaviour.

Why do we say that culture changes people's dimension of consciousness?

For example, in ancient China, according to the traditional culture, it is improper for men and women to touch each other's hand in passing objects, women are beautiful in a reserved manner, women should smile without showing teeth. Under these feudal cultural backgrounds, unmarried women would not study how to talk with strange men about the weather or have lunch together when they only stayed in a boudoir. They have no expectation of studying on how to associate with men, because there is no sense. In their consciousness, it is forbidden to associate with the opposite sex, for unmarried women.

In a similar way, between the Chinese girls who are influenced by traditional ideology and the girls who are relatively open, their dimensions of consciousness on communicating with people of the opposite sex is different. In our daily lives, this discrepancy is expressed in a way when the relatively traditional party has no experience or the other party has more experience or is more experienced. Judging from the way of consciousness and the subconscious, this is different size of dimensions of consciousness or blankness of consciousness dimension.

There is another concept, which is Chinese always call a person just entering the society a blank paper, which is also vacancy, which means that newcomers into society has vacant consciousness about social experience. They have no detailed information about the concept of society.

Because of the influence of systematic culture on the subconscious of Chinese, in Chinese's dimension of consciousness, there is a natural concept of system. Chinese instinctively know how to apply the system to benefit them, or how to obey or escape from the restrictions of the system on themselves, to avoid penalty on them from the system. These are all influences of systematic culture on Chinese's dimension of consciousness. In contrast, Western people live in an environment different from the Chinese's, so they have no concept of system.

In China's systematic culture, the family system is the system with which Chinese would have the earliest contact and is the system the Chinese are mostly fond of and best apply.

In addition to applying the existing consanguineous relationship to make out the system, the Chinese also create their own systems through establishing sworn relations with friends, teachers, adopted father, adopted mother, which are all typical Chinese styles.

To be honest, the author of this paper has no deep study on foreign culture but has read many books and watched foreign TV series for several decades. In those books and TV series, there is no one example presenting the phenomenon of establishing sworn relations with friends, adopted father, or adopted mother. Even the author of this paper never heard the words of sworn brothers, adopted father, and adopted mother in foreign works.

Certainly, sworn brother is just a small role in current Chinese culture, but the systematic culture having greater influence on Chinese is family culture in which the most representative is the relation between parents and children. This relation is a core relation in family systematic culture, and it is a leading relation in family as well as the main contact between members in the family.

Almost every Chinese has heard such ancient sayings as 'All his friends and relations get there with him', 'It is the custom for a son to pay his father's debts', 'The son should avenge his father', which are interpreted again and again in literary works like movies, TV series, books, etc. They almost become eternal themes.

Due to the influence of systematic culture, the Chinese have a different thinking mode between that of foreigners.

Confucius developed the systematic culture in China, or to say, Confucius transforms systematic culture into a systematic cultural product that is specific and is able to be implemented.

The ideology of Confucius and Mencius and feudal ethical code are specific to individuals. Certainly, Confucius was the first to propose this system, just like the Windows system was firstly launched by Microsoft and is widely applied to computers. Windows is used for computers specially, but the social management system of Confucius' ideology is rooted in every Chinese and is the operating system of every Chinese dynasty.

To my point of view, the acceptance points and advanced things of this operating system have the following advantages:

1. This system defines everyone in the society specifically.

There is clear affiliation and social definition in either administration or daily life, enabling everyone to know what powers and obligations they have. This could help to avoid social contradictions to the greatest extent and help everyone know what should be done and what should not be done. In normal operation of the system, social disruption would not occur.

2. This system was equipped with endowment insurance and free compulsory education since the Chinese feudal society two thousand years ago.

Chinese have the culture of bringing up sons to support parents in their old age. It is necessary to be filial to parents in feudal system. It is illegal if the sons do not provide for their parents, and in severe cases, the sons can be judged with death in the charge of disobedience. Therefore, in the feudal system, the sons must be filial to parents and provide for parents. The family transfers the inheritance to the son, while the daughter belongs to her husband's family after she is married and has no right to the inheritance. This is called 'a woman follows her husband no matter what his lot is'. After the son inherits the heritage, he must support his parents and worship their ancestors. This is called inheriting the lineage. When the son and his wife have no children, it is called the last of family line and is the most unfilial behaviour. It is a very severe thing in feudal values. Having children is to have the function of endowment insurance. This is to ensure that the elderly will be looked after properly and make a stable and harmonious society.

Since the son has the function of endowment insurance, skills and talents of the son are the most promising that his parents can have rich and better lives. Therefore, the parents would educate children from morality, talent, and knowledge since the children's babyhood. The parents would prefer suffering hardships for their whole life just for creating a good study environment for the children and for making the children become nation pillars. A child is better unborn than untaught. This is equal to the function of free compulsory education. Not only in ancient China, but also the modern Chinese are never bored with it.

The above are the greatest benefits to ordinary Chinese from this system. In addition, this set of functions of endowment insurance and free compulsory education is very successful and plays great effect until today when influencing daily actions and thinking mode of the Chinese. For this reason, the author of this paper does admire Confucius's works and contributions.

This system is undoubtedly the most advanced and practical social management system in natural economy condition where men do farm work and women engage in spinning and weaving. Chinese created Chinese ancient culture and far surpass Western culture by such advanced system. This success is entirely owed to systematic culture and the Chinese's understanding of the system and life.

Certainly, systematic culture was not created by Confucius but is an integrated concept and systematic ideology that is handed down from the ancient times.

The works that Lao Tzu did for systematic culture are overall and conceptual description and exposition, while Confucius is a worker dedicated to practical application of systematic culture.

Therefore, Lao Tzu's influence on and contribution to the Chinese systematic culture is ineffaceable and decisive. In short, Lao Tzu is the one who studied basic theories of the system, while Confucius is the one who worked on practical application of systematic culture. From the point of technology, basic theories would never be out of date, but practical application would have to be improved constantly along with development of productivity and variations of contradictory nature.

Although systematic culture is very advanced, there are obvious deficiencies in Confucius's social management system for current society, due to changes in the times and environment. China's economy and technology as well as productivity are hampered in development and are surpassed and invaded by Western countries, just because the Chinese are restricted by this systematic culture.

Actually, this is not a fault of systematic culture, but China needs to update the application program of systematic culture, like the Windows system which would be always updated in a few years, from 95 to 98, 2000, XP, and Win10. Since the hardware facilities are changing and hard disk is expanded and CPU is accelerated, even though the old system is in good condition, it has to be rectified to adapt to development needs of new hardware.

The reason is the same for the social management system. Because of changes and increases of market economy, industrial reforms, and Internet, today cannot be compared with the era two thousand years ago when men did farm work and women engaged in spinning and weaving. However, the Chinese still continue to use the operating system that was designed by the ancients two thousand years ago. It is definite that China would be backward and have obstacles in development of economy and productivity. However, with proper rectification, social management system would play its enormous social effects and functions.

19. Ancient thinkers share the same theme and philosophy

About 2007

As the Buddhist texts go, we should have superior enlightenment and wisdom to face all things around us. What is superior enlightenment? To see the nature through the surface of the things. What is the nature? Motives and purposes, thinking mode, and basic principles.

We are in the bustling street. We see all the flowing people who come and go. We see this fantastic world. The busy people are actually doing the same thing—living, or more specifically, living a better live. That is the nature of things, or it is the nature of the ordinary people, the nature of common people. It is what they are living for.

Actually a thinker or philosopher has true purposes and thoughts. Maybe we read several days and nights for books that he writes, but if we conclude it, it will be left as a sentence or an idea, which may be the final purpose. And many of his words and ideas and speaking are centring on this purpose and are the concrete solutions and methods.

And his thinking mode or the main logic will be only one, or he will have only one basic structure, which is to take people to that place.

We know that there are endless routes from A to B; that is to say, thinkers and philosophers have an endless way to get to the ideal purpose.

As time goes by and productivity develops, the continuous development changes conditions of human society. What people need most is to take different routes and take different methods. Although we may have taken a different route from the ancient thinkers, that does not mean that we abandon them at all. Roads are many, so if we still go for that goal, we can say that we are still sticking to the same truth and the same road.

Ancient thinkers or ancient civilisations of China are different from the Western's. Compared with that, there are huge or natural distinctions between China and the West. It can be traced from time immemorial to see the distinctive and natural difference between Chinese culture and Western culture.

According to my opinion and understanding ability, the Book of Changes and the Inner Classic of the Yellow Emperor and the other ancient philosophies Tao Te Ching, the philosophy of yin and yang, Confucianism, and the later Diamond Sutra that came into China have fundamental influence on the thoughts of Chinese scholars.

But my opinion is that these books and the philosophy of yin and yang do not belong to the author only, an ordinary person who can write such a classic book and form these ideas and concepts.

I even believe that it belongs to prehistoric civilisation; it is the intention of God. In the circumstance that has low productivity like before, people still make their living by hunting and fishing. How could they form the idea that we modern people cannot even understand? I think that unscientific and illogical.

Tao Te Ching, Confucianism, Diamond Sutra, I think they can be understood after meditation—not just understanding it from the words that can be translated into understanding slang, but understanding the purpose of the writer and the purpose of the writing. To them, their ideas and concepts are not very complicated, and we can even say that to some extent, there are some similarities.

An old Chinese saying goes, everything is the same. It is what I am trying to tell you. Each philosophy has a different form, but they have the same goal.

Actually the final purpose is the simplest and the noblest and the most vulgar. It is like turning a circle and getting back to the original dot.

It looks like going to the original dot, but it is not that simple. It has a higher level, and it is like the spiral stair.

Each philosophy has the same ultimate goal, which is to liberate human beings and the world. But to liberate human beings and the world will start to liberate the country.

So, Chinese ancient philosophers and thinkers are talking about the whole set of concepts of governing a state.

20. The philosophy of yin and yang and social system

About 2007

The philosophy of Lao Tzu appears the softest and the most feminine, while individualism in the Western culture appears the most masculine.

Each category of Chinese culture is closely related to Lao Tzu's Tao Te Ching, including Confucianism, which is just the application of Lao Tzu's philosophy in the feudal society!

More importantly, Chinese harmonious society is another modern manifestation of Lao Tzu's philosophy, and its nature lies in femininity!

The typical manifestations of femininity are conservation, peace, content, muddling along, and even sabotaging!

Egoism in the Western culture definitely focuses on masculinity, centralising individuals and maximising personal interests, and its main features are offence, aggression, enterprise, and struggling!

Since femininity is superior to masculinity, the country of China was parcelled, invaded, and defeated by the Western countries featuring individualism after going through the flourishing feudal governance!

After all, however, China may be defeated by the Western culture's masculinity, if it can't totally get out of the feminine limit. The nightmare that eight-power Allied forces captured Beijing would come in the end!

Actually, according to the philosophy of yin and yang, neither femininity nor masculinity is imperfect at all. Just like the combination of man and woman, we may feel regretted, imperfect, and anxious, whether there is no man or no woman in life.

The Western countries appear so masculine that it gives us the impression that the people there are all foolish or stupid! China shows such feminineness that Chinese people look so sissy and worthless, just like fake eunuchs!

One country should show its femininity when the strong is needed and appear masculine when the soft is required! So how does a country integrate femininity and masculinity together well?

In the social system, the society runs in order, people abide by behavioural conventions and follow the social regulations. Such a society is where feminine social system shows its advantages!

While each individual is active, energetic, and diligent in the masculine, so working hard manifests the masculine society's strengths. Human beings are primarily selfish, so when will they become energetic, diligent, and hard workers? It is when human beings are working for themselves that they work diligently and energetically.

So what is working for individuals themselves? It is extremely selfish, centring on individuals, doing all for themselves and their benefits and ignoring their wives, children, parents, and even their own countries; that is, personal interests are placed in the highest situation. Such is the Western capitalism, whose nature is to protect personal interests. The laws, morals, and ethics in the Western countries all serve their personal interests.

Such is the typical combination of femininity and masculinity in the social system.

So the question is how to combine the behaviour of following social rules and obtaining personal interests. That appears in the perfect social system.

It is definite that femininity and masculinity can be perfectly combined with each other. The conception of separating ownership from management is the result of the perfect combination of following social rules and obtaining personal interests.

Only if it is not only applied to the state-owned enterprises and capital but also used in the social system will the conception will it show its maximised effectiveness. The conception is able to make a difference to the whole world if applied appropriately.

Masculinity refers to the sky, persistence, aggression, enterprise, innovation, warmness, heat, brightness, conquering, man, the male, the left, and the government. Femininity means the ground, softness, conservation, defence, tradition, coldness, darkness, obedience, woman, the female, the right, and the citizens. The two concepts are the two parties in the unity of oppositeness, interdependent and indispensable, such as the different parts of a car.

Masculinity is motor, providing power. Femininity is the brakes, offering brake power. Motor and brakes are equally important. The car will be damaged and the people will die, if a car is only equipped with strong motor without brakes. Both time and oil are wasted and no movement is made, if a car only has good brakes without a strong motor.

In the area of politics, government serves for the people, and the balance of yin and yang is the people's support of their government. Otherwise, the people's fighting against their government is the unbalance of yin and yang, if the government's policies harm the people's interests.

As for the field of culture, such is the case as well. Culture refers to the centralised manifestation of the outlook of life and social thoughts of an entire nation towards a country, a society, and even the universe.

Judging from the psychical analysis, it is the centralised reflection of the people's subconscious. It is also the restatement of a nation and a country. Politics and economics are just expressive forms of culture, but culture can be expressed by a variety of other forms.

Culture decides human beings' patterns of thoughts; in turn, humans' patterns of thoughts decide different political patterns and then affect the economy. Certainly, politics and economy can also make an effect on human beings' philosophy and viewpoint and then help to change culture that is widely recognised as ideological education.

What is the yang-qi of a nation?

1. Elites' patriotism, that is, graduates' and the senior intellectuals' patriotism, appears masculine, featuring destruction, corruption, and harmful elements. The prevalent corruption in China is the typical reflection of the lack of masculinity. If a man is short of yang-qi, he is afraid of exposure in the light. So is a country. Publicising possessions is unrealisable, so it is obvious that there is too much yin and too little yang in China.

Meanwhile, as the balance between yin and yang, democracy and autocracy also should be made balanced; otherwise, man will die if the fever is too serious.

2. A nation's yang-qi is also reflected by men's collective characteristics. For example, whether a man is afraid to die or not, whether he does have a sense of justice, whether he is aggressive or not, or whether he does have the desire to conquer.

But how does a man have such characteristics? The external environment, mainly including political environment, economic environment, the gender environment, etc.

These environments are interrelated and inter-affected, which lead to the creation of a national integrity, that is, a national yang-qi.

One or two things don't matter at all, so it is no problem that there are one or two henpecked husbands in one nation. But the nation will be ruined if most of its male people are henpecked.

Property law, a combination of yin and yang, is the inevitable result and legal safeguard of separating ownership from management. Under the condition that the feminine and masculine social system doesn't change, property law introduced the culture of femininity and masculinity.

If you intend to make clear that property is the basis of masculinity, the property and possession as well as the range of each individual's personal interests should be made clear. The state representing its people can be considered as a private individual, and each person is a private individual who is required to be the most productive, that is, make the most of masculinity. That is to say, the range of each person's personal possession should be made clear; so should the range of proprietary rights, including the range of the people's possession represented by their state.

The relations of different possessions between wives and husbands, between fathers and sons, between family members and countries should be strictly divided, seriously protected, mutually nonaggressive, non-interferential, and individually dependent. Thus, each person may show his enthusiasm for labour. Because human beings are selfish, they can work tirelessly and determinedly for themselves, and there is no way to make them work so hard except the method mentioned above. That is to say, if a person's personal possessions and personal interests are protected well, he has the possibility to do his best.

Such is a state. How could a state council's lack of proprietary rights make an important decision for its state? Proprietary rights can be set aside while great national events are dealt with. Is that money?

How do its people obtain interests if a state fails to deal with international events?

A state centres on the maximum of the national profits. Individuals focus on the maximum of personal interests. If it works, the wealth of a whole nation can be accumulated.

If Chinese people intend to revitalise our nation, they should realise masculinity and individuals' interests, including parents, wives and husbands, fathers and sons, nations and individuals.

Certainly, the Chinese is by no means the lack of femininity. Ying-qi has the effect on the growth of various plants and animals. China's ying-qi is reflected by the public ownership of the state system in China. The public ownership sector of the economy makes clear the limit of individuals' affairs and the cultural events, independently and in charge of political rights, respectively.

61

However, the public ownership sector of the economy also has the functions of justice and balanced growth towards the solution of national important events. As is written in the Tao Te Ching, it can be concluded as the effect of more damage and less compensation. How feminine! How kind!

According to the ancient philosophy in China, the 'nature and humanity' ideology is necessary if human beings intend to obtain the permanent harmonious state, and utopia or communist society was put forward by Marx. The 'nature and humanity' ideology is the reflection that human beings' behaviour abides by the objective laws of nature.

What are the objective laws of nature? It refers to the inexorable law concluded from all things that happened to human beings, natural surroundings, related to the nature of human beings and the events made by human beings since the beginning of recorded history.

Regarding the laws of human beings' social system, what is the most suitable lifestyle that human beings should lead is the most appropriate and effective law.

1. Law of the jungle—it is not only an objective law, but also objective truth, that is, those who bow before it survive and those who resist perish.

2. Human beings need the permanently peaceful life.

How to lead a permanently peaceful life? The answer is a harmonious society keeps the permanent peace.

How to reach the permanent harmony? A true permanently harmonious society features the forced control and the relevant power serving harmony. Otherwise, the peaceful state may disappear immediately without the state of the long-term peace.

So how does the strong power stay for a long time? Only public ownership and its capital have the power to keep the permanently steady status.

Marx intended to use public ownership to keep the strong power, in turn, apply strong power to the construction of a harmonious society. However, Marx totally ignored the objective laws of the law of the jungle and human beings' nature featuring selfishness.

He aimlessly and optimistically painted a rosy picture of socialism, ignoring the basic conditions, that is, human beings' ugliness, selfishness, and greediness. The result is that almost all socialist countries have been ruined.

On the contrary, the capitalist system set up on the basis of human beings' selfishness and greediness seems rather successful. Tao Te Ching is the softest and the most feminine law, while the survival of the fittest is the most masculine law. Femininity is totally lower than the masculine.

Governing the state and being a man should be equally focused on. Centralised power of a country follows the laws of the king; policy of benevolence is the feminine way to control a state. Governing the state by masculine means is to discard the weak and the coward and to support the strongest figures.

The above two aspects are not contrary at all. Thus, I hold that the education of the law of the jungle should be reinforced as the harmonious society is being constructed.

Improve the education of the law of the jungle. People's resentment of the rich is the most ashamed rubbish in our country.

Masculinity and femininity can be compared to the bones and flesh of human body. Bones are too hard to be made bend, so it belongs to yang. Muscles are soft and elastic, so they are called yin. Bones and flesh compose the human body, enabling humans to rise on their feet and walk freely.

The law of the jungle presents the national spirits, called yang, and bones. Harmonious society shows the yin of the national spirits, that is, flesh.

In Western society, they believe in the law of the jungle and never think about harmony; they only have bones without flesh, so they are so strong and so aggressive.

Chinese traditional culture focuses on harmony and friendliness and says no to the law of the jungle, so each person is required to take care of himself or herself, hiding the creative and personality, which is called sticking to the rules. Chinese people only have flesh but have no bones. Once in a while, several proud heroes, standing out from the crowd, were born but ended up with miserable treatment, such as Yue Fei, Han Xin, Qu Yuan, Yang Hucheng, Lin Zexu, Peng Dehuan, and so on. Don't mention the old times, and such is the case in the modern times.

Thus, after investigating both Western culture and Chinese culture, the best social system, culture conceptions, and moral standards are shown below:

There is the law of the jungle in the harmonious society.

The perfect combination of yin and yang equals the system of flesh and bones.

Chinese socialism has developed to the present modern times when there is the best opportunity to realise the corresponding social culture, social system, governing thoughts, and moral standards.

1. The concept of harmonious society has been deeply rooted in the hearts of Chinese people as a cultural basis.

2. Chinese citizens generally recognise the Western culture and hold that the thought of money is supreme, and the law of the jungle has been widely accepted by the Western people as a preferred social basis.

3. Chinese should find out some proper words and accurate forms of expressions from the two sorts of concepts so that femininity and masculinity can be legalised, moralised, and habituated.

4. The integrated society of the law of the jungle and harmonious society is characterised by the essential and fundamental thought of the law of the jungle, which provides the entire society with great creative and intensive vigour, fully stimulates human beings' vitality and enterprise, and overcome the human beings' weakness, including ugliness, selfishness, degenerations, and laziness.

The negative effects and social conflicts resulting from the law of the jungle should be absorbed and assimilated by the concept of harmony to create a peaceful world. The public-owned national capital is helpful to accomplish the harmonious task. That is also the most significant of the state-owned capital.

Human beings' minds are always straightforward. For instance, people may take it for granted that the law of the jungle is reasonable and totally ignore the justice and harmony in society.

People argue that Taoism is the magic power to govern their country. By doing so, humanity may totally disappear or be discarded, and all people may be willing to be ordinary so as to keep a harmonious, friendly, but nonsense society.

Apart from the miserable wives, Chinese parents also frequently mention the word 'conscience'.

In the human rights–centralised Western countries, the relationship between parents and their children is friendship. Especially after their children are grown up, such relationship will become more obvious.

Parents show great respect towards their children's human rights and rights of property. In return, such children do for their parents.

Parents and their children are definitely independent from each other from the perspective of economy and character.

Parents are responsible for their own behaviour, and so are their children. Parents are never in charge of their children's behaviour, and neither are their children. If there are some feelings between parents and their children, they are the purest in the world involved within business meanings or disguised patterns.

On the contrary, Chinese people appear totally different. The relationship between parents and their children is the utter commercial relation.

Children are the commodities of their parents; the caring and love from parents to their children are the concrete goods, though there are no prices pronounced. Thus, parents need not pay tax.

Judging from the way to educate their children, Chinese parents often ask their children, 'Who is good to you, Dad or Mum? You see, Dad and Mum care so much for you, so you should know how to express your thanks to us one day!'

As for a son who treats his mother rather badly after being married to a lovely girl, the common remark from the Chinese audience is 'The conscienceless man, cruel as a wolf!'

There is a recognised commercial relation between Chinese parents and children. Parents give birth to their children and bring them up so that their children are able to look after them after many years, that is, raise children for themselves.

Therefore, in the rural area, Chinese parents hate their daughters so much, since most daughters will live in their husbands' household after their marriage and won't live with their own parents, while most sons will live with their own parents. A huge number of female babies have been aborted and abandoned because girls have no function of looking after the aged.

It is when the productivity was far behind in China that Lao Tzu put forward his systemic cultural thoughts, so his arguments were quite right in the past. At that time, people were rather poor and innocent and just walked out of the jungle, transforming into real human beings from the savages. Then each person was born militant and wild with the strong ambition of snatching the social resource. The masculine thought featured by the law of the jungle is considered as common sense, the basic culture, and the basic social environment in the ancient times.

The softest and the most feminine systemic culture of Lao Tzu quite fits the masculine and original social surroundings led by the law of the jungle, which also gave birth to the significance of ancient China's culture.

The principle of systemic culture is the principle of socialism that takes the strong social resources—army, country, land, and state-owned capital—as the solid foundations and then adjusts the social and international relationships as well as the social conflicts. The most effective role of systemic culture is to create a balanced society. The more intensive the social conflicts appear, the more effective the system's functions are. Those are a country's functions.

Because a large amount of rich national resources are employed as the adjustor for a society, every sort of social strength is just a weak individual that is too small to notice. Though social conflicts are so intensive, there is no strength that is strong enough to fight against a country.

However, why does a capitalist society speak highly of human rights, freedom, democracy, humanity, donation, and conscience? The reason is that there is no ability or institution in a capitalist society that can be used to solve the social conflicts in the lower layer. So some verbal forms of hypocrisy have to be employed to obtain spiritual victory.

But the national capital of socialist countries is mainly used to solve the social conflicts in the lower layer. Therefore, there is no need to worry about the intensification of social contradictions in a socialist country. There is also no form of social strength that can be against the state. Whether capitalists or the poor citizens are all considered as the chess pieces on the chessboard, the statesmen in a socialist country can apply the state-owned capital to control the entire society and serve the people. Thus, the statesmen in socialist countries are the happiest people on earth, the most rewarding people in the world, and the most different people broadening the most significant historical missions and the serious responsibilities. Socialist society is the most promising one, as an ideal society.

Politicians of capitalism are all wretched. They are all capitalists' puppets who have no thoughts of their own and are totally controlled by others.

While statesmen of socialism are true statesmen, they have the power to make full use of rich social resources to realise their political dreams. They can easily take the law of the jungle as their own cultural conception and moral regulations, enabling citizens to show off the best of their productivity and enthusiasm towards labour. The simple reason is social productive, the most effective and the most advanced, which can also prove that the social system of socialism is the most advanced, the path which the previous revolutionaries led us to believe was the only correct way, and the Communist Party is the most proper. Otherwise, how does the party take its power?

What's more, the social conflicts resulting from the law of the jungle can be settled easily by handling the state-owned capital without any concern. It can't be realised in the capitalistic society. It is the absolute advantage. It is also the primary benefit of socialism. It is the solution to the problem.

Femininity refers to obtaining man's purpose by wits and human beings' weakness. Masculinity means to achieve one's goal by treaty, force, power, and violence.

Femininity is equal to realising one's aims using human beings' weakness, which is seeking the short-term interests and ignoring the macro directions, great witness, and a whole new view of issues. Masculinity means the realisation of individuals' goals by making good use of cravenly clinging to life instead of braving death.

One centres personal interests, the other stresses on force. One uses tricks, the other applies actions.

Both femininity and masculinity have their own weakness. If they can be combined perfectly and applied flexibly, femininity and masculinity will make an invincible magic weapon.

But in the aspect of strategy, femininity should be taken as the starting point to avoid the unnecessary and huge scarification. In the aspect of tactics, masculinity should be employed to force the enemies to give in, conquering without a single fight. Force can be used to settle relevant issues, unless it's absolutely necessary.

Exogamy is a typical example of the application of femininity to reach universal harmony in the world. Getting married and giving birth to children is the most harmless and the most effective means of warfare.

After all, human beings are poor creatures. Except by means of war, there is no way to settle some significant problems, such as the American Civil War.

The Taiwan issue should be eventually settled by the conquering of troops from Mainland China. The Hong Kong problem should be thoroughly solved by replacing the jurisdiction of Hong Kong with police and judicial officers of Mainland China. Anything else is nonsense, a waste of time, and simply a stall.

The terrorism and the devils of Sunni and Wahhabi must be absolutely smeared, completely resolved by beating them into a mess. Anything else about religious freedom, human rights, slaughter, extinction, and humanity is nonsense that makes things become increasingly worse.

21. The essential difference between Chinese culture and Western culture

About 2007

Chinese culture is mostly represented by the ideology of Confucius and Mencius, while Western culture is mostly represented by the ideology of the Darwinist law of the jungle, democracy, freedom, and human rights.

However, the ideology of Confucius and Mencius and human rights are a manifestation of things. As we see cars running on the road, as well as bicycles, what's the difference between them? It is very superficial if it is only distinct between price, appearance, and function. Only if they look into the substance of things can people really make comment on it; otherwise, there will be no practical significance. The appearance of things is changing anytime, and the nature of things does not change. Cars are transport in which power is generated from the internal combustion engine, while bicycles are human-powered transport, which is the most essential difference between cars and bicycles.

There is also an essential difference between Chinese culture and Western culture, in which Chinese culture is a kind of culture that treats the whole country, region, family, and clan as a system to adjust the relationship between people.

The Western culture is a kind of culture that is individual-centred and puts personal interests and needs as well as individual rights and obligations as the research object and the central task to adjust the relationship between people.

Briefly, Chinese culture is a system culture and Western culture is an individual culture.

22. Chinese culture is a system culture

About 2007

I think the Western countries should have a better understanding about the concept of system than Chinese or the Oriental, even that there was no word like 'system' in ancient Chinese language. In ancient China, the nation, society, and individual harmony in a good system are called nature-human integration or harmony between yin and yang, without mentioning the concept of system while the actual meaning is the system.

The concept of system is not complex. As far as I know, system is an integration composed of many parts to complete a certain function and be able to assist and control each other. Bicycle is a system, car is a system, aircraft is a system, production line is a system, a computer is a system, and computer software is also a system.

But it is the excellent and advanced point of Chinese ancient civilisation to research the whole country, universe, and society as a system. Chinese ancient civilisation was ahead of other countries and civilisations by around a thousand years, which exactly relied on the system culture of Chinese tradition.

It leads the ancient Chinese far ahead of other countries, but because of its great success, Chinese people still follow this system culture and social institutions inherited from the ancient sages, while other countries are in the industrial revolution and changed from the natural economy to the market economy. The system culture promoted Chinese social civilisation. But later, because its users didn't adjust the system in time, the system that formed thousands of years ago had seriously hindered China's economic development, technological advances, and the development of productivity and eventually led to the eight-power Allied forces and the invasion of foreign powers.

It is not the fault of the system culture itself and system concept; instead, it is the users of the system, those in power that did not really comprehend the principles and concepts of the system. The system can be continuously adjusted and improved and with the ability to accomplish certain functions. The Chinese Confucius and Mencius system is to bring the Chinese society into a relatively stable and conservative position. However, with the development of productivity, the development of commodity economy, and the increasingly fierce international competition, the kind of conservative and stable system should be upgraded and the operation direction of the system should be adjusted to make the social system towards the development direction of promoting the development of productivity and fully adapted to the jungle of international competition, thus China can get the opportunity and social system to exceed the West.

69

Why is the traditional Chinese culture a system culture?

Traditional Chinese culture is Confucianism, Buddhism, and Taoism, i.e. Confucius and Mencius culture, Buddhism culture, Taoism culture, and the philosophy of yin and yang.

The system of Buddhism is not very obvious, while the Confucius and Mencius culture and Lao Tzu ethical culture as well as the philosophy of yin and yang are purely system cultural.

There are several features of a system:

1. The holistic view integrates the whole country and society as a whole to research and unify, dispatch and arrange for a variety of social resources.

2. The system can be regulated and given feedback. When there is a problem in system operation, the underlying system can give feedback information to the management centre and the system can be adjusted by the management centre.

3. There is a certain purpose of the system, which is like a boat always with a sailing direction. Where he wants the people on board go is very clear and not aimless.

4. There is a clear division of work for the system components.

5. The system requires each part in harmony and unity.

6. The system excludes the people who corrupt the stable social system.

The following are several characteristics of the society under the guidance of traditional Chinese culture, and these are the basic characteristics of the system.

1. The holistic view integrates the whole country and society as a whole to research and unify, dispatch and arrange for a variety of social resources.

All the lands in the world belong to the emperor, and all the people on the lands are the courtiers of the emperor. The Chinese ancient emperor has supreme authority and is second only to heaven. The Chinese ancient emperor can decide everything of the country which he rules. In the Confucius and Mencius culture, those who challenge the authority of the emperor are all considered to commit treason and heresy. It is precisely because the emperor has so much power that the emperor can handle the overall situation of all things domestic without any restrictions and constraints.

2. There is a clear division of work for the system components.

The system administrator is the emperor, who governs the people through courtiers.

In a family, the husband is the administrator and the wife is the one under administration. And in a family, the husband is the administrator and the child is the one under administration.

The emperor, husband, wife, and children have their own clear division of social work and social position through moral and legal force to strengthen the management.

3. The system requires each part in harmony and unity.

How to achieve harmony and unity in Chinese feudal society? Because of the despicable humanity, everyone has the trend to maximise the benefits while the feudal society arranged the code of conduct for everyone, which is called Taoism.

The emperor requires Taoism—kingcraft. An emperor without kingcraft is called tyrannical, and it's reasonable for his subordinate to eradicate or kill him and take his place.

The courtiers also have their courtier rules—loyalty to emperor and patriotism—that the courtiers have to die if the emperor commands. Therefore, loyalty is always the highest evaluation criteria for Chinese ancient courtiers.

The wife—Female virtues require women to chastity and virtuous. In ancient China, the demands for women to be obedient to the husband are very stringent, whoever they marry, and a husband can divorce his wife, but the wife only has to endure to the dissatisfaction of her husband.

Children—Filial piety is a very famous ethic in China and there are twenty-four filial models to regulate and discipline children's behaviour.

Brothers (fraternal duty)—In feudal society, the brothers are requested to be friendly and helpful to each other; the story of Kong Rong's 'Humility of a Pear' is a very famous education of fraternal duty in China.

In fact, the fundamental means to keep harmony in society in ancient Chinese culture is the inequality of the social status, and the one in a low status should be subject to the high-status managers. It can be said that everyone has a manager and a very clear codes of conduct and norms of behaviour for themselves, of which are enforced through legal and ethical to achieve the purpose of social harmony.

4. The system excludes the people who corrupt the stable social system.

The behaviour of those who do not obey filial piety and female virtues, and mislead and are insubordinate to His Majesty is considered to be a felony in the feudal society, so that the entire social systems and social power will eradicate and eliminate them regardless of the law or morality.

5. The system can be regulated and given feedback.

This is deeply rooted in the Chinese mind and that to go to the capital city to appeal to the emperor and stop the sedan chair of courtiers to accuse injustice are the most classic materials in traditional Chinese artworks. Thus Chinese people have the petition complex, which is an act that people have strong resentment against local officials and demand the system administrator to come forward for system adjustments. It is always a hot topic for Chinese people that grassroots people can win the case against the evil forces of people in high and powerful positions.

6. There is a certain purpose of the system.

The system is like a ship, and it always has the sailing directions. Actually it is obvious where the state system wants to bring the country to. The purpose of Chinese Confucius and Mencius system is to let the whole society in a state of rural life, which is smooth, quiet, and in an orderly way with a population increase. It is the situation described by Lao Tzu: 'To make the country smaller and the people scarce so that even though there are a variety of instruments, they do not use these; to make people attach importance to death, rather than to distant migration; although there are boats and vehicles, do not always take them; although there are weapons and equipment, no place to go embattle and war; to bring the people return to the ancient natural state of tying knots for recording. As a result, people can eat well, dress beautifully, live comfortably, and have happy lives. Between countries, there are only just a few kilometres so that people even can see and hear each other without intercommunication from birth to death.'

The philosophy of yin and yang, Confucius and Mencius doctrine, and moral philosophy actually come down in one continuous line, and their dominant ideas are exactly the same. In a manner of speaking, the philosophy of yin and yang as well as moral philosophy is a kind of idea, while the Confucius and Mencius ideas and doctrine can be treated as the specific application of this culture concept in the social system.

Lao Tzu's thought deems that the country should be governed by morality, and Confucius's thought is about the specific application of this idea.

The kingcraft, female virtues, filial piety, loyalty to emperor and patriotism, being faithful to the husband to the end, the twenty-four filial models, etc. are all Taoism summed up by Confucius and Mencius, and all these are identified with Chinese past dynasties' kings and used to govern the country, as well as the basic concept and basic national policy of governing the country.

In the philosophy of yin and yang, yang is equal to heaven, rigid, enterprising, attack, innovation, heat, light, conquer, man, and male, as well as the leftist and the government. Yin is equal to earth, flexible, conservative, defence, old-fashioned, cold, dark, obedience, woman, and female, as well as the rightist and the people.

It strengthens that yin should submit to yang in the specific application of Confucius culture in the social system.

Emperor equals yang, courtier equals yin, and courtier absolutely submits to emperor.

Husband equals yang, wife equals yin, and wife absolutely submits to husband.

Father equals yang, son equals yin, and son absolutely submits to father.

The philosophy of yin and yang divides all things between heaven and earth into two kinds of one-to-one corresponding things: yin and yang according to their properties. And in these things, there is a primary and secondary as well as the opposite and complementary relationship. The philosophy deems that everything will be okay if it strengthens and clears this kind of relationship; on the contrary, the mess that reverses yin and yang will appear if it breaks this kind of relationship.

Confucius used this concept in society and cleared and strengthened the relationship between humans to yin and yang and subordinate relationship. He established the orbit and code of conduct for each one, which was not allowed to be damaged.

The basic theory of traditional Chinese medicine is the Inner Classic of the Yellow Emperor, which is not only an ancient book, but also a book of systems theory. The Inner Classic is a theory that treats the human body as a system to study, and many systems of it can't be fully explained by present technology on anatomy, while they have been proved to be very effective by practice.

So the traditional Chinese medicine culture is also the system culture. In a word, traditional Chinese culture is the system culture.

23. Western culture is the individual culture

About 2007

The most representative of modern Western culture are the United States Declaration of Independence, Universal Declaration of Human Rights, and Amendments to the United States Constitution.

Law is the most basic tool to adjust the relationship between humans, and it's also the most basic rules of the game; it decides the nature of things.

Viewed from the name, the Universal Declaration of Human Rights is the declaration of individual rights. All of its content is a kind of social norm formulated around the power owned by individuals in society.

Only one item in the Universal Declaration of Human Rights refers to the relations and obligations between humans, while this obligation is also formulated to ensure the rights of others not infracted by the actions of the parties.

Therefore, the Universal Declaration of Human Rights is a code of conduct, and all the contents are formulated with the starting point of personal interests.

The United States Declaration of Independence is even more like this—the first sentence of the opening is the emphasis on individual rights: 'All men are created equal; the creator gives them some unalienable rights that include right of life, right of liberty and right of pursuit of happiness.'

All men are created equally; it is a right concept from the microscopic view of an individual. It represents an equal relationship between humans from the spiritual level, while Western civilisation can only guarantee the equality from the spiritual level, and the equal relationship between humans from the material level is impossible. Its meaning is only used to limit the relationship between humans, while it doesn't mention the relationship between humans and society and humans and nature at all.

'The creator gives them some unalienable rights that include right of life, right of liberty, and right of pursuit of happiness.' The emphasis here is on three objects: 'right of liberty' and 'right of pursuit of happiness', while 'right of pursuit of happiness' is actually adjectival and used to describe survival and freedom. In fact, survival and freedom of each person aims to pursue happiness naturally without emphasis. Only when he is a masochist can he see another kind of happiness, because he feels that masochism is also a kind of happiness too, and the others have nothing to do with this,

74

because happiness or unhappiness is a thing only known by the litigant himself instead of charging by others.

Rights of life and liberty are the objects emphasised again and again by the Declaration of Independence and Western civilisation, and they are proud of them. These two rights, right of life and right of liberty, are both totally individual rights and don't mention others at all. It refers to a person having the right to survival according to his own way of life and living according to his own will, and it doesn't mention the relationship between individual and society as well as individual and nature at all.

Amendments to the United States Constitution—except for election and tax, the content is all about the clauses that protect individual rights and doesn't mention public power and social constraints on individuals at all. 1. Guarantee freedom of speech to express personal political views and right appeals.

2. Individuals have the right to carry guns to protect individual property and rights.

3. Home residency is the most proud of rights for Western countries: Wind can enter, rain can enter, but thousands upon thousands of horses and soldiers of the king can't enter.

4. Right of personal property and residence safety, right of suspect, etc.

Therefore, the main purpose of laws of Western countries is to conduct legal protection around the individual private rights. Morality can be said to be the basis and extension of the law; morality is able to rise to the law under a certain condition, and it's a code of conduct of people that spreads around the law, so social rules of the Westerners, including law and morality, all serve for personal interests.

Culture is the sum-up of the performance of law, morality, and ideologies in daily life and literary works. Therefore, the Western culture is a personal culture that only emphasises the individual rights while ignoring and weakening the universal connection and interrelationship between humans, humans and society, and humans and nature.

24. Why must individualistic culture go with system culture?

About 2007

Chinese traditional culture is system-based, while Western culture is individualism-based. The success of Chinese feudal society lies in the system-based culture, while the prosperity of the Western world today depends on its individualism-based culture. Present socialist system in China is the combination of system-based culture and vague individualism-based culture.

It was the outbreak of weaknesses of system-based culture when China was attacked by the eight-power Allied forces, so the world needs everlasting peace and system-based culture to unite the universe, eliminate differences among people, as well as maintain equality.

However, the greatest drawback of system-based culture is the contentedness with temporary ease and comfort. It is actually a decadent idea like Lao Tzu's recovery to one's original simplicity, making no attempt to make progress as well as destruction of productivity.

It is competition that makes human society progress, and the horror and threat of wars that forces men to advance. Therefore, if human society is unified, there would be no war or threat. As a result, men will have no opponent and become content with village life, eating their head off, seeking temporary peace, and unproductive as advocated by Lao Tzu. In this regard, competition among countries is meaningful and should not be eliminated or abolished.

With the existence of differences among countries, people feel angry towards backward countries that are regarded as a dog in the manger. It is the anger from the strong to the weak. The earth belongs to earthmen, not the locals. If the locals hinder the earth from development, backward nations will be attacked by civilisation.

That is the demand of civilisation for land and living space as the demand of rutting beast for a mate. As a matter of fact, men are animals, but men's demands can be packaged by consciousness and covered and ornamented before being shown to the public.

However, men are animals in essence, and they strive for objectives simply out of animal instinct. People of backward civilisation are rutting beasts, and land resources are their mates. They start war to seize resources. It is reasonable to launch a war out of anger. It is the law of nature to attack benighted and backward countries or dogs in the manger, which is just and a necessary path for human society development.

Likewise, China was attacked by the eight-power Allied forces because of its backwardness, which was an unjust shame and invasion for the Chinese. From the perspective of the development of human history, however, it was just.

As people say, every progress of human history must be made on their own. God won't help you. All progress of human society must be treated with immeasurable blood and life.

Some obvious truth must be understood by means of bayonet and head. As an ancient Chinese saying says, refuse to be convinced until faced with grim reality. It is exactly correct.

Men always think they are right and they never make mistakes. Their ancestors have lived like this, and it must be correct if they live life this way, for which they even would like to pay their life. Men may not be aware that this seemingly correct conduct has hindered the development of others and stood in the way and been a stumbling block to others without their knowing. The earth belongs to all earthmen just as the American continent does not belong to the Indians. By far, people have accepted this fact. Based on this logic, if one country someday can defeat the Americans as the Americans defeated and drove the Indians like herds, can we say the American continent no longer belongs to the Americans but another nation? As a Chinese saying says, history does take interesting turns.

Strong enough as it had been to rule the world, China was still invaded by the eight-power Allied forces. If it had happened to China, it would happen to any nation.

Ancient Chinese remarked that things are constantly changing and no dynasty is immortal. No nation can be always strong, so temporary strength is regarded as civilisation and truth. Nations of temporary strength all feel good about themselves with national vanity, believing they are the boss.

The Chinese had long had such feeling, but most of us suffer from inadequate knowledge on history or refuse subconsciously to accept the fact that they had been the boss before.

For this reason, such a feeling is nothing fresh or novel for the Chinese. There is nothing to be proud of. Temporary superiority will, like morning dew, vanish as the sun rises.

Therefore, it is of no significance for men in this competitive game. Now we come around back to the start, it's the supreme truth to recover one's original simplicity. For men, especially ordinary people and common people, what do they want? It is physical things like life, money, wife, children, house, and car. As for all kinds of ideas, doctrines, power, fame, status, nationality, liberty, fraternity, and equality are simply means with which we realise our objectives.

It is the objective rather than means that separates winners from losers, combined with GDP, people's living standard, money, and power. Such superiority is temporary and provisional that it can last for decades or a much shorter period of time.

As a matter of fact, human society is temporarily kept from large-scale war with the presence of balance of terror. No one can be sure how long such balance will remain. As long as there are differences among countries and estrangement among people, it is just a matter of time as to invade and be invaded, rule and be ruled, as well as destroy and be destroyed because the root of conflicts or the devil is deeply rooted in our mind.

This is the death instinct in human consciousness, discovered by Freud. If such instinct is released, it is to kill. We can often see the news of serial killing. Killers kill people who have no interesting relationship with them or for reasons that are inexplicable and eccentric to us. These people are usually quite normal and even have seemingly perfect families.

I think these people can be generally divided into two categories. One is born with a defect that makes his subconscious primitive impulse different from normal people. The other kind may have suffered from stimulus before and such stimulus is kept in his subconscious and completely changes his impulses. These desires are expressed differently from those of normal people in structure.

Such impulse and desire can be found in everyone. They are not absent in normal people, but normal people can have them controlled within a certain range while there are people who can't control such impulse and desire. In a sense, this kind of hatred and death instinct to eliminate people is out of men's self-protection.

In most cases when people think someone or some people have caused them serious damage, people typically have two reflections in view of the condition of the other side. When the opponent is very strong and we feel powerless to or cannot resist, we tend to fear, panic, and run away. The most common comment is becoming terror-stricken at the news or turning pale at the mention of a tiger. Who had no fear faced with SARS and bird flu? Even the medical staff fell short, not to mention our ordinary people who are unable to resist. That is why all were scared and felt threatened.

78

When we suffer from serious damage caused by things weaker than us or they threaten our survival, we will generate the death instinct to destroy them. Of course, such weakness is not absolute but relative and conditional, such as weakness at that time. When we find help to make us strong, we will also generate the death instinct to eliminate the other side. This is what is usually seen as revenge or vengeance.

Revenge is a common theme in movies and novels as well as an eternal theme for mankind. It often happens in our daily life. Hatred can be big or small. It can be as small as bursting people's bicycle tyres secretly or stealing a chicken and as big as world war, genocide, and terrorist attack. They have no difference in essence in view of psychoanalysis, a release of human death instinct.

War is the abreaction and manifestation of human death instinct in the form of military combat for victory or loss. Genocide is the abreaction and manifestation of human death instinct in the form of troops massacring civilians. Terrorist attack is the abreaction and manifestation of human death instinct in the form of a few armed attacks on civilians. Despite the different forms, they are abreaction of death instinct in essence.

There is, of course, a difference between chicken stealing or bursting a bicycle tyre and war, genocide, or terrorist attack. People stealing chickens and bursting bicycle tyres only have to convince themselves, while terrorist attacks require planners to arouse the death instinct of more people. War and genocide require planners to arouse the death instinct of the vast majority of people of a country before they can use the state machinery to slaughter.

People hate those who steal chickens, burst bicycle tyres, engage in terrorist attacks, genocide, and war. But I have to remind people that these people are just like you and me. They are not different from us in essence. The only difference is that their death instinct is aroused by some people or some things that have controlled their will and action. Objectively speaking, these people have caused injury and harm to us, the world, and the social environment and natural environment indispensable to us. We have full reasons to hate them.

In other words, there will be a lot of people against me. You may say you have high moralities and will not steal chickens or burst tyres, not to mention engage in terrorist attacks or genocide.

There is a Buddhist tenet, as a man sows, so let him reap. I don't believe in retribution, but I believe that everything in the world exists for a reason and there are causes and effects. People's death instinct cannot be aroused or released for no reason. As an old saying in China says, the miserable man must have his defect that causes the misery.

I don't know if those who have been revenged for death instinct ever thought of why people's death instinct targets you instead of others. Is this accidental or certain?

Stolen chickens may be carried off by animals and a burst bicycle tyre may run on a nail, which can belong to accidents. War and genocide, however, are organised in a planned way. They can never be an accident.

For this reason, the promotion of system-based culture, establishment of system, and suppression of individualism can make a country strong, stable, orderly, harmonious, and unified. But too much stability will lead to the loss of vigour and momentum to strive forward. As a result, all people will recover one's original simplicity.

Advocating individualism-based culture can spur the creativity and vitality of all social members, but it will also lead to social disorder and disharmony in the meanwhile.

It challenges us on how to make a combination and flexible use of the two. To put it simply, the country carries out state capitalism in some realms while encouraging individual capitalism in other fields. State capitalism is conducted in the grand framework while individual capitalism is advocated in micro areas. State capitalism can be found in passive work and individual capitalism in active work. State capitalism is applied to fields that can make money while individual capitalism is applied to areas that do not make money.

Why?

Because the society needs harmony, maximum-range adjustment of the interest, political and economic relationship among people is required. Such adjustment requires power and capital guarantee. Because of natural selfishness and hopelessness of human nature, no one is willing to give up their vested interests without power suppression and benefit induction. No one is willing to help others selflessly. Individualism-based culture and individualism cannot overcome this. Individuals with vested interests in individualism-based culture can always distort justice with money.

Small government and big capitalists that are advocated by some economists can perfectly illustrate this point. The government requires money in all businesses, while small governments have no resources in their hands at all. They have to watch big capitalists look in everything and wait for their discussions. How could you make me believe the government would make big capitalists sacrifice their own interests for the purpose of justice and fairness? Can the government adjust the interests of big capitalists whenever they want? With no power and capital guarantee, how can you say you can safeguard the rights and interests of the vulnerable groups, justice, and fairness?

In a society of state capitalism, the state machine is not fed by individual support nor threatened by any individual threat. In addition, it can mobilise a large amount of state-owned capital to do anything justified to maintain fairness and justice.

When maintaining state grand capital framework and structure, we can maximise the implementation of individualism-based culture, protect individual interests, and inspire individuals to active creativity. This is the right way.

The combination of individual culture and collective culture constitutes the current Chinese pattern.

Public ownership shall be developed in the resource-based field and the field dominant with state-owned capital, providing maximum financial support for the state with the public capital and achieving effective and scientific governance of state and maximum fair and justice.

The private ownership and individual culture shall be widely applied in the non-resource-based field and the field not appropriate for the state-owned capital.

Either the public ownership or the private ownership, and either the individual culture or the collective culture is used to serve and maximise the interests of the people.

Regime and the state machine can really serve the interests of the people, which is the manifestation of the ancient Chinese saying 'harmony between heaven and people' and social harmony.

25. Chinese feudal system culture and state capitalism system culture

About 2007

I. Feudal System Culture

To my way of thinking, in order to ensure that a system normally works,

1. each component should function in accordance with certain requirements; and

2. all components must be coordinated and unified to play a role.

I think the former manifests itself in society in the form of obligations and functions. Take machines for example. Gears are obliged to turn for the benefit of the entire system; so does the screw used to fasten machine units together. There are even more obligations when it comes to human beings. All of us have to work to increase social wealth; men are duty-bound to raise a family as breadwinners, while women should bear children to carry on the family line. These are the basic obligations of men and women in a feudal society.

The latter, as for me, represents power. Gears in a machine are subject to the whole system. As required, they must stick to their specific positions and stay put, or else, they cannot rotate. The screw should hold the original position and cannot loosen; otherwise, it would fail in clamping units. In the Confucian feudal society, fathers have the power to govern their children, which is called filial piety. Husbands have authority over wives, and it is regarded as a virtue. As for emperors, they have much more power. The system established in the feudal society could only be maintained and enforced by political power.

Under the natural economy of the feudal dynastic system in which men did farm work and women engaged in spinning and weaving, the above system, beyond doubt, once yielded huge social benefits and energy. As a result, a far more advanced civilisation was created in ancient China than that of the rest of the world.

Nonetheless, after lasting for over two thousand years, this system obviously is not compatible with emerging science and technology. In other words, new technology generates new hardware, which cannot be activated by the old system. Then this system now becomes an obstacle.

Actually, the first sentence in Tao Te Ching has made it pretty clear: 'Tao that can be told is not universal and eternal Tao.' Those specific approaches that can be expressed in words need constant update along with the development of productivity and the emergence of new things. This is how Tao works. No improvement, no Tao.

The Confucius and Mencius doctrines and all maxims in Tao Te Ching may be adapted, changed, or even abandoned in accordance with specific conditions. However, the thinking method that people use to pursue the correct path has gone through a few changes in all ages.

But it is just a way of thinking to solve problems and an approach to make policies, rather than a specific policy and method. Methods and strategies that can be described in words are not eternal Tao. Tao means that things can change and need to change as the condition varies.

Some contents of Lao Tzu's ideas, Confucian thoughts, and their specific plans are indeed decadent, for instance, being content with the status quo. But in another sense, these thoughts represent the pursuit of ordinary people. As a matter of fact, they usually lack ambitions and crave comfort and pleasure. It is correct to consider it as the ordinary people's wishes, but totally absurd as a strategy of running a state by the statesman.

After the application of two thousand years, the Confucius-Mencius system needs to be improved to a large extent. It is never behind the times to manage a country systematically, effectively as a whole, and to mobilise all kinds of social resources properly and reasonably so that the society can advance normally, highly efficiently, quickly, and harmoniously. Such basic theories are the changeless, eternal Tao.

II. State Capitalism and System Culture

What kind of new social management system is needed in the current social institution? It depends on the development situation of our society nowadays as well as the principal contradictions thereof.

What are the social conditions at present?

1. Selfish human nature

Every man looks out for number one, and God serves us all. No matter in society or in daily life, everyone engages in something to satisfy his/her own desires or to have his/her demands met. This is the truth. Maslow outlines a pyramid that shows personal hierarchy of needs according to human desires. His theory includes the basic needs for survival and safety, as well as a higher level of self-actualisation. However, each type of desire aims to meet one's own needs; few people volunteer to do something only out of altruism.

2. Not all men are created equal in society. Some children are born rich, others impoverished. Some are intelligent, others slow-witted. Some live in villages, others in cities; some live in socialist countries, others in capitalist states. Some are boys, others are girls.

We all have different backgrounds and our own desires and needs. The idea 'all men are equal' is no longer fresh news. Though this slogan has been preached since ancient times, in real life, people are unequal.

People share different understandings of equality. A variety of people agitate for such catchwords as equality at all times and in all countries. There is gender equality, equality of opportunity, equality between rich and poor, etc. Equality is a dream of mankind since ancient times. People always pursue it but never have the dream come true.

In my opinion, gender equality, equality of opportunity, rich-and-poor equality are all lies and appearances; that is to say, the seeming equality is in fact unequal.

In my view, true equality comes from the essential and basic equality, namely, the equality of capital. Equality of capital is the most substantive equality and the most equal equality. Without it, other types of equality are false and deceptive.

What is capital? People in the capitalist countries have the clearest and the most thorough understanding about it. In recent years, China has also gradually learned about the concept of capital. But there are a large number of people, including Chinese and foreigners of the capitalist countries, who do not really understand what capital is. Some even have misinterpretation or misunderstanding of capital.

Capital is neither bloody as many people think nor the enemy of the working people. It is not sacred and omnipotent in some people's eyes. Capital does have magical powers, but it is a governable tool. Capital is profit-driven enough to serve whoever controls it. It does not make sense to judge it in terms of goodness and badness or beauty and ugliness. Flexible use of it can bring benefit to the common people; on the contrary, people shall be plunged into an abyss of misery if capital is out of control.

As far as I can see, capital is an infinite thing of beauty that coexists with the sun and the moon. It conforms to the philosophy of yin and yang, moves in circles in company with the universe, and never ends.

Why do some people hate capital and capitalists to such an extent that they prefer to get rid of it? It is because capital is not under their thumb, but in the hands of capitalists. Capital services the capitalist instead of them. Capital is reduced to a powerful tool and an accomplice used by capitalists against them. Hence, they hate capital and capitalists.

Marx's communist society requires people to drum up political power. It is a correct and advanced idea. But confined to the social environment at that time, many specific Marxist approaches need improvement. A lot of theories call for constant development and modification.

According to my perception of Marxism and based on the practice in China for so many years, communism should be understood as a doctrine of joint property, rather than a creed of shared labour. The character 'chan' in the Chinese counterpart of communism should be defined as property or capital instead of work or production. Therefore, it is more precise to call communism co-capitalism or state capitalism.

Why do we understand it in this way? What are the difference between co-production and common property? Co-production means that all people work together as manpower.

Common property represents a system in which people are all capitalists and work together, though the results may vary with each individual. It is because the fact that workers labour together does not necessarily lead to common prosperity, but common poverty in most cases. China's practice proves it to be the truth. Working together is equal to the communal pot and common poverty.

Joint property is in total contrast to co-production, because it is a continuous reproduction process in an endless succession, so we are both workers and capitalists. We work for ourselves and also share out bonus on our own. Property moves in a never-ending cycle. With compound interest, money begets money, and there is more and more wealth. People shall live better lives just as what we wish for.

State capitalism establishes a system of national governance with the basis of state capital. It is also a huge system taking the state as a unit. It takes the power and economy as the main pillar and the source of power.

The harmonious society is achieved through the adjustment of relationships between man and man, between man and society, as well as between man and nature so that human beings can fully obtain material and spiritual satisfaction.

Apart from meeting their own material needs, individuals need to improve their mental level and spiritual realm in order to reach the requirements of God. Humans shall abandon the devil, cult, crime, hatred, ignorance, barbarism, evil, and dirtiness. Otherwise they will fail to reach the requirements of God, resulting in self-destruction or destruction by God for no value of existence.

26. Chinese like spheres and Westerners like cubes

About 2007

Chinese are under a situation: only when the situation changes do they adjust themselves to a favourable direction. However, facing the same situation, foreigners are blockheaded and content to remain where they are. Why?

China has a long history. All historical things educate modern people to win by wits and strategies, for example, there are many strategies in 'Thirty-Six Stratagems', various wars, novels, biographies, and many Chinese legends, and every war uses strategies.

All these tell Chinese that it is not wrong to get something by strategies. In contrast, if one person could get something but not give a try or other people could do but he can't, he will fall behind. Chinese culture and traditional ideology is the culture that wins from existing regulations and restrictions.

What are regulations and restrictions? It is the culture that the emperor is the emperor, the minister is the minister, the father is the father, and the son is the son, the husband is the husband, and the wife is the wife. Chinese not only maintain the system, but also reach their purpose; this exactly is Chinese's intelligence or wisdom.

Under this kind of systematic culture, system is above rules; that is to say, power is above law. Building your own system means you can defy rules or make rules serve you.

Under this kind of systematic culture, China unconsciously builds its own connection network and system. And it continuously makes efforts to maintain this kind of system for the purpose of excluding other people, possessing privilege, and building a sense of security.

Actually, emperor and minister, father and son, husband and wife is a basic system framework built for this nation by Confucius, and as national policy, ethics, and laws, it could not be amended. Moreover, power and interests form and dominate the system. Power could change the distribution of power and interest in the system; this is a function of this system, which has existed from the feudal society.

The originators of ancient Chinese culture, that is, Tao Te Ching and Book of Changes, are about philosophy of change. This is a gift God gave to the ancient Chinese. Foreigners' IQ probably is lower so that they could not accept profound culture, only accept the simple one.

There is fundamentalism in Islam religion and Christianity. The fundamentalism of Islam religion is Wahhabi, which is the ideology of IS and terrorism.

When facing a new situation and environment, they could not change themselves to adapt to the new environment. Contrarily, they insist on ancient rules and deal with things according to thousands of years' pedagogy. This is fatuity, also an evil, and it is necessary to amend and renew the system of culture and ideology.

27. On American culture of individualism embodied in American movies

About 2007

Movies are the primary representation modes of contemporary culture; despite the fact that the channels of cultural transmission and modes of cultural representation become increasingly diversified, movies still bear the most significant influence on the transmission of masscult.

Movies often tell a complete story within one or two hours and enable people to appreciate the story within the shortest possible time and in the most relaxing ways, and different people can get exactly what they want from the same movie. That's the so-called 'there are a thousand Hamlets in a thousand people's eyes'.

People with poor intelligence can hardly gain a thorough understanding of the connotation deeply embedded in the movies, but they are probably moved by the fascinating settings and plots.

From the perspective of psychoanalysis, people's experiences of certain things are bound to leave their traces in and have some effects on the subconscious and ultimately change people's view towards certain things. People cannot remember every single experience since they have experienced too much ever since they were born. But every single experience that they remember definitely has influence on them. The overall combinations of the influence of all experiences on people are what constitute people's subconscious, such as people's true views on these matters.

Some experiences have great influence on people, while others just happened and faded away. Experiences do not have to be directly experienced. All kinds of experiences can have certain influence on people's subconscious. It is just a matter of degree.

Experience gained from books and newspapers as well as movies belongs to experience, and doing something on your own is also a kind of experience. So armchair strategists are as confident as a much-experienced veteran in terms of battles, since their subconscious tells them that they are experts on such matters. In fact, however, people's awareness always stands at a distance from the truth, and some are in complete opposition.

It is just like Marx regarding himself as an expert in capitalism, yet his knowledge on capital was nothing, as correct as an old waste collector. He should not have talked about exploitation, let alone exploitation theory.

Let's get down to business. A good movie contains fascinating settings and profound connotation, both of which can have certain influence on the subconscious of the public.

Indeed, I have been thrilled by American blockbusters many times. But the more I see, the stronger the feeling of their absurdness and superficiality becomes. They are simply nonsense.

The eternal theme of American movies is an immortal hero who saves the whole world. What is it that has been called individual saving the whole world? This individual could be an unknown ordinary person, a taxi driver, a baked roll maker, a retired veteran, a pilot, or an actor. An accidental experience made him the only one who could save the whole world. Then he, after suffering from numerous hardships and adversaries, shouldered his unshakable responsibility, miraculously defeated the conspirators and all evil forces, and successfully saved all human beings, at least saved a country, earth-shaking things like that.

What's an immortal hero? That is, this hero can never be killed. And he could always come with superpower especially in the moment of emergencies. For example, a baked roll maker could dismantle bombs, fly an airplane, and break a code or things like that. Finally, he won the beauty and enjoyed the happy ending. That's the end!

This is what is typically referred to as individual heroism or liberalism. American people pin all their hopes on an individual hero. When they are faced with certain crisis and their lives are at stake, whoever can save them becomes their individual hero.

Therefore, it is well justified to say that Western culture is completely individual culture. Americans hate organisation and system, and they are hostile to any kind of bond and division.

The essence of system culture is the dependency on organisation, system, division, connections, and cooperation. The petition culture in China is a typical example of system culture.

People from the underclass suffer from uncomprehending wrongs and turn to the organisation, system, connections, and power to uphold justice. It seems that the petition culture in China is in an incomparable position in relation to the individual hero in America, and the differences strike like one in heaven and the other in hell, one being a doormat, the other, saviour— one a mouse, the other a lion.

However, from another point of view, two fists can hardly defeat four hands

90

and even a hero has to take the underdog status when his rivals are in large numbers. A ferocious lion is not necessarily a winner, faced with packs of wolves.

Organisation and system finally defeat individuals. This is common sense and is also the truth.

With system culture put into better use, China can still enjoy a prosperous future. An inappropriate treatment with this kind of culture would get Chinese people nowhere. The key is how to make use of the system appropriately.

28. The reason why communism could be successful in China is Chinese traditional culture's cohesiveness with communism

About 2007

Communism suffers defeat all over the world, but in China it could last till now, which is not coincidence but due to the cohesiveness between Chinese traditional culture and communism. Both of them are the systematic culture with global outlook, while the Western culture totally belongs to individual culture.

What is systematic culture? It refers to the culture with global outlook to make the country and world as a whole to research and modify. The Chinese traditional culture is to take the responsibility of the whole world, which is cohesive with communism.

Nowadays, when we mention these words, it seems far from us. But in the bottom of our hearts, the emotion is buried, which is the culture in our lives.

Currently, almost all the people, no matter illiterate or those with doctoral degree, no matter the vendor or the high official, are always busy every day. All the people are pursuing profit. This is the nature of human beings.

We always hold the view that the world is vast and the world is strong, but for us, the power of individual is rather small, which is like sand in the Yellow River. We could do nothing. If the stupid think like that, there is nothing wrong; but if the talented people are also with the same idea, it would be the tragedy of the society.

In our life, we always meet many unreasonable and unpleasant issues; generally, we always try our best to change it within our ability to make it go with our mind, while we always try to avoid those we couldn't touch, unless under force. We have no choice, thus we will search for the solution to change it, for example, to appeal to the higher authorities for help or make a lawsuit.

Actually, all the things involved with people all over the world could be changed only with the proper method, which is Taoism.

As there is always a balance in the bottom of everyone's heart, so everyone knows which is favourable and which is unfavourable. No one is fooled, and the lie could cheat others for a short period but not for a long time.

So those could really benefit the people will finally be accepted by people. And lies and fatuity will finally be abandoned.

The world with lies and fatuousness will bring pain and trouble for us. Those with high IQ will always find solutions if they want to change the lies and fatuousness. No matter how strong the lies and fatuousness are, justice will always defeat evil. And wisdom will always defeat fatuousness and lies. The key is not to change the world, but whether if they want to change the world.

In Buddhism, there is a saying 'express one's desire or hope'. But the desire or hope could not be expressed by all people. Those with common wisdom had better with the heart to earn money. It is useless for them to express the desire or hope. All they can do is change themselves, let alone change others.

Premier Wen Jiabao said in China it is not the lack of one who looks up to the sky, which refers to taking the responsibility for the world. In China, we don't lack it. Those with high IQ should express their heart, which is the heart to change the world, also referring to looking up to the sky.

Chinese classic culture, moral culture, and the Confucian culture are all with the faith of looking up at the sky. The only difference is that some is deep and some is shallow. Self-cultivation, regulating the family, country, and world is the faith of Confucius, but it is the faith that could be reached by the ordinary people.

The moral culture of Lao Tzu is the looking up at the sky of a gentleman, which is also the faith of high IQ.

No matter which kind of looking up to the sky, they refer to the overall view and systematic view of country and world, which is to change all the unreasonable elements of the world, to eliminate the evil and fatuous from the source. Make the society, country, and world operate in order and sound development. The ancient people could make the wild boar into dishes which are indispensable in daily life nowadays. So what could not be changed in daily life? The only problem is whether you want to do it or not, whether you dare to do it or not, and how you do it, but not whether it can be done or not.

I don't encourage those with ordinary IQ to regulate the world. More often, they have failed before they begin. I admire the spirit of those people but don't agree with their behaviour. People with ordinary IQ will always review questions with a one-sided view. Letting them regulate the world will only bring problems and with no good result. No matter if they are right droppings or left droppings, they are only droppings.

Communism is a systematic theory. The whole country is a whole part to modify, regulate, feedback, and control; all those are systematic ideas.

Communism truly changes the country into a machine, and everyone is a part of the machine. Just like the relations of emperor and officials, fathers and sons. But they are with different types.

How does the national machine work? How to modify it to benefit the largest profit of the people, country, and nations is the question those who look up to the sky should consider and research. And it is also related to the profits of each of us.

We are living in this environment like the fishes in the lake. The quality of lake water is like the living environment of us. And the political and economic relationships are our living environment. If those relationships have severe contradiction, like the fish living in the water which is severely polluted, even if they are not dead, they could not live for long, which is intolerant that those with low IQ will suffer the largest damage.

How to modify the political and economic relationships of the country is the question researched by those who look up to the sky. Moral philosophy and Confucius' ideas are the unique culture of China, which is the typical integral and systematic social management theory. It is the totally the same as the communist ideas. That's why communism could be developed in China but suffer defeat in other places.

Ancient China was famous for its systematic culture. And in the future, it could also lead the world with the systematic culture. The key is how to modify the system and how to realise the largest profit of the nations and country.

1. The kingdom is owned by the emperor in Chinese feudal system, as is indicated in the saying 'all the lands under heaven belong to the emperor with all the people on the land being his servants'. The emperor is also known as son of God, representing God and empowered by God with the divine right. So the emperor rules the country on behalf of God. The system is public ownership in this sense, except that the interest distribution mode is different.

2. The feudal emperor has the kingly way, taking the world as his responsibility and considering the whole world as a system for unified coordination and management. Communism shall take advantage of public ownership, managing the world in a coordinated and consolidated way.

3. A lot of cultural ideas are interlinked because of similarity in material and management system. People can adapt to the new social change just with a little improvement, naturally accepting communism and the Communist Party.

94

29. Contradictions in human society are caused by people's different perspectives in viewing things

About 2007

Certainly, this viewpoint is not a sermon, but instead, it is the supreme wisdom and perfect enlightenment as it is mentioned in Buddhist sutras. It refers to the most objective, essential, and accurate understanding of things. He will not blindly worship something because of a sage's words, and he will also not abandon his understanding of the truth of things because it is not accepted by the common people. The reason is that there is only one truth, and different conclusions can be drawn from different perspectives towards the same thing, just as blind men and an elephant in an ancient fable. In fact, the reason why we have different opinions towards the same thing is that we are in different positions and points of view. The ordinary people can only look on things with their own angles and positions, which is all they can do. They are not capable of seeing things from different perspectives. People with more wisdom and intelligence are more likely to see things from diverse perspectives. Seeing things from different perspectives means looking on the same issue by assuming oneself is someone else in a different position and environment in a different time, as conclusions on the same thing may be completely different in different conditions.

As for a leader and a powerful man, he who can understand more is likely to be able to make use of the power of more people so as to reach his purpose and avoid the damages and obstacles from others. This is a basic condition for success. This measures the cognitive value of the world merely from the perspective of whether an individual is successful or not.

My purpose of studying the philosophy of life is not just limited to the individual success, because an individual's success is not just the success in career. The ability of making more money can be called a success, but it is only a small one. A person also needs the comprehensive success and the world's success.

In my opinion, an individual's comprehensive success not just refers to the achievements in one's career, and an individual also needs a comprehensive satisfaction healthy body, happy family, good living environment, and unthreatened security. The comprehensive development and satisfaction is the individual's real comprehensive success. The world's success means different countries and districts of the world live in peace with each other and respectively achieve their own development and satisfaction.

Maybe many people will doubt it and refute me, and they may think this is only a fantasy or illusion. But actually I think this is not as far as what people have imagined. Our present life is full of sufferings, pressures, competitions, slaughters, and various kinds of contradictions everywhere, which is true indeed. However, according to my understanding of the society and the world, sufferings and contradictions in human society are all caused by our incapability of comprehensively and objectively understanding the society and the world. Different countries, nations, districts, and individuals have their own views of the world, and a lot of these views are contradictory and conflicting with each other.

Actually, we may have different colours, languages, and financial situations from different districts, but we are basically the same when we initially come to the world. We have basically the same animal instinct. We have the same emotions, pleasures, and the same instinctive impulse. Regardless of the white race, the yellow race, or the black race, when we accept the same environment and live under the same conditions, our basic viewpoints are basically the same.

To my point of view, the same objective thing in the world has only one truth, though different conclusions may be drawn from different perspectives. But what I want to say is what the truth of a thing is, the sum of different conclusions drawn from different perspectives. This is the real truth of things. Just like CT in medical science, only with an all-around check from different levels and angles can we find out the truth and essence of things.

All contradictions in the world derive from the contradictory parties' different perspectives in looking at the same thing, which leads to their contradictory conclusions. Meanwhile, the two parties both persistently think they are absolutely right, thus leading to drastic contradictions, conflicts, and even slaughters and wars.

Almost everyone believes they are right and righteous, and no one will initiatively admit he is Satan, even including Hitler himself, the recognised Satan of the world. During the Second World War, most Germans and Japanese believed they were saving the world instead of destroying it.

Thus, if we can let all people understand the integrated essence and truth of all things in the world, I believe people will draw coincident conclusions and results. The reason is that at the moment of our birth, the subconscious of all people is basically coincident. People's purpose in the world is actually the same. In fact, everyone has the desire pattern expounded by Maslow. The demand pattern of everyone is gradually satisfied from the primary demand at the bottom to the self-actualisation demand at the top without end.

It is true especially for the common people. People need security, enough food and clothing, sex and love, and the realisation of the self-value.

People hate wars because wars threaten their demand at the bottom security demand. Security is the demand of human at the bottom. However, the world we are living in is not peaceful and tranquil. We need a good living environment and investment environment, so our first concern is security, and the insecure environment is absolutely not the place we are willing to live in. Of course, there are also many adventurers, conspirators, and war maniacs in the world, but their emergence is caused by another social factor rather than completely by their inherent bellicose and bloodthirsty nature.

In psychoanalysis, anyone who loves or hates something has a reason. All things that happen in the world are causal.

Hatred is not the normal reaction of all normal people towards irrelevant things in the outside world. It emerges because some behaviour of some people seriously affects others' life, happiness, and benefits, and there are no other proper normal ways to deal with it. As a result, such an instinctive impulse of destroying others emerges. In this sense, hatred is a kind of desire and instinctive reaction out of the pursuit of protection for its own security.

So the contradictions in human society are caused by the different views on the same thing. We need to unify people's perception of all things, as there is only one truth. We need to tell the truth, rejecting the lies, cheating, and deception.

Right is right, wrong is wrong, black is black, white is white, and fact is fact. Never compromise, fear, or give in.

Only the truth can really solve the contradictions in human society.

30. The essence of war is the cannibalism led by elites

About 2007

Social elites have a distinctive feature, i.e. they can accept the advanced culture and think earlier and faster than common people and apply it into social practice. Besides, they cannot only absorb and use the advanced culture by themselves, but also influence and lead the common people to accept and absorb it. The political revolution actually starts from culture and thought. Conflicts in politics are actually the conflicts between two kinds of culture and thought. By spreading their ideas, elites are able to establish their organisations, political parties, and mass organisations. In this way, they can organise their supporters to fight with their opponents divergent from their thought and culture. Apart from the conflicts in culture and thought, those conflicts are likely to tend towards wars and slaughters.

The American Civil War is a conflict between the two different kinds of thought and culture, slavery and capitalism. China's war of Kuomintang and the Communist Party is a conflict between the culture of communism and capitalism. In fact, any war happening in the world is essentially a war of culture and a war of thought. There are always some people who believe their original social system is proper and their original cultural thoughts are correct, because culture determines social relations, and social relations determine people's vital interests. Instead of saying that they are protecting their vital interests, they are more of protecting their existing belief and culture. Instead of saying that they go into wars for the benefit of themselves, they are more of going into wars for the purpose of maintaining their own belief and culture.

From the contemporary perspective, the American Civil War was to liberate black slaves and offer those rights and freedom. However, during the Civil War, the slave owners in the South fiercely fought with the army of the North, which explicitly demonstrates this issue. In the eyes of the blacks, the North army was not there to liberate and help them, but instead, the North was to make them lose their jobs they relied on. Thus, in order to protect their livelihood, they dashed ahead to fight with the North army.

Because at that time, the blacks hadn't received the culture of freedom, democracy, and human rights, they still insisted on their original belief and culture loyal to slave owners and at the service of slave owners. This kind of loyalty and service had formed an inherent culture, which was handed down and taught from age to age, so they firmly believed in it without any doubt. Thus, to let them completely abandon their original thought and culture immediately without receiving the brand-new culture and idea would

98

extremely annoy them with the complete overturn and challenge of their subconscious. If they did not protect their original culture and thought, they would sink into the helplessness and fear of the unknown—the unknown challenge and helpless fear of the future fate. It is just because of their anger and fear of the lost culture and thought that they picked up guns and rebelled.

The war in which Sun Yat-sen overthrew the Qing dynasty is also a war between two cultures, a war between capitalism and feudalism. In this war, what role did the common people play? Ah Qs. Those who overthrew the Qing dynasty are Ah Qs led by revolutionary elites, and those who protected the Qing dynasty are Ah Qs led by feudal official elites. In history, we refer to these two kinds of Ah Q by completely different names. The former is called revolutionary warrior. The latter is called feudal reactionary force.

This is a political fraud. Frankly speaking, common Ah Qs don't know what they are fighting for or who they are fighting for. All in all, they just fight with the idea that the world will belong to them if they win. However, the ignorant Ah Qs are not aware that they were not included in the so-called us. They were just cannon fodder and chessmen anytime and anywhere. The world always belongs to elites.

The world is not peaceful, and wars occur everywhere constantly. And ignorant Ah Q is being killed or exploded all the time with even various ways of death. Some Ah Qs kill another group of Ah Qs, and then they are killed by another group of Ah Qs. Meanwhile, no matter what parties they belong to, they insist they are incomparably righteous and they are the embodiment of justice till death. Even if they are bombed into ash, they still treat it as glory which can illuminate their ancestors and leave a good name forever.

Above all, the essence of war is a cause where different elites lead two groups of ignorant people to kill each other and certain elites get the benefits in the end.

31. The responsibility for world peace lies in elites

About 2007

In society nowadays, there are numerous contradictions around the world. Instead of saying that they are conflicts of thought, they are more of conflicts of culture. The concept of thought is much narrow than that of culture. Thought may refer to one or several ideas, but culture is all-inclusive, which is manifested in every detail of our daily life, in our smiles, gestures, expressions, etc. Culture is a kind of systematic thought.

Culture and thought are actually both windy and dispensable. Whatever culture and thought we hold, we can still survive in the world. But what's the significance of human survival? Just fighting for favour or seeking to prevail over others? No. In contrast, the purpose of fighting for favour or seeking to prevail over others is to live, or to live better. Different thoughts and cultures are only slightly different in aspects of living style and living quality. Some are backward and some are advanced. On the world's scale, there are not two individuals whose thought and culture are completely the same, just as there are not two completely same leaves in the world. There is always a difference between two individuals in thought and cultural level, which is the root of the contradictions in the world. If the thought and culture of all people were exactly the same, people would be able to understand each other and communicate well with each other, and thus, no fights and wars would exist.

The fights between people are caused by their difference in culture and thought, which leads to the dispute and divergence in benefit distribution of everyday life. Once such difference and divergence universally exists in two districts or two social classes; political storm and wars will be generated if it is intensified to a certain degree and raised to the political level. That will be the tragedy of all human beings and the tragedy of the whole world.

However, seeing from another different perspective, with the development of technology, popularisation of education, universal improvement of the quality of all people around the world as well as the development of the Internet, people are able to gradually reach a consensus in their divergence of culture and thought through reasonable comparison and normal appeal. I believe whatever colour we are, wherever we are, and whatever language we speak, there is one thing for sure: the fundamental subconscious and original impulse of people all around the world are the same, because this is the inherent system of people. In humans' original impulse, there are some fixed instincts: some are ruthless and some are weak. When people do anything as they want without taboo, their ruthless nature will be shown.

Numerous evils such as aggressions, plunders, slaughters, and extinction of races in human society have explicitly demonstrated it. To be frank, if there was no balance of terror of nuclear weapons and if nuclear weapons were only mastered by one regime, we couldn't imagine how many wars would happen and how many people would die. Even now, humans still haven't broken away from the shadow that nuclear weapons might destroy the earth. Actually, everyone in the world is living under the balance of terror, but some people are aware of it and some are not at all.

But on the other hand, there is also the instinct of weakness and being afraid of death. This may seem ridiculous to some people. But I think everyone is afraid of death; everyone wishes to spend their lives safely, peacefully, and happily. It is just due to this kind of desire and impulse that humans are likely to truly move towards civilisation.

As an ancient Chinese saying goes, safety starts at home. To live a life safely and light-heartedly is really a kind of happiness, which is actually what every normal and sane person on the earth wishes for deep inside their heart. A sane and normal person will not kill another person or be killed by others just for a piece of bread.

Culture and thought is just a kind of idea and information, which can be exchanged and spread in various ways, including peaceful and non-peaceful ways. Besides, to some extent, its exchange and spread always start from theories. In fact, any countries, any nations, and any sane people can conduct cultural and thinking exchanges with each other by certain means, and through the communication, they can understand each other, borrow from each other, trust each other, compromise with each other, and help each other.

However, the separation of different regimes and languages leads to people's misunderstandings, suspicion, hatred, and oppression. In such misunderstandings, suspicion, hatred, and oppression, conspirators just make use of the selfishness, greediness, extremes, and narrowness in human nature to make waves and gain profits.

In reality, there are sober-minded elite in every nation and every country. If all of them can achieve compatible culture and idea on a spiritual level, the world can realise the real peace.

32. The change of culture starts from elites

About 2007

In fact, Chinese property law is just a kind of prelude of the Cultural Revolution, and it is a symbol which lays a foundation for the new round of cultural revolution in China.

It is just because culture has a kind of acquiescent and hidden property that culture is usually in a condition that the true face of Lushan is lost to my sight, for it is right on this mountain that I reside. Usually people are not willing to think about the right or wrong of existing facts, because the change of existing culture will involve the interests of many people, which is nothing else but removing mountains and filling seas for common people. It is impossible for a person to remove or change anything on his own, and blind confrontations will only lead to cruel sufferings or death for justice.

But I think to change culture is not unreachable or as difficult as reaching for the sky. The key issue lies in methods.

Though people have some bad habits such as selfishness, scholasticism, and satisfaction with things as they are, they still have the nature of pursuit of brightness and success as well as unwillingness to lag behind. No matter how selfish and greedy a person or a group or the social elite class in power is, they will think it over when it concerns the overall national interest, welfare of descendants, and their own achievements or ruling status.

If a country or a nation's culture needs to be changed, it will be a fruitless approach to start changing from the common people by calling on them through obscurantism by means of the so-called democracy.

The reason is that people at the bottom of society are more likely to have the narrow and extreme thinking mode. Actually, though democratic society seems to be fair and just, it is unscientific after all. If people at the bottom of the society and people in the leading class have the same political rights, the narrow and extreme ideas and thoughts of the people at the bottom may completely submerge rationality, scientificalness, and advancement.

The reason is that they cannot realise culture at all, and they cannot realise the constraint and control of this subconscious on their words and deeds. All their words and deeds are the servant and megaphone of culture. However, a major cause for the success of the elite class is that their brains' comprehensive analysis and logical judgment ability are generally superior to the common people. Thus, they are able to achieve the leading position and advantages in the field of politics, economy, etc. Besides, the real elites of society are the first to understand and accept the advanced culture and thought. The social progress is essentially the cultural process led by elites, and the social change is actually the cultural change led by elites. Therefore, I think an excellent social system should let elites who are capable of representing people's interest hold power and administer state affairs.

1. A country's prosperity and development needs elites to hold power and establish national policies. And such elites should be a group rather than several individuals.

2. People in power must truly represent people's interest, their fundamental and long-term interest, and so to speak, it refers to the spirit of three representatives. However, if elites can't represent people's interest, it will lead to a disaster.

33. What are Chinese doing?

About 2007

In recent years, economic development in China rapidly improved. Besides, apart from building substance civilisation, the objective to build harmonious society and spiritual civilisation was announced recently. Chinese culture and logic are quite different from that of foreign countries so that it's always hard for foreigners to understand what we are doing now and expect what we will do in the future. Chinese seem different from foreigners forever. Some people are even scared about fast development of China. After reading this thesis, you will get an absolutely clear idea of Chinese, Chinese culture, and society development direction. Maybe we can see China and its development from a different angle.

In the past, I often published some critical writings on the Internet to make analysis and comment on something happening in China. Government seems to pick up thought from civilians published on the Internet. In other words, civilians influence development of China by means of the Internet.

The same as the Soviet Union did, China failed to take an effective method on management of state-owned enterprises. Chinese state enterprises get into hard condition within a period of time. However, this situation seems to be turned after government made separation of ownership and management right. State enterprises are released from heavy load and achieve stable profit, giving support to stabilise Chinese government in turn. With substance civilisation achieved, the new goal is to build spiritual civilisation. They think building spiritual civilisation is the unique way to solve deeply rooted social contradiction problems and build a harmonious society so as to achieve maximum fairness and justice.

To achieve maximum fairness and justice is still a goal far away, before which there are many things to do and many difficulties waiting for us to conquer. How this goal will proceed needs our witness together.

It's believed that if other countries refer to the Chinese development model, learn from our experience, and make some modification according to their current situation, they will do better than China. Western countries should know better how to make profit, manage, keep to rules, and keep to principle.

34. Chinese economic achievement is attributed to the implementation of new ideological culture and political system

About 2007

In my opinion, China is developing well in all directions, which should be attributed to new ideological culture and political system. It's still not perfect but it has been improved a great deal and live up to standard basically.

Many people say that China is a giant without thought and culture of its own. But actually it's not like what they say. What is current situation China staying in?

Based on public ownership and state capitalism offering political support and material support, China is a new human-civilisation society under political power with an aim to solve deeply rooted social contradiction problems.

This concept is subtle since things related to it are quite complicated. In China, it can be only done but not said. The policy to put aside disputes for economic development is seen as a Chinese feature and developed Marxism. However, nobody can tell where those so-called features come from. Opinions shown here just stand for me. These personal points of view are not related to others.

Harmonious society expresses our ideology and culture, and state capitalism expresses our political system. According to present strong productive forces, harmonious society must be based on state capitalism.

To achieve harmony is not to be said only. The achievement of it needs political and economic support. I used to publish some writings on the Internet to explain how a socialist country exploits the superiority of socialism.

How does a socialist country exploit the superiority of socialism? The way is in China: Based on public ownership and state capitalism offering political support and material support, China is a new human-civilisation society under political power with aim to solve deeply rooted social contradiction problems.

How to develop the superiority of socialism in socialist country? It lies in the cultural ideology and political system currently practiced in China.

Take public ownership and state capitalism as the political security and material security to construct the brand-new harmonious society of human civilisation under the power guarantee and with the purpose of solving the deep-seated contradictions.

105

35. How a socialist country develops advantages of the socialist system

April 2004

Socialism and capitalism are two different social systems which have different guiding ideologies and core principles for adjusting interpersonal relationships. Those that can improve the development of the society in a capitalist country can only be taken as a reference rather than as true saying to follow. Just as treating different diseases uses different prescriptions, taking wrong medicine will only be just the opposite.

The core principles for adjusting interpersonal relationship between socialist system and capitalist system are different; so are their paths of development. To understand their paths of development, we must firstly understand their core principles. In my opinion, the guiding ideologies and core principles of a capitalist system are as follows:

According to their own conditions and the environment provided by the society, every individual in a capitalist country produces their own desires for life and the society and then produces their own life goals and directions in life. In the capitalist society, everyone is respected and encouraged to go forward according to their own goals and directions, but everyone must be responsible for their own behaviour. The society will not interfere with anyone nor assume any responsibility. It only provides minimum basic protection for everyone. Everything depends on their own, and the life rule of survival of the fittest is followed in the society.

The guiding ideologies and core principle of socialist system:

Socialist system is a social system in which people are masters of their own affairs. After people hold the state power, starting from the fundamental interests of the majority of the people, by adjusting the political, economic, and other social relations, they are striving to produce the social relations between man and man, man and society, man and nature and social environment that can meet the social needs of the majority of people and conform to their interests, and to further improve faster and more rapid favourable development and maximise their spiritual and material satisfaction. As a result, there will be a better world in which harmonious unity, mutual promotion, and common development between man and man, man and society, man and nature are achieved. The relationship between man and the society in a socialist system is different from that of a capitalist system.

The relationship between man and the society in capitalist system:

106

This is the most original, basic relationship between man and nature since life exists. It is a relationship between an individual and the society, generated by imitating the relationship between animal and nature in nature. It only wears a civilised overcoat, but in essence, it is of no difference from the one between animal and nature.

The capitalist society, however, is a social system centred on the individual. When people are born, the society will give everyone a small surfboard with democracy, freedom, and human rights. Everyone can hold the small surfboard, and ride at their own will in the sea of bitterness. The distance one can ride only lies in one's own abilities. Only a few people can ride out of the sea of bitterness and come to the island, such as the big capitalists in this time. Some people get lost in the sea and become those who oppose and harm the society. So in a capitalist country, the high crime rate is very high; especially the malignantly intentional crimes are horrible, causing great harm to the society. In order to arrive at some island or the other bank of victory, the vast majority of people, full of helpless fears in the law-of-the-jungle struggle, paddle until they die, sinking to the bottom of the sea.

The relationship between socialist system and the society:

Socialist system adjusts interpersonal relationship according to the rational aspect of human nature and from the macro and rational height. It develops social systems by meeting the interests of the majority. In other words, the minority whose interests are different from those of the majority must make concessions for the majority so the whole society can be harmonious. When social systems are developed, in order to safeguard the interests of the majority, a few people must sacrifice their interests. That is to say, it is a social system where most people exercise dictatorship over a few people. When the interests of the minority conflict with those of the majority, the minority only have three choices: (1) they persist in safeguarding their own interests wilfully and arbitrarily while ignoring those of the majority. The majority will exercise dictatorship. (2) They can change themselves, join in the society, make concessions for the majority, and keep the harmonious relationship and unity between man, between man and society, between man and nature. (3) They can leave the society and the country for another society and country to live in.

The principle of socialism is to consider the whole society and the whole country as the most advanced means of transportation. It is like a huge aircraft carrier, taking all the people in the society to the bright world and to victory. Everyone in our society is a spare part on the carrier; it asks each of the parts to keep harmony with the whole carrier. All people should take concerted action, make concerted efforts together to the bright world and to victory. Thus, a socialist country, if properly adjusted, can create infinite social benefits, overcome all difficulties, and achieve any goal.

Since the socialist country uses reason and science in adjusting the relationship between man and society, it adjusts the relationship globally and generally, which is the charm and superiority of a socialist system. Therefore, compared with capitalism, it is an advanced social system. When developing any system, considering any problem, we take the priority of sociality, overall, majority, and historical orientation, and then consider humanity, individuality, uniqueness, and locality. Of course, we do not completely ignore, sacrifice humanity, individuality, uniqueness, and locality but put their interests in the secondary position. Without violating the overall, we should also take humanity, individuality, uniqueness, and locality into full account. However, we cannot sacrifice the interests of the majority because of humanity, individuality, uniqueness, and locality. Only in this way can we give full play to socialist superiority, not be dominated by external factors, make clear judgment, and resist any interference of bad thoughts generated internally or externally.

Socialist society regulates social relations among people by taking the society as a whole, paying attention to the harmony and unity among all persons in this society, the society, and nature so as to achieve the social realm and social relations with harmony between heaven and people. We can avail of the harmony with nature and society through self-regulation and self-effort. Society serves for everyone, with individuals also contributing to the society; therefore, man and the society, man and man have formed the harmonious, rational, and peaceful relationship in which people take what they need and contribute what they can do. When the individual interest clashes with community interest, the individual can maintain harmony with the society through self-change. When the interests of the majority conflict with the social interests, we can maintain the harmony of both interests by changing the relationship between man and society through the adjustment of political and economic order.

As for the socialist aircraft carrier, because there are no successful examples, we only try, test, and debug it according to its principles. We do not reach the normal sailing state, so various defects and contradictions will appear in the process of debugging. As members of the society, we should understand and tolerate defects and contradictions. After all, our starting point which is to liberate all mankind is good. It is inevitable for us to take some detours. As long as debugging the carrier is completed, it will sail formally. We can quickly catch up with any one of the world's advanced developed countries; I believe we all can see this day. This is not out of reach but just around the corner.

With the development and popularisation of information technology, the central government can realise its unified management of the finance in state-owned enterprises. However, only recently the requirement can be met, and it is the right time. With the popularisation of Internet technology and the enhancement of our productivity, the production relation of our socialist country also needs to be made with corresponding adjustment, which is consistent with the great theory that relations of production must conform to the development of productivity.

1. Political power in the hands of the people can solve our security problem.

2. The united finance management of the central government, the central government investment can solve the problems in funds, employment, and development.

3. China's positive, mature socialist market has been basically completed and is gradually connecting with the world. With the market, the operation and management of our enterprises can resort completely to the market, allowing the reasonable, healthy competition in the market to determine enterprises' decline and prosperity. There is no need of being too worried about them.

If the above problems are solved, all other ones will be easily solved. The socialist aircraft carrier can smoothly sail and run faster and faster. We will be more and more powerful and become the most powerful country in the world soon. All the problems, such as lay-off, unemployment, the gap between rich and poor, the gap between urban and rural areas, the problem of Taiwan, and the issue of the Diaoyu Islands will be conquered without a single fight.

Considered from the perspective of the problems in real life, since the economy in a capitalist country can be developed, the capitalist system is really good in a sense and worth learning. This is undeniable in spite of its drawbacks.

On the other hand, the big-pot system and the old mode of planned economy were implemented in our country in the first years when the PRC was established. It was the fact that the low productivity at that time was exposed. Based on the above two points, we can make the following analysis.

Why did the big-pot system and the old mode of planned economy fail? What can the socialist market economy implemented in China recently and the economic system performed in a capitalist country have been telling us?

It is people that achieve all the good systems, so we must firstly understand people for the success of our career. We should know what people are, under what circumstances we can be the most enthusiastic and creative and create the greatest social value, and what people really need. All the systems are completed by people, and their purpose is to make people have a better life.

We can make a comparison of the capitalist system with the market economy performed in China after we carried out the policy of reform and opening up to the outside world and the old mode of planned economy so that we can find out their fundamental difference. What did the society provide for the labourers with the big-pot system and the old mode of planned economy? Let's recall the situation at that time. Everyone's salary was basically fixed. They could get a similar salary regardless of their performance at work. Individuals were not encouraged to other things, except their own work by the government. The houses were provided by their working units, and the state was responsible for all the expenditure on going to see doctors and children going to school. What's more, consumption was controlled by the state. In this model, the state was responsible for nearly all the problems of workers in their lives, so workers did not need to assume any risk nor the right to do so.

What did the society with market economy and capitalist system provide for labourers? It provided free trade and commercial competition. What did the state provide for those private enterprises and self-employed people? It provided policies and regulations. Similar to a capitalist country, everyone who plunged into the commercial sea is given a small wooden board of conducting any commercial activity within the scope of law. Those self-employed and private entrepreneurs are responsible for all their commercial actions, and the state does not provide anything else. Why has China's private economy flourished?

So are the capitalist countries. They also give each citizen a small wooden board of conducting any commercial activity within the scope of democracy, freedom, human rights, and law and let them ride freely in the boundless commercial sea.

During the early period of China's socialism, the state provided people with the real things—housing, education, medical care, and salaries. However, what market economy and capitalist system have brought to people is the vague, abstract concept of conducting any commercial activity within the scope of law, rather than any real things. Why do people still scramble for them? Aren't they crazy? No, it is true that market economy and capitalist system do not supply people with real materials but give people an environment for individuals to develop freely and to realise their own value and personal ideals. In this environment, people may fail, but they are more likely to exert their potentials, achieve their personal ideals and maximum value, and get more opportunities to develop.

In view of this, to make every worker exert their maximum labour productivity, what they need is an environment that can stimulate their potentials, rather than the limited material conditions. This is the experience that has been summarised by Chinese people with their blood and tears since the development of the cause of communism. This is a profound lesson to bear in mind by every communist at the initial stage of socialism.

However, the environment for the working people in the socialist country is different from that of the capitalist country. Why? A capitalist system serves for the capitalists, so what it provides is the environment in which capitalists can exploit more surplus value.

On the other hand, the environment in a socialist country serves for the common working people, and for their more beautiful, harmonious, prosperous, peaceful life. Because of their different service targets, the content and significance of the environments are quite different.

I. Educational Environment

Education is of decisive significance for individual, family, race, and state; it can directly determine an individual's social status and productivity. The average education level of a country determines the strength of a country, prosperous or declined. The education received by an individual during the initial twenty years since he or she was born impacts all of her or his life. The educational environment refers to the educational condition that the society can provide for every citizen. The vast majority of capitalist countries regard education as an industry that can increase in the gross national product and commercialise it. As to the effects of education on individuals, it is indeed valuable. Education is a tool that can produce more productive labourers for capitalists, and its purpose is to satisfy capitalists' need for talents who can make more benefits for them. That's just so. They also have compulsory education, but the knowledge they give people is only the basic knowledge that a labourer should have. They impose high tuitions and take strict control of the education in operation, management, business, trade, production skills, which may pose a threat to their social status. The common people cannot afford it, so they can only work as advanced productive tools and are exploited. It is very hard for them to become bosses.

However, the employment environment in a socialist country is quite different. The state is one in which all the working people master their own affairs, the regime is one which serves the people, and the education institutions are established for people to create more excellent workers. All of them should be serving the people rather than the machinery for capitalists to produce the exploited generation after generation.

Thus, the educators and education institutions in a socialist country should do research on such a question: how to impart the knowledge that can improve the productivity to the ordinary people in the simplest, cheapest, rapidest, most widely spread, and most effective manner. To improve the gross national product is the work of entrepreneurs, rather than the task of educational institutions. They are two different things and cannot be confused. The educational institutions set up by the people are aimed at serving the people with their heart and soul. They are not the machinery used to directly improve the gross national product and increase the economic growth rate. This is the biggest difference between socialism and capitalism in education.

II. Employment Environment

The easiest and most effective way to solve unemployment issues is to create new enterprise and establish a new plant. These will create more surplus value and profit. The capitalists will establish new enterprise and a new plant in a capitalist society. It is the politician's responsibility to deal with unemployment rather than the entrepreneur's thing. It will surely raise contradiction in the capitalist countries. Government needs to solve the problem of employment. Capital is controlled by capitalists, whose purpose is to earn more money instead of considering the problem of employment. So solving the problem of unemployment and development in capitalist countries is fluctuating with market changes, and government has no rights to intervene directly.

While the socialist country is in public ownership as the main body of the country, the situation is completely the opposite. Politicians should all have the assets of state-owned enterprises, can directly solve the employment and development problems, where the need to solve the employment problem is where to invest, and where the need to solve the problem of development can arrive where to invest. Of course, the investment is in order to profit, but it can also solve the problem of employment and development. Profit is the most important, employment is the auxiliary function, killing two birds with one stone. But in many of our state-owned enterprises, despite the losses to the state loans, wages will continue to have the order reversed; this behaviour is one of the simplest economic mistakes our politicians make on state-owned assets, resulting in waste of capital, not producing its due benefits, not realising the due function.

However, at the beginning of reform and opening up to the outside, as discussed in other articles of the author, the central government did not really hold the economic power of state-owned enterprises, so it was impossible to achieve what I have said—solving the problems of employment and development directly. The superiority of the socialist system did not play its due role in solving the issues of employment and development. Consequently, lots of related problems arise, such as triangle-relational debits, lack of vitality, loss of state-owned assets, losses, embezzlement, corruption, illegal charges, disunity among people, etc. I have even published an article on the Internet to make the following suggestions to the government: the central government should immediately take over the state-owned enterprises, give up the right to manage the state-owned enterprises, and close hopeless and lost enterprises. The state-owned capital should be used in the place in most need rather than wasted in those enterprises that make losses. The government should directly solve the problems of employment and development and carry forward the superiority of the socialist system.

III. Security Environment

It is said that the security problem is a simple and old problem that officers and soldiers catch a thief. Since the country existed, the security problem has been focused on by all the dynasties and governments in the slave society, the feudal society, the capitalist society, or the socialist society. It seems nothing special. But if we think so, it may be completely wrong.

In fact, security problems are various social factors including politics, economy, ethics, morality, and education that are reflected in the behaviour of people, and all the various conflicts between man and man, man and society are also reflected in the security issues. The security problem seems to be about officers and soldiers catching a thief, but actually it is to solve all the conflicts on the contradiction between man and man, man and society in various fields. If the essential problem cannot be solved appropriately, thieves cannot be caught. On the contrary, they will be more and more. If the essential problem can be solved appropriately, thieves will be less and less; eventually no thieves need to be caught. The real thieves are not in the streets, nor in the mountains, but in the hearts of the people. The shortcomings in the political system and defects in the economic system or the shortage of education and the bad social environment will lead to moral and ethical conflicts. To a certain extent, they will affect social order and social stability.

If we fail to realise this point and are blind to catch the thieves, maybe one day, when you suddenly wake up, you may find all the people around you are thieves. What should you do if even you become a thief unconsciously?

Kind people find it difficult to make a choice.

The thieves who break the law and commit crimes should be caught. It is an issue worthy of studying and thinking over on how to eliminate the thieves from the basic system, stop them from the source, and eliminate them in people's hearts. There are fundamental differences between the socialist system and capitalist system on this issue.

Why must we build a harmonious society? Why is public ownership better than private ownership? Firstly, I need to clarify a problem, that is, the state capitalism and the individual capitalism.

In state capitalism, because all the people in a nation cannot effectively manage the state-owned assets possessed by all people, nor effectively maintain and increase the value of the state-owned assets, they authorise the government and the state under the leadership of the Communist Party of China to exert the ownership right of all the state-owned assets on behalf of them.

The property law of PRC clearly stipulates that all the state-owned assets possessed by the country shall be exerted by the state council. Thus, China currently is performing state capitalism.

State capitalism is an advanced form of socialism and communism. And it is the only right, feasible organisation form and the only one proven by practice.

Other organisational forms of socialism and communism are fantastic, utopian socialism, and communism. They can only bring disasters, terrors, and evils to mankind. We have experienced them.

The individual capitalism is one led by the Western countries, the core of which is advocating private capital. The individual capitalism has its advantages and disadvantages. It is of significance in overthrowing and replacing the feudal dynasty. However, the wheel of history does not stop here, the science, human beings are making constant development in technology, culture, and civilisation. The serious drawbacks that existed in the society of individual capitalism are more and more obvious, so individual capitalism is bound to be replaced by state capitalism.

36. Strengthen management on government to the public assets of government

Advice on Repairing Corruption of Officials

April 2004

Corruption in official workers not only happens in China, but also happens everywhere in the world. In a socialist country like China, officials should insist on the principle of serving for civilians, but the corruption behaviour works the opposite to basic principle and country law. It's believed that corruption behaviour can be eliminated. However, many corruption cases happening around us are worth our meditation. We need to find the root and destroy it completely, since it causes a negative effect on the image of party and socialism. If we compare socialism to a mansion, corruption is like borers and termites that chew on it and will finally destroy it if we cannot eliminate them in time.

Because corruption is behaviour by an official, it's related to politics. Meanwhile, corruption is also an economic issue, and it's related to economy. Therefore we plan to analyse from the angle of politics and economy in an attempt to find the essence and root of corruption.

Analysis from the political angle:

China is a socialist country in which total assets of all state-owned enterprises belong to civilians. The Communist Party of China represents civilians to manage assets. In other words, the Communist Party of China represents civilians to exercise ownership and management rights. The head office of the Chinese government is located in Beijing, but officials who manage public assets are from the local government branch. The government distributes their rights to its branches. Distribution can be classified into two types: ownership and management rights. Meanwhile, the government uses party discipline, national law, regulations, and system to limit the range for given rights. It's regarded as corruption when officials disobey party discipline, national law, regulations, or system in order to illegally occupy ownership of assets that belong to the public. If officials keep to party discipline, national law, regulations, and system, no matter how much profit they make, it's not corruption. In essence, corruption is behaviour to deny the leadership of government.

Analysis from the economic angle:

When analysing from the economic angle, distribution can be also classified into two types: ownership and management rights. Management rights allow owners to manage production and organise economic actives. For companies, any action for management needs management rights. For factories, raw material purchase, product sale, and payment obtainment need management rights. Management rights can be needed for fulfilling duty as general manager, making profit for company, or for working as a go-to. In broad sense, any behaviour to receive income on behalf of the government needs management rights. For example, tax income, road maintenance fee, education expense, and fine all need management rights. However, if we consume public assets, it needs ownership. For example, extra bonus, allowance, item transferring, car purchase, house purchase, restaurant expense, and travelling all need ownership. Ownership is needed for fulfilling the duty as chairman to consume cash.

Apart from management rights given to local government and officials, much party discipline, national law, regulations, and system are used to limit the range of ownership. It's regarded as corruption when officials disobey party discipline, national law, regulations, or system in order to illegally occupy ownership of assets that belong to the public. From the economic angle, corruption is a kind of infringement since they use extra ownership beyond the range given by government, to embezzle public assets.

Ownership and management rights sound familiar to people who study economy, but they are not familiar to most civilians since they are seldom talked about in daily life. These concepts will be easy to understand through the following examples.

They are various business beings in our society because of the influence of the reform policy. The simplest one is self-employed entrepreneurs. They open a barbershop or a grocery store to sell living items, clothes, cats, and shoes. People call them small boss. Capital and production tools all belong to them or the family, so they have full ownership. They have rights to manage their own business legally, free from interference, so they have full management rights. All in all, self-employed entrepreneurs have full management rights and ownership of their companies.

A bigger one than self-employed entrepreneurship is private enterprise, which is a bit bigger than self-employed company. Private enterprises have different sizes, such as a small one with only few workers and a big one with hundreds of employees. Here we classify private enterprise into two types:

1. management rights are incorporative with ownership

2. management rights are separate from ownership

That management rights are incorporative with ownership means people who invest in business manage a company directly. In this condition, the chairman usually takes over the position of general manager as a part-time job. Generally speaking, this kind of company does not have branches. It's usually small-sized, since no matter how excellent the chairman is, the employees he/she can manage directly are limited. The employee number usually ranges from ten to twenty. In such a small-sized company, the chairman or director owns assets of the company, so they have ownership. Meanwhile they take part in management, so they also have management rights. That's the incorporation of management rights and ownership. In such companies, financial personnel are usually relatives of the chairman.

With further development, it's possible for the company to be expanded and have its own factories, sales departments, branches, and so on. Besides, branches are usually distributed to different places. Under this condition, it's their choice to take part in management or not. The chairman can distribute rights to employees who are not shareholders but are good at some important skills by putting them in positions like sales manager, plant manager, branch manager, or head office manager. They do not invest in the company and have no ownership, but they have certain management rights allowed by the chairman. That's the separation of management rights and ownership.

In all types of companies, the chairman is likely to give full rights for production, sales, and management due to the trust in employees, but no chairman will give full rights for financial affairs and give absolute freedom to financial workers with no monitoring measures. Besides, no chairman will employ a chief financial officer he/she doesn't trust at all.

These things discussed above are part of basic common sense in modern enterprise management, which is not hard to understand. In the discussion above, it's regarded as corruption when officials invade and occupy ownership of public assets that government represents civilians to exercise. However, what gives chances for corruption to happen over and over again? The answer to that question is associated with understanding for ownership of economic society, which is mainly represented by recruitment right for financial personnel in the company.

In all types of companies including self-employed entrepreneurship, private company, and joint company, the financial personnel are always appointed by the owner of the company directly. The financial personnel are employed to manage, calculate, and sort out the capital of the company. The owner of the company gets a clear idea of financial condition through the financial personnel. Therefore, the financial personnel can be compared to the eyes and hands of the company owner. People who control the financial personnel can control the flowing of capital and know the overall financial condition. How much capital is lost, how much profit is earned, who should pay more, who should pay less, which debt needs to be lagged, which debt needs to be paid at once, when and how company should spend capital, purchase of house and purchase of car—all are operated by the financial personnel.

Control to the financial personnel is equal to control of the whole company. Importance of the financial personnel can be compared with military leadership in war, which determines the success.

With military leadership as strong support at the back, people can do many huge affairs, like overthrowing the government, eclipsing sun and moon, making exploitation, bullying civilians, doing things without rule and restriction. They can keep superior and subordinate in the dark, go opposite to the government, and make the world not different from hell. Military leadership in economic life cannot influence the world directly, but the effect caused is similar.

It's believed that many people have heard one popular thought, 'where there is a policy, there is always a byway to cope with it'. That shows that military leadership is in the control of government. However, in economic life, military leadership has been out of control of government. People inferring from that thought have full ability to be immune to policy from government since they have strong economic power. The government has to refer people with economic power to put policy into practice, so they have nothing to fear.

It's seen that performing ownership of state-owned assets is really important. The government has enough reason to put it in a place equal to building of military force for more attention paid to management. When we go to the tax bureau to pay tax, we often see the slogan posted on the wall: 'Tax is the pulse of a nation'. It's absolutely true. Apart from tax, all state-owned assets are the pulse of a nation and need a special institute appointed to manage carefully.

However, management of ownership of state-owned assets is ignored in China. Ownership and management rights are distributed to lower branches instead of a special institute managed by the government directly.

The concept about ownership and management rights is not as obvious as traditional military leadership. Only after society production reaches a certain scale and the economy develops to a certain degree will it show up. It doesn't exist in slavery society, feudal society, and even junior phase of capital society. It's a concept of rights and economic relationship between people after the economy is highly developed.

Since our country was transformed from a feudal society into a socialist society and missed the process to get the economy highly developed that happens in a capital society, it's understandable that we do not have a clear idea of concepts based on a highly developed economy.

118

The analysis is made on a relationship between corruption and economic leadership.

There are two bottom-line conditions for corruption to happen:

> 1. Corrupt officials have the chance to get capital that belongs to the public.

> 2. Corrupt officials have a way to prevent their illegal behaviour from being found at once.

Corruption will be unlikely to happen if one of the conditions cannot be met. Therefore, corruption will be prevented on condition that we destroy one of the necessary conditions.

Features of corruption behaviour are concluded as follows:

> 1. It's confidential behaviour.

> 2. It's behaviour tightly connected with profit.

> 3. It's collective behaviour instead of individual behaviour.

Corruption refers to behaviour that aims to occupy public assets. It can be classified into two types:

> 1. Financial personnel take advantage of their position to occupy public assets.

> Generally speaking, it's individual behaviour that is comparatively easy to detect and solve.

> 2. Official leader takes advantage of his/her position to occupy public assets.

This kind of corruption is abominable and invisible. It's usually a collective behaviour that is deeply hated by civilians. In theory, discussion will focus on this kind of corruption.

In a normal financial system, movement of capital needs to be operated by three persons: leader, financial personnel, and cashier. Without any of them, movement of capital cannot be done. In other words, corruption cannot be done if any of them disagree to cooperate. Therefore, any corruption case of the official leader must be a collective behaviour. Personnel and cashier have guilt of duty dereliction even if they announce they know nothing about it.

Even if the Chinese government has granted accounting law to regulate responsibilities and behaviour of financial personnel, it's still hard to achieve expected justice by using accounting law under current social situation.

1. Financial personnel are alone and helpless. They are just junior employees in the charge of leaders.

2. They need to feed family, get married, and gain status in the company, all of which they need support from leaders. Leaders have top rights for finance, administration, and HR management. Those rights are what leaders deserve and a reflection of the regime. Without those rights, leaders cannot be called leaders, and regime cannot be called regime. Naturally, the fate of financial personnel is determined by leaders.

3. Many leaders employ and promote people they trust as financial personnel. In that way, financial system means nothing but hot air, and conscience will be the unique element to decide how leaders behave.

Measures taken by the government like building anti-corruption bureau, encouraging civilians to report on corruption, and organising a detective group to reveal corruption are all subsequent measures. If criminals give chances easily for others to find the evidence, they are the fools instead of the leaders. Corruption that can be seen by every civilian around is more robbery than corruption. Therefore it's difficult to solve a corruption case for leaders.

In my opinion, it makes more sense to prevent corruption from the angle of basic system, since subsequent measure is never ended. As long as we improve basic system to prevent it, it can be really eliminated completely. In China, what leads to corruption is the drawback existing on the management of public assets. Capital flowing is necessary for a developing economy, but it also gives chances for a corrupt criminal to occupy flowing capital illegally. Capital flow is necessary for a developing society, but we need to ensure no possible capital flow into the personal pocket in the process. To solve this problem means to solve the corruption issue.

Reasonable capital flow needs support from both entrepreneurs and officials. Management action and rights owned by them promote economic activities happening in society. Civilians give rights to government, and government distributes the rights to local officials to manage capital flow. People compare money to water, and those officials operating economic activities are hard to keep hands dry after touching water-like money. Those officials with wet hands are cases of corruption. Here is a method that can give chances for them to promote the economy but keep them away from water.

Like we discussed before, leaders have to escape from monitoring of financial personnel and cashier if they want to succeed. However, financial personnel are on the weak side in this defence battle. They are alone and helpless, which leads to failure in the fight against corruption.

President Mao used to point out, 'Our principle is to ensure government leading the gun, instead of the gun leading us.' Economic construction is not different from the real battle, and it's a silent battle in the dark. Many colleagues are lost and reduced to criminals with guilt to the public.

What makes them lost? That cash is like thousands of soldiers and endless bullets. They can be used for improving the economy, but they can work the other way to corrupt our officials.

As for capital, the government has to realise it's a coin with two sides. Besides, it's essential to keep capital in strict control. As long as we can make sure the financial personnel comply with government and national laws, corruption can be eliminated completely. Like the discussion made previously, financial personnel are alone and helpless in the face of corruption. Therefore, in order to solve this problem in essence, it's suggested that the government should manage financial institutes independently and set financial personnel of state-owned companies as officials so that they can keep away from the influence of corruption. On condition that financial personnel have enough strength to fight against corruption, this problem can be solved.

Politically, by taking measure, the government can centralise power on finance, which will help strengthen people's democratic dictatorship to protect exercise of government policy from opponent measures.

Economically, by taking measure, government gets feedback from financial institutes around the nation so that they can give instruction on any mistake that will destroy the government's image in public. Therefore, it's necessary to take this measure.

When appointing financial personnel, it's suggested that the government should pay attention to the following points:

1. Independence given to financial personnel cannot influence economic development.

Firstly, financial personnel cannot be restricted by anyone except government force, and especially cannot be restricted by leaders. Only independent work can reflect true financial condition so that the government can take correct measures to improve and adjust the current situation. Only independent work can monitor the leaders' work to ensure there is no corruption. Only independent work can really exercise government policy correctly to ensure that civilians can get the welfare they deserve.

However, independent work doesn't mean that it's allowed to influence normal economic development and doesn't mean that it's allowed for financial personnel to interfere with the action of leaders that are reasonable.

Except the right of leaders to appoint financial personnel, any rights of leaders work as usual. The only thing different is that there are some eyes around leaders for monitoring to ensure legitimacy and rationality of the leaders' work. Any action of leaders to operate finance will be monitored. Meanwhile, innocence and loyalty of leaders will be witnessed by financial personnel. With government's monitoring, leaders will have more motives to work hard legally.

2. Financial personnel need to receive necessary training to master financial acknowledge, understand relevant government policies and regulations, and master basic skills to fight against economic crimes. Finance is professional work, which must be based on enough financial knowledge. Therefore, financial personnel need to be proficient on financial knowledge.

New-generation financial personnel represent government and civilians to monitor the leaders' work. They need to check if any action of leaders complies with party discipline, national law, policy, legal regulations. They have to report to the government if they find anything suspicious. Therefore, they have to be familiar with policies and regulations from the government.

3. Financial personnel need to be relocated periodically.

People compared money to water. Theirs is a popular Chinese saying that flowing water is always keeps fresh and an often operated door can avoid being destroyed by a moth. It's hard to ensure that financial personnel won't be influenced by corrupted leaders around them. Therefore, it's necessary to relocate the financial personnel periodically, and by the way, they can test the performance of previous financial personnel to check authenticity and reliability of their work. By doing that, the government can get feedback from financial work in time to ensure they won't be influenced by corruption.

Financial work is complicated, but the work target is limited, inflexible, and dogmatic. Any financial personnel can do it well as long as they are given some time to get familiar with the local condition of the working place. What they need to do is just to operate data the way they do as usual. Therefore, periodic relocation of financial work is feasible.

From the political angle, building a financial team can help centralise government power and strengthen people's democratic dictatorship so as to prevent corruption from happening in China. Meanwhile, it shows the superiority of socialism and helps gain faith from civilians, which gives strong economic support to the communist government.

From the economic angle, building of financial team protects legal rights of civilians and standardises economic behaviour of state-owned companies and government branches, which paves the way for economic development based on socialism.

In addition, standardised management on state-owned assets maximises the faith from civilians, which enables us to get ahead with our reform strategy. As long as political power, financial power, and military power are in the charge of government, we can have strong support to try any method that is likely to improve our economy.

37. State-owned enterprises can catch up with and surpass the world multinationals

Complete Separation of Management Right and Ownership

April 2004

Now, the operation form of enterprises in China is varied, such as individual enterprise, private enterprise, collective enterprise, state-owned enterprise, joint-venture enterprise, wholly foreign-owned enterprise, joint-stock enterprise, etc. But what enterprises they are, Chinese or foreign, enterprises to the bad or Fortune 500 enterprises, there is one thing in common—to make money. All aim to make money, increase the enterprise's capital, and maintain the value of the capital. Enterprise means hope; that is, starting a business aims to make the enterprise better, more promising, and richer tomorrow. To sum up, all are for making money.

It is known that the survival is for the fittest, for the enterprise in the market economy that only the strong can survive and the weak are necessarily eliminated, which is a ruthless and exact fact. Only recognising this point can the enterprise survive.

Facing the cruel and marble fact, how can the enterprise become strong to remain invincible, grow constantly, and resist all kinds of waves? These are the problems that the enterprise should consider.

All successful businesses have two things in common:

1. The money that the enterprise makes can really be packed into the investor's wallet and handed in to the owner of the enterprise.
This sentence is easy to understand. To the investor and the enterprise's actual owner, the purpose of investment is to make money for self, not for others. Only investors really obtain generous return. The founder of the enterprise has the responsibility to make the enterprise survive. If the investors and founders think greater return will be obtained if they continue to invest, they often invest larger projects with the returns, enlarge production, or expand the operation scope. Conversely, if the investors and founders of the enterprise cannot obtain the return and even suffer loss, they will weigh the pros and cons and adopt corresponding countermeasures. For example:

> a. If they think they can gain the return temporarily and make a profit instead of suffering a loss after they change the management strategies and adjust the enterprise, they will carry out internal adjustment within the enterprise.

b. If they think they can endure the temporary defeat of the enterprise and the enterprise shows benign development and will produce generous returns in the future, they will maintain the status quo.

c. If they think bad management of the enterprise is caused by insufficient investment, such as advertising investment and equipment renewal and the status quo will be changed after continuing to invest, they will often continue to invest.

d. If the owners of the enterprise think the enterprise cannot make profit and market and the external environment have changed, they will often sell the enterprise assets, withdraw the investment as much as possible, and close the enterprise in order to reduce the loss.

2. The enterprise is managed by the person who is the fittest.

As per the analysis in another article, after the enterprise expands gradually and the staff surpasses a certain scope, the owner of the enterprise is not able to directly manage more people so that they can share corporate responsibility and authority with others.

In a popular way, the boss of the enterprise will not directly participate in the actual labour and let the people help them make money, and they just count the money after the enterprise is developed to a certain scale.

This sounds a bit of something for nothing, but you cannot understand in such a way at any cases. The behaviour that the boss takes out their own money to invest is also considered a labour and a kind of advanced mental work. Boss and investor are labourers, just for which China's constitution is modified again and again.

Investment behaviour, on the one hand, can make the boss create thousands in wealth but, on the other hand, can also make the boss suffer loss beyond retrieval. The money that the boss makes under the bullets in the market and unprofitable risks is legitimate income and is protected by the law. Hence, even though the boss does not participate in the operation and management of the enterprise directly, it is understandable that their income is also legal.

Next, we will introduce the relationship between the benign development of enterprise and actual managers after the enterprise's management right and ownership are separated. After the separation, the owner of the enterprise has the right to appoint anyone to help him or replace him to manage the enterprise. This person is the actual operator and manager of the enterprise as well as the owner of the enterprise's management right.

Rationally speaking, not considering other factors such as emotion, politics, trust, etc., only from economic benefit, what kind of person can replace the owner of the enterprise to manage the enterprise? To put it simply, the person who can bring the maximum return and profit can replace the boss to make more money. The person who cannot do well must step aside as a result of relentless market economy, especially ruthless international market economy. In order to survive and become the first, an enterprise should make such a choice.

So what kind of people can create huge economic benefit? What kind of people has the best ability to make money? Such persons are those who have experienced theory and practice. Regardless of race, colour of skin, language, everyone is equal in the market economy, and the fact can speak.

Now, we will analyse the state-owned enterprises from two points above.

Who is the owner of state-owned enterprises? All Chinese people are the owner, and the Chinese Communist Party on behalf of the national people performs the ownership of state-owned enterprises.

Who is the manager of state-owned enterprises? It is our party. The leaders of state-owned enterprises, especially large state-owned enterprises, are led by the party and even appointed directly. We do not hear that the boss of private enterprises, and even the American boss, serves as the head of large state-owned enterprises.

So, it can be said that state-owned enterprise takes the form of integration of management right and ownership, which is similar to the operation and management mode of small private enterprise with about twenty on staff.

It is certain that the existing mode has its inevitable reason.

1. The Communist Party of China, on behalf of the people, to perform ownership and management right, has the right to manage all the state-owned enterprises in any form.

2. To control the ownership and management right of state-owned enterprises in such form also reflects people's power. Directly using administrative means to regulate state-owned enterprises is the product of planned economy.

State-owned enterprises are owned by the state and all the people, and the ownership should be mastered by the people, which are the iron facts and unshakable forever, so the central government must protect and control the ownership of all state-owned assets with every means and absolutely can't let go.

On the other hand, management right refers to the leaders' production labour to operate the enterprise. For the factory, it means buying raw materials, organising production and processing, selling the products and recovering the payments for the goods, which are operative behaviour and the reflection of management right. Management right is embodied in a general manager's duty to help the country and enterprise to make money, workers' behaviour, and consumption of state-owned assets, such as extra bonuses, subsidies, practicality, buying car, house, inviting a person to have a meal and holiday for tourism, etc., and the boss and chairman's duty and spending money.

Therefore, after management right is completely separated from ownership, management right means the worker's behaviour. However high the position and power are, you are the worker if without ownership and you must act according to the boss's face and rules and regulations. Otherwise, there will be many people to trouble you, which is the mode we need.

However, our party represents the interests of the working people. Most party members are born workers and peasants, rather than bourgeois, so working hard is our strong point. Compared with the big capitalists of those multinationals, operation and management are our weaknesses. Hence, it has some difficulty for the party to operate and manage the enterprises directly. While for those large multinationals, after the ownership is separated from the management right, those big capitalists can make own capital increase gradually and manage the enterprise well without direct involvement in the operation and management of the enterprise, from which we can draw lessons.

So in order to make the state-owned enterprises give the vitality into full play, the author suggests the following adjustments:

1. The ownership of state-owned enterprise is completely separated from management right, the financial institution is specially set up by the central government to treat the financial cashier personnel as state civil servants receiving unified management by the central government without receiving the management of leaders of the enterprise, and they should report the operation status of the enterprise to the higher authorities of the central government to prevent all state-owned assets from damage. The central government shall have the right to transfer the capital of the enterprise at any time and correct the enterprise leaders' wrong economic instructions so as to firmly hold the ownership of the enterprise.

127

2. The management right of state-owned enterprise is open, as the author points out that the management right is the reflection of a worker who works for the country and enterprise to make money, but can be replaced at any time. Their work is weighed by the performance.

The leadership doing well or badly can be reflected in the financial statement. To say it simply, who operates and manages the enterprise makes money and working for the people is not important, because this is just a form of representation.

The most fundamental factor to determine the nature of enterprise is the money handed in to whom. If the money is handed in to the big capitalists, the enterprise serves for the big capitalists. But if the money is handed in to the people's government, the enterprise serves for socialism. This is the most fundamental decisive factor and the most valuable thing.

Compared with previous modes, the following are benefits in having such a way:

1. The person can devote their talent for the enterprise and people intently.

The leaderships of enterprise will be affected in three factors in the existing mode:

    a. The leadership should be held responsible by the superior. This is obvious because they are selected by the superior leadership.

    b. The financial management is within his duty. If he makes mistakes as the result of inducement of money, the leadership should resist the temptation of money.

    c. It is the leadership's duty to take responsibility for the enterprise.

There is an old saying that a man may not spin and reel at the same time, but our leadership does three things at one time, so they will feel the heavy pressure and difficulty. While after the management right is separated from ownership, the leadership is only responsible for the enterprise. Certainly, the behaviour should be legal. The only standard to weigh the quality of work is how much money the enterprise makes and the benefits for the enterprise, nation, and people. If doing well, he is the hero and will obtain the reputation, status, and money. If he is doing badly and making mistakes, he will step aside and be replaced.

However, the enterprise's finance does not belong to him, so he has no opportunity to illegally seize the money.

The leadership of higher level can transmit administrative order when he violates the rules. But he is not appointed by the superior but from social open recruitment or election, so he devotedly dedicates his talent to the enterprise and people.

2. The central government directly controls the enterprise's finance to strictly supervise the leadership's economic behaviour so that the corruption behaviour can be prevented and the status and image of party is maintained in the eyes of people.

3. The surplus fund is directly transferred to do more things for the nation and people.

4. People's democratic dictatorship can be consolidated and strengthened after the central government really controls national economy.

If the state-owned enterprises can carry out the adjustments above, they can catch up with and even surpass the level of large foreign multinationals in the organisational structure and have the power to compete with them in the international market. Besides, the superiority of socialist system can fully be displayed, and the advantages of various population groups can be mobilised to make them serve for economic construction of socialism.

The root cause for the insufficient vitality of state-owned enterprises is the mutual diversion and interference of management right and ownership, which are hard linked together. Therefore, the fundamental way to solve the state-owned business enterprise's insufficient vitality is the complete separation of management right and ownership, to realise benign development.

38. State-owned enterprises can solve the problems of employment and development

On the Use of Profit of the State-owned Enterprises

April 2004

State-owned enterprises, as the name suggests, are the enterprises that all the people own. These enterprises have always had the problem of insufficient vitality, and even some enterprises are considered by people as baggage because of many problems left over by history, such as triangular debts, too many retired workers, too-heavy enterprise's burden, bad enterprise benefit, etc. However, state-owned enterprises are not a burden but a cornucopia that can create numerous employment opportunities and much wealth.

As the author mentions in other articles, there is no essential difference among state-owned enterprises, private enterprises, and foreign multinationals, all of which aim to make money, increase surplus value, obtain the highest profit at the lowest cost, and keep and increase the value of capital. The differences among them are investors, beneficiary of enterprises, and money to whom. State-owned enterprises give the money to the country, private enterprises give to the boss, and foreign multinational groups give to the capitalist. There is no difference in other aspects, and it also should not have.

There is something in common between how to make the state-owned enterprises full of vitality and how big capitalists increase the wealth.

Firstly we can look at how the big capitalists operate and manage their own enterprises. It is very simple that big capitalists manage the enterprise's wealth macroscopically, not microscopically.

Big capitalists may invest in ten or a hundred or more enterprises, so how do they manage these enterprises? It is very simple that they just need to invest and create these enterprises. Certainly, they are very cautious about the investment. After they determine investment in the industry and think the industry is promising, they will invest. Otherwise they will hold the money to wait for the timing. After the enterprises are created, they will recruit managerial talents to help them manage the enterprise and make the enterprise operate normally. They will not directly be involved in the operation and management of the enterprise and only strictly supervise the finance to make all the money in their wallets. Except for the normal flow capital and staff's wages, the rest all belong to them. Big capitalists only need control the direction of investment and finance to make tens of thousands of people to help them make money, and they will close the enterprises that lose money or have no hope and withdraw the capital to invest in other

130

aspects. This is the basic principle for big capitalists to make money. It seems to be very simple to say it, but it is not easy to do it.

1. How to determine the investment project is not easy for the common people to understand. It needs a smart mind and the eye of a politician, or it will cause huge loss if a wrong investment is made.

2. The person managing the enterprise's finance should have vision, experience, and knowledge. Whether the financial personnel are loyal, will do false accounting, will escape with the money, are corrupt and will betray the company, or have a working ability are a series of complicated problems, which is not easy for everyone to confirm. Any errors may result in huge loss and investment failure.

3. How can incentive mechanism be used to inspire the managers of enterprise to make money? On the one hand, it should prevent them from betraying the company, and on the other hand, it should let them give full play to their enthusiasm, which is really a troubling thing.

So the capitalists should have conspicuous and admirable points to manage dozens of enterprises based on individual ability.

We look at state-owned enterprises again. The author finds that state-owned enterprise has something in common with big capitalists' subordinate enterprises that the owner of the enterprise does not directly manage the enterprise. Why say that?

Big capitalists have ownership of the subordinate company, but they do not directly get involved in the enterprise's operation and management.

Party central committee has ownership of China's state-owned enterprises, but it does not directly get involved in the enterprise's operation and management.

Therefore, the economic relationship and the management idea of two kinds of enterprises are the same.

In theory, the state-owned enterprises can draw lessons from successful big capitalists and large multinationals in management mode. Besides, state-owned enterprises have more advantages than large multinationals.

1. The state-owned business is an economic entity supported by the country. Even if the private enterprise has a greater scale, from the points of economic strength and resources, the advantage can't compare with state-owned enterprise.

2. The credit of state-owned enterprises is much higher than that of other enterprises, which does not need more explanation because state-owned enterprises have the support from the country. The credit is the most important intangible asset in the business.

3. The loyalty of financial personnel in state-owned enterprise can be controlled by the nation. If the country arranges a special institution to manage the finance, the financial personnel's loyalty can be controlled at the highest level with any administrative means, while the financial personnel's loyalty in other enterprises cannot be ensured through the nation's administrative means.

4. The state-owned enterprises are not invested in by one person, but by a nation and all the people jointly. So compared with those single capitalists, state-owned enterprises have more advantages.

Because the investment model of state-owned enterprises is the same as the capitalists, they can draw the lessons from the successful big capitalists' management concept to serve for our state-owned enterprises when the state-owned enterprises meet difficulties in the process of actual operation.

If we can understand, all the things are not complicated. Making money or boundless money is far beyond the common people and they will not dare to think, but it is little complicated for the investors who have money. The problem is whether we have the courage to want and do.

According to the investment theory of big capitalists and multinationals, the author puts forward the following plan for reference. If the plan can be realised basically under everyone's efforts, state-owned enterprises can theoretically create countless chances of employment and social wealth to move so many ordinary Chinese out of poverty and into riches.

Under the existing condition, where do the new jobs come from?

If the nation sets a new factory and enterprise, it needs a large number of new workers. On the other hand, if an old factory is closed, it is certain that the workers in the old factory will lose the jobs and become laid-off workers, which is simple to understand for everyone.

Therefore, in spite of the bad benefit, bad operating condition, and even loss, the nation still provides subsidies to the large state-owned enterprises to pay for the workers' salary in order to reduce unemployment and social pressure.

The nation's macroeconomic regulation and control mainly refers to the project examination and approval system. When the local governments or enterprises need to invest in new projects, they firstly should write the report and apply to the related department and apply the loan from the bank after the examination and approval.

The author thinks this mode is complicated, passive, and has holes, which is not conducive to investment and employment.

According to the author's points of view,

1. No matter from the economic law or actual problem, the finance department of state-owned enterprises should perform unified management by the central government. The profit created by the enterprise should be allocated by the representative of the owner of enterprise—the central government. In other words, except for the salary, premium, and capital flow, all the money made by the state-owned enterprises should be allocated by the central government.

2. After obtaining the money, the central government should actively and purposefully set up new enterprise and factory and invest in a new project according to the report of all the enterprises and central macro planning.

3. For those enterprises with loss, the central government should assign a specialist for assessment. If there is no investment value, it should close the enterprise immediately and turn over the remaining assets to the country. Enterprises that suffered long-term loss are not allowed to persist, which is a waste of money of the people and country.

4. The central government should use all means to strictly control the financial leaderships' loyalty to the country because they hold huge capital. If there is fraud, it will cause a huge loss to the party and people.

5. The central government only pays the wage and bonus for local government and leaders of enterprise according to a certain proportion based on the money made for the people. Certainly, it should provide appropriate guidance and help in operation and management for them.

6. The central government hands in the actual operation and management of the enterprise to the local government and leaders of enterprise and law. As long as the business behaviour is lawful, it should not ask anything and interfere and should give them complete management right.

In fact, in simple words, people give the money to the central government, and the central government uses the money to set up better and more profitable enterprises for the people, to truly improve the people's level of life, and close the loss enterprise and non-performing enterprises.

Macroeconomic regulation and control is important, but it is not as direct and quick as direct investment. Government's macroeconomic regulation and control is an indirect management for the capitalist countries that have no ownership of the enterprise and cannot directly invest. In the socialist countries, there is no need for managing state-owned enterprises. The survival of state-owned enterprises is directly controlled by the nation.

Of course, people give the money to the central government, so the central government should pay attention to investment efficiency. But it is normal business to be successful or to fail, and not every investment can be successful. We also cannot require the government to achieve 100 per cent success rate of investment. Eight successful projects in ten can be considered as a basic success. It should summarise the unsuccessful experience, withdraw the remaining money, and continue to invest in other projects. If the investments fail one after another, it needs reflection. To sum up, efficient use of funds to make the capital flow quickly is the best resolution to resolve China's employment and development.

Where there is need to develop, there are factories to set up. And where there is need to shake off poverty to get rich, there is reasonable investment. The regime should serve for the people and state-owned enterprises can achieve.

Chinese government is not the expert in capital operation; hence a lot of mistakes of low level are made. Capitalist countries, with hundreds of years' experience in capital operation, run better than China. For some reason, they have never thought to do it like this and why they do it like this. China's development mode is seen, so you can know the concept of national capital and problems from another perspective.

39. Active labour, passive labour, and the state-owned enterprises

About 2007

Labours are different from each other. We have to do labour every day and go to work and come back from work, which makes us bustle about every day. But the labours are different in categories, job division, and wages; in addition, we have realised no one studies them as theory, which are active labour and passive labour.

Definition of Active Labour and Passive Labour

The most representative people are the train conductor and the hawkers on the street.

The labour of the train conductor is passive. The labour of the hawkers on the street is active.

The active labour is the one where the fruits of labour have a direct relation to the worker's subjective consciousness.

The passive labour is the one where the fruits of labour don't have a direct relation to the worker's subjective consciousness.

The labour of the train conductor is the most typical passive labour, whose fruits of labour have no direct relation to their subjective consciousness of the work, which mainly means their labour attitude and enthusiasm. No matter if the attitude of the conductor is bad or good, you have to buy the train tickets. Few people will change their decision to take a bus or plane instead of a train because of the bad attitude of the conductor. People often feel happy for their having bought the right ticket. A reasonable person will not be too mean on the rudeness of the conductor.

So the business volume of the ticket conductor is decided by the supply and demand of the market, which has no direct relation to their performance. Their business achievements are not controlled by themselves, so they are called passive labour.

The hawkers on the street are exactly the opposite. Their turnover has a direct relation to their subjective consciousness. We can realise that the reason why the passers-by will buy his things after observing them is their active attitude to do business and initiative to greet customers. All these have caused the trust, interest, purchase desire of the guests, and they will buy their things. If the hawker is vicious, no one will buy his things except for necessity otherwise. So whether the hawker can attract customers, whether he can deal with business and his own work emotion will both affect his turnover. So we call it active labour.

Active Labour, Passive Labour, and the State-owned Enterprises

I remember that in the Cultural Revolution, all of us proposed to cut the tail of capitalism, which means to eliminate the private enterprises and individual labour completely.

Nowadays, in addition to some state-owned monopolies, the other competitive state-owned monopolies are all basically annihilated. What is the reason? That's because most of the workers in the state-owned monopolies are doing the passive work, while the workers of other enterprises are doing active work. Because the owner of the private sector takes the active labour, the whole enterprise is regarded as the active labour.

Human nature is selfish, greedy, lazy, and indolent!

Because of the ugliness and hypocrisy in human nature of the state-owned employees, they can only make a show of authority in the field of state-owned enterprises. They may find them at a loss when they meet with the company of the active labour.

So the private sector cannot be eliminated, and the state-owned enterprises simply cannot do the active labour. Thus, the state capitalism must coexist in state-owned and private enterprises. Neither of them could eliminate nor replace the other.

The existing state-owned enterprises can afford much more disposable funds for secondary distribution and public utilities, such as military, infrastructure, basic scientific research, transfer payments, and so on.

It's necessary to spend the money. The taxpayers will not agree to spend their money on those, but it is suitable for the residual value to do these. With the funding, our country will not be subject to the capitalists, and they can do something of justice, reason, and science, which is also the basic logic and principle of Marxism.

Although Marx said a lot, I think all of it is nonsense. He did not have any practice, and the only valuable thing is that socialist politicians can do something with the residual value of state-owned capital. It is superior to capitalism. That is to say, the state capitalism is the only advantage of the Marxist theory, which is the socialism improved by the later generation. The rest is all fantasy.

However, active labour and passive labour can be transformed with the development of productivity and the improvement of management level.

Some active labour can be converted to passive labour.

For example, the Fordist form of labour, which is a pipeline operation, forces workers to complete the work in accordance with established requirements. It is a typical case that converts active labour into passive labour.

The store clerks of McDonald's, KFC, and some other brand stores will be mandatorily asked to entertain customers in accordance with certain standards by their boss. On entering the McDonald's door, you will hear someone saying, 'Welcome, this way, please!' I feel that they greet in a fake way, but those are the mandatory standards of their boss. Clerks are forced to show initiative, but in fact it is passive.

Therefore, the state capital can march on to the areas of private capital gradually in the case of suitable conditions and eventually oppresses them into a corner. However, it may take a long time, and you need to accumulate a lot of experience on that field. But it can be achieved finally.

40. Harmonious society and capital equality

About 2007

Every individual in this world needs his own living space. It is the purpose of the harmonious society that every individual could have his own freedom to the largest extent and does not have conflict of interest to the largest extent.

How do we realise this? It needs an invisible hand to adjust and control people's demands, desires, and behaviour all the time. What is this hand? That is the absolute and utmost equality and integrity. How do we realise this?

My personal view: the largest inequality is the inequality of capital rather than inequality of human rights. But it is incurable because of the selfishness of humans.

People only know two things; one is money and the other is gun. Maybe it is profitable or has no choice, or human beings will do anything under the lawless situation. People are born to consider their own petty profits instead of others. This is human nature, and humans are all ugly.

How do we make society consisting of ugly people meet the needs of the majority? How do we make the majority live happily but not affect other people's interests?

The society should try its best to provide an equal, reasonable, and good living space for the people who can't make money. There shall be a strong power to restrict the people who are evil, brutal, and powerful. Uproot them when necessary.

Let the world achieve true fairness and justice.

Under the situation of capital inequality, putting forward the equality of human rights is totally a flicker and defraud. The capitalist and the poor are absolutely unequal. The so-called equality of human rights between the capitalist and the poor is like a spiritual heroin and anaesthetic.

How do socialist countries realise the equality of capital?

Here is the simplest example. There are two enterprises: one is private and the other is state-owned. The capitalist and leaders of state-owned enterprises do the same work, and so do the workers, provided that the two enterprises have the same turnover and profits. The boss of a private enterprise pays 80 million a year to himself, and so does the boss of a state-owned enterprise.

This yearly salary is a legitimate income for the boss of a private enterprise, which is protected by law. This yearly salary is a corruption for the boss of a state-owned enterprise, which will be punished by law. But there is no difference in nature; they make money from their enterprises.

The corruption of socialist countries is illicit, but it is legal in a capitalist country. Hence, from this perspective, socialist countries are incorruptible thousands of times more than capitalist countries. The capitalist countries guarantee the inequality of capital by law and strong power. The state capitalism system of socialist countries guarantees the inequality of capital by law and strong power.

State capitalism belongs to the state, not the private boss in state capitalism. The bosses of state-owned enterprises are appointed by the state. The income of the boss is state-certified and paid by the state. The bosses of state-owned enterprises do not have the ownership of state-owned assets; they only are advanced wage earners who seem to do the same work as the bosses of private enterprises. However, the most essential things of enterprises are totally different. One has ownership and one does not, one is a boss and one is a worker, one could get the salary he wants and one's salary is paid by the state.

Theoretically, under the state capitalist system, the surplus value of the state-owned enterprises is divided to the state to the largest extent, and the state will divide the money to people in another way, while the bosses of the private enterprises possess the surplus value to the largest extent. This is the most basic theory of Marx.

Marx's so-called exploitation theory is valid under the theory of state capitalism. But it is not invalid in the field the state could not be involved in.

Do the capitalist countries make money in some fields and absolutely not make money in other fields? What fields? This needs asking to economists.

Here is a simple example: government capital could win benefits in the state-monopoly field and industry-monopoly field, such as steel, oil, energy, telecommunication, and so on.

It will be defective to use state capital to run a barbershop. Why? This is my theory: active labour and passive labour.

It will be profitable for the active labour of state capital, and it will be defective for the passive labour of state capital. Therefore, the private enterprises do active labour, and the state-owned enterprises do the passive labour in my theory.

Harmonious society is a social system with scientific management of all devils, heresies, evils, uncultured behaviour, dirtiness, oppression, absurdity, and integrity of human nature and producing by social operation militarily, politically, economically, essentially, and at source.

State capitalism, that is, the capital equality of communism, is the basic material insurance for harmonious society. The harmonious society has to be built upon state capitalism.

41. The deep analysis of the Tao Te Ching and the Diamond Sutra and Confucius-Mencius culture

About 2007

In my opinion, the deepest influence on Chinese culture should be the Tao Te Ching, while the thoughts of Confucius and Mencius are the specific form of the Tao Te Ching in the feudalistic productivity period.

It is said that after Lao Tzu wrote the Tao Te Ching, he travelled around the West and left the Diamond Sutra for India.

It's just a rumour, but the Tao Te Ching covers completely the Diamond Sutra in terms of dominant idea; the Diamond Sutra is a kind of understanding and explanation of the Tao Te Ching. It is one aspect of understanding and explanation. It explains clearly in a certain aspect, making people easier to understand. Frankly speaking, no one in China can really understand the true intentions and thoughts of the author of the Tao Te Ching.

42. Tao Te Ching

About 2007

It is a philosophical classic that focuses on the philosophy of governing a nation and the whole world from a macro point of view. And it can be also said to be a set of methodologies or thinking patterns.

But later I knew that Taoist school regarded it as a classic of Taoism, and they applied the dominant ideology and methodology to their own bodybuilding, which resulted in the famous Taoism kung fu in China—shadowboxing. Shadowboxing is quite familiar to most households in China and enjoys a much greater recognition than the Tao Te Ching.

Referring to Tao Te Ching as part of philosophy is based on the fact that it does provide a set of unique methodologies that can be used not only for a nation, the whole world, or even universe, but also for individuals, enterprises, and most of the existing systems.

The Tao Te Ching is the specific representation of the philosophy of yin and yang with explicit literariness. The philosophy of yin and yang is its dominant ideology.

Lao Tzu integrated the philosophy of yin and yang into the complete set of theories on national navigation. Yet the usefulness of the Tao Te Ching is not just limited to national navigation. It can be used for every single matter around people and all matters in the world. It is the most influential book to Chinese people, especially to their thinking patterns.

And what's more, what was embodied by Confucius does not go beyond the scope of Tao Te Ching. Confucius-Mencius ideology just specified the contributions of the Tao Te Ching to the construction of politics, feudal system, and administration and navigation and made them available in every specific and detailed matter.

Many Chinese scholars suggest that the Tao Te Ching is too profound to comprehend when making some comments on the book. Actually, an interpretation of Tao Te Ching should never be confined to the translation of its literal meanings. Instead, we should try to infer the author's dominant ideology and appreciate his intention of creation.

The author's intention in creating the Tao Te Ching is to illustrate at some length the administration methodology and dominant ideology of a nation as a system, or say, as an autocratic system or a regulable national system. Or to be specific, it is the thinking patterns of administrators of a regulable system (particularly of nations).

What have been proposed in the Tao Te Ching are some specific methods and suggestions, serving as just references that should not be interpreted from the literal meanings. As we can see, the first sentence of the book made clear the stance of the author—everything in the world is in constant change. Ways of governing a nation or specific resolutions for certain problems that can be expressed via language and writing system are bound to be readjusted and rearranged according to specific social contexts with the passing of time, changing of situations, or the development of productive forces.

As an old Chinese saying goes, we should listen not to what people say but how they say it. The opening remark of the author made clear his intention.

A detailed analysis of the content in the Tao Te Ching will be provided in later sections. Here, the dominant ideology in the Tao Te Ching is to allow the king or leading group to administrate and coordinate within a nation as a system. When coordinating, administrators should let nature take its course and give judicious guidance according to circumstances so as to integrate members of the system into a united force to resolve conflicts for the purpose of reaching the harmonious state within the system where man and nature are of one soul and coexist peacefully in everlasting prosperity.

43. Confucius-Mencius ideology

About 2007

If we say that what's in the Tao Te Ching is all about thinking patterns and conceptualisations, then Confucius-Mencius is mainly about specific cultural products. Since Confucius-Mencius ideology is the embodiment and realisation of the concepts for a nation as a regulable system, it contains mainly the specific proposals put forward according to the there-then situation of productive forces and production relations:

1. The supremacy of imperial power

2. Dominance of the king over his subjects

3. Dominance of the father over his sons

4. Dominance of the husband over his wife

as well as the derived specific methods of each kind of ideology.

We can leave alone the other details for now. Four rules can serve to include all men and women, old and young in the society into a large system.

The kings are born with a mixture of multiple powers such as military, political, and economic power and serve as the administrators of the social system. What's more, Confucius and Mencius pushed the kings into a mythological position where they are not only political administrators, but also sons of nature, dragons, leaders, and managers of people's spiritual world, as well as governors appointed by God to be on his behalf. And many ethical codes have been established to consolidate the dominant status of the kings in political and spiritual ruling and administrating based on that.

Feudal ethical codes represent the formal establishment and confirmation of the holy status of kings in administrating and governing, as well as psychological hints. While officials at different levels under the leadership of the king are just the maintainers and executers of the system with which the king exerts his political power. From a political point of view, the political system can only work within the domain of the national political administrative system and people's political behaviour and cannot govern people's everyday life directly.

The doctrines of Confucius and Mencius also regulate father-son relationship and husband-wife relationship and guide people's daily life into the orbit designed by Confucius and Mencius. Such relationships are maintained and supported by political system and are compulsory.

Besides, Confucius and Mencius also advocated filial piety, strengthened the subordination in father-son system, and made it more vivid; and the advocating of three obediences and four virtues (specifically, obedience to father before marriage, to husband after marriage, and to son after husband's death; fidelity, physical charm, propriety in speech, and efficiency in needlework) is to strengthen the subordination in husband-wife system.

Therefore, the doctrine of Confucius and Mencius is a rigorous system involving all members of a society and covering all social problems!

44. Diamond Sutra

About 2007

There exist lots of books on Buddhism, yet among them the most well-known one is the Diamond Sutra.

Buddhist sutra includes the Mahayana and the Hinayana. As far as I am concerned, only the Mahayana amounts to the title Buddhist sutra and constitutes the true intention of Buddha since it focuses on holistic research within the psychological domain of the whole of mankind, while the Hinayana just focuses on individuals as research subjects. In comparison, the Hinayana places more emphasis on individual behaviour and ethical cultivation while the Mahayana tends to be influence and work for social system.

In my point of view, Buddhist sutra and the Tao Te Ching depict the same thing, just from two different angles. They resemble each other a lot in terms of the theme conveyed and techniques employed, and Tao Te Ching has relatively more detailed and diversified expressions.

In Buddhist sutra, people with great wisdom are called Buddha, while in the Tao Te Ching, they are called gentlemen. Buddha is wise people, while Taoism is the great wisdom.

One talks about wisdom from the perspective of humans, while the other approaches it from matters. All matters are conducted by humans, so the core of the two turns out to be the same.

In Buddhist sutra, people with wit and wisdom are asked by the Buddha to take saving all living beings as their own responsibilities. And they are required to save all living beings by the roots and take them out of misery, not just solve a certain problem temporarily.

As the productive force changes, people have increasingly improved productive force. As a result, people's individual awareness range and social demands as well as the conflicts and misery they are faced with keep changing all the time. That is to say, when the productive force is very poor, what people want most might be something to eat and some clothes to put on; as the productive force improves, people begin to demand personal rights and development space, hence the emergence of the slogans and concepts of democracy and human rights.

With the development of productive force and improvement of people's awareness, people have needs at much higher levels. Just as what's in

Maslow's hierarchy of social needs, the society also develops gradually from lower levels to higher levels.

With the improvement of people's living standard, apart from food and clothes and certain material foundation, people have more needs in self-actualisation and need to love and to be loved. The harmonious society is exactly an embodiment of self-actualisation in loving and being loved. To love and be loved is actually a kind of social security at a higher level from its essence and profound significance.

Therefore, what Buddha needs to do is in constant change with the development of productive force. Yet the purpose is the same—to save all living beings by the roots and take them out of misery instead of to solve the problems temporarily. That is what Buddha needs to do and what is conveyed in the Diamond Sutra.

45. Comments on the Tao Te Ching and Diamond Sutra

About 2007

The author of the two books is an incredibly great person. He wrote the two books not for all human beings, but for those with outstanding intelligence and amazing comprehension abilities.

According to the current situation, the two books are probably only for 20 per cent of the entirety of mankind—the leaders and the powerful ones. People with average intelligence find it impossible to understand the true intention of the author. They only misunderstand what the author said, following the literal meanings, or they cannot understand it at all. The act of looking at the two books as something for fun, without any idea of the content is, if not acceptable, at least not disastrous compared to the acts of distorting the original intention of the author and randomly speculating, which may hurt others and themselves as well.

The administrators of a society, ranging from the king of a nation, the leader of a government, president of a country, to the authority of enterprises, often have certain control (more or less) over people's destinies and living environment. Their decisions determine the fate of the country, and the Tao Te Ching is written for them. They are the elites of the society, the administrators, the leaders, and the organisers. What does the Tao Te Ching tell us anyway? It is required that the elites of a society, the administrative level, decision-making authorities should be strategic and virtuous. They should govern the country, the local place, as well as the enterprises with strategies and virtues. Here, Tao and Te are not what we mean morality in daily discussion.

The two are totally different concepts. Tao in Tao Te Ching refers to the correct, rational, and perfect ways of handling things. Te refers to the accomplishments and performances established following the Tao—the ways. Tao appearing in what was referred to as an enlightened and great king and an unprincipled dim-witted ruler means exactly the same as ways and strategies. That is to say, this king had the appropriate ways of governing a country or he knew nothing about it at all.

With appropriate ways and strategies, a nation, local places, and enterprises can enjoy a full-scale reconstruction and an everlasting prosperity. They will stand as long as the earth, the moon, and the sun exist.

Without appropriate ways and strategies, a nation will decline and be destructed, plunging people into misery and sufferings and enterprises into bankruptcy with the evil forces in charge.

Governing a country, the same as managing an enterprise, requires ways and strategies. Then where do ways and strategies come from? They are from accurate, objective, and rational methodology. They are derived from the insights into the genuine and objective regularities of the country one governs and the enterprise one manages after scientific, attentive, thorough, and objective research and study based on the prior knowledge and the current situation. They are the accurate conclusions drawn and the best projects put forward.

This requires profound knowledge and extremely amazing organisational and thinking capabilities so as to have incredible courage and incisiveness, to accurately locate his or her own position and direction, to draw conclusions that lead to the most appropriate objectives and methods, and finally, to lead people out of dangers and towards brightness and relief.

46. The essence of the Tao Te Ching lies in its implications for political authorities to rule with the characteristics of water

About 2007

The essence of the Tao Te Ching lies in its implications for political authorities to rule with the characteristics of water. They should behave like water—willing to be at the disposal of people and to be modest, to nurse and nourish all living beings, to make them prosper with wisdom, to gather strong power (the power of being the source of everything) beneath the soft appearance, to enjoy an everlasting prosperity and nourishment of everything—so that they can accumulate abundant virtues and wealth to make these benefit for thousands of generations to follow.

To gain prosperity, it is required that either the leader of a country, the minister, the governor of a province, the mayor of a city, the director of a factory, the county commissioner, or the boss of an enterprise should love his country, local place, enterprise, and factory wholeheartedly and attentively try to solve various problems existing in the world, the country, the province, the city, the factory, and the enterprise, to lead them towards prosperity and brightness and to enable people within these places to live and work in peace and contentment and to enjoy individual and national wealth. Such is how a country, a local place, an enterprise, and a factory can gain management strategies and moral support to make the country, the public, and the boss wealthy and the employees content. Such are merits and virtues!

The love and Tao mentioned here do not necessarily refer to the act of punishing the evil. To lay off extra employees in order to save all other employees' interests is also a kind of goodness, merit, and virtue.

47. An accurate understanding of the decadent ideas in Lao-Tzu theory and some suggestions for improvement

About 2007

There exist many decadent ideas in the Tao Te Ching, yet it should be noticed that any ideology was produced and put into use within a certain social context and background. Lao Tzu theory was put forward in accordance with the there-then social environment and productive force to the end of adjusting relations among people in society.

When was the book being written? It was during the Spring and Autumn Period and the Warring States Period when China was transforming from a slave society to a feudal society and battles were everywhere, plunging people into endless misery and sufferings. Seeing all these, Lao Tzu had a mixture of feelings. What people were in desperate need of back then was peace and security, and to lead a quiet life was the most luxurious wish and biggest consumption for them.

Therefore, the Tao Te Ching put forward by Lao Tzu is actually for political authorities. Lao Tzu held that they should conquer the unyielding with the yielding to reach the end of the whole world as one big family and that man and nature are of one soul. They should also nurse and nourish all their subjects like sunshine and raindrops do with the earth so that they can build a harmonious society.

In yin-yang theory, yang means destruction, abolishment, forging ahead, innovation, and fighting, while yin denotes cultivation, breeding, protection, reservation, contentment, and adjustment.

With the progress of different developmental stages, the progress of productive force to a certain level and social conflicts being accumulated to a certain degree, external forces will make it necessary and urgent to reform, and the society then needs revolution. If the authorities cannot see the true social conflicts or timely adjust relations among people, they are likely to resort to the means of war to resolve social conflicts. What belongs to yang in terms of wars include the idea that either you die or I die, being completely done with someone or something, to remove someone or something by roots, and to solve the key issue for the solution of the whole problem. So in summary, the means of yang are aggression and destruction. It is just like urban reconstruction. Without knocking down and destructing old houses, how can new buildings be built? The act of knocking down old houses requires the most extreme means of yang. Then new houses are built and residents move in, becoming host and hostess to manage the houses and make them prosper. That's the process where yin works.

The current phenomenon of women in the dominant position while men are in a much weaker position can be traced back to the most deeply rooted, most ancient, and original theory of Tao Te Ching.

Lao Tzu advocated the employment of yin at an extreme end to solve all problems. However, as time passed, things changed gradually. The ancient Arcadian scenario in which men ploughed and women weaved faded away. Gone are the days when men undertook farming while women did all the housework and brought meals to their husbands day after day and year after year. It was the Western guns that woke up Chinese people from their fantasies and pulled them from their sleepy state back to reality. What is reality? It is competition—endless, fierce, and damaging competition.

Competition exists everywhere, among humans, among different areas and countries. It does not belong to Chinese only, and it is not what humans want in nature; instead, it is an obligatory course posed on us by external forces.

Those left behind are bound to be bullied, and a typical example was the burning down of Yuanmingyuan. To avoid lagging behind, we must compete. To be number 2 or number 3 assures no security. We need to compete to be number 1.

The balance of yin and yang as well as the harmony of celestial and terrestrial forces for the growth of all living things are present in the ancient Chinese philosophy of yin and yang, which emphasises both feminine and masculine. Therefore, the traditional Chinese culture needs to add and reconcile with the Western masculine culture, playing their roles in a scientific and correct way.

The current mode of social operation in China is a combination of Eastern and Western cultures, and the organic product of communist culture and democratic culture. They play their strong points in different areas to serve for the people and their fundamental interests, effectively and scientifically promoting social stability, social justice, scientific national management, as well as stable and rapid economic development.

48. Truth that can be expressed with language never lasts long

About 2007

Tao Te Ching: Chapter 1

'Tao' and 'Te' are different from 'morality' which is usually mentioned by us.

Tao Te Ching is not a book talking about ethics.

'Tao' refers to the way of dealing with problems. More precisely speaking, Tao refers to the most correct, cleverest, and humane way of dealing with problems with the lowest social cost and the best effect. Tao means an ultimate method of considering all big and small problems through careful consideration.

'Te' refers to the social benefits produced by the implementation and promotion of Tao, which is the best way.

'Tao' and 'Te' mean achieving good social benefits through implementing the most correct method, which is the moral praised highly by Lao Tzu. Certainly, morality in an ethical sense is included in it, but the moral is not limited to morality in an ethical sense.

It is the first chapter of Tao Te Ching and also general introduction.

Lao Tzu emphasised, 'Tao refers to truth and a changing thing. It cannot stick to convention. Otherwise, Tao does not exist.'

From the method and strategy of governing a country, national policies, policies, laws, and regulations developed by gentlemen (namely, state leader and leading group) are determined by practical situations. In case the situation changes, the thinking mode, key work, and contradiction nature of the gentleman have to change at any time. Otherwise, a disaster will be triggered by wrong national policies.

It is very simple to understand. At the beginning of revolution and during the period of Japanese rampage, the gentleman had to highlight the contradiction with enemies and the opposition party and made his countrymen see the direction of revolution clearly and harbour a hatred for treason, invasion, oppression, flinch, and so on.

All in all, the purpose of hatred was to establish a new people's regime. Therefore, hatred was Tao at that time because it could stimulate people's desire of destruction and slaughter. In that case, the people's regime could be established only through destroying and slaughtering enemies.

However, domestic contradiction turned into the contradiction of economic construction after the revolution achieved success and aggression in all directions was pacified. No one can make money by means of hatred. It is Tao of economy and money. Tao of hatred should be ended. Tao does not exist if people knowing nothing about Tao of economy take the helm of the state, issue confused orders, and wage a war randomly. Without Tao, a country will disappear and fall apart like Eastern Europe. China would have ended in the same way if Deng Xiaoping did not make vigorous efforts to turn the situation and separated from them.

Economic construction is Tao of business, which has no colour and class. What a gentleman should do is to combine Tao of business with national conditions and perfectly blend them instead of concentrating on economic construction with outdated struggle and Tao of hatred. In this case, Tao does not exist.

At present, Tao refers to perfectly combining Tao of business with national conditions with great wisdom, which not only consolidates the regime, but also develops the economy. Through looking at the card in his hand and others' hands, a gentleman enhances advantages, avoids disadvantages, achieves success one way or another, uses both hard and soft tactics, and achieves the goal to ensure healthy development in all aspects.

The Tao Te Ching is theory specially aimed at system. The state is a system that Tao Te Ching pays most attention to because whether a monarch has Tao is directly related to the life, death, happiness, and health of the people.

The state is a system. In particular, a despotic state is a system that can be regulated and controlled to the fullest. China's feudal dynasty is a national system of autocratic centralisation according to the systematic thought of Lao Tzu.

Socialism and communism are a national system of new generation and an autocratic national system that can be fully regulated and controlled. In such a national system, whether the gentleman (namely, state leader and leading group), the key figure in the control centre of the system, has the way of running the state is directly related to the operating condition and safety of the whole system.

If controlled well, a national system can fully release the potential of each individual in society. Each individual can fully display his value and get the maximum return. In the meanwhile, our country can be far ahead of other countries.

When driven, a car runs faster than creatures with two legs. Cars are the method of a system state while two legs belong to the way of a democratic state.

If controlled badly, contradictions will be constantly aggravated. Full of chaos everywhere, a state will fall apart, collapse, and disappear in the end.

Apart from the way of running a state, all kinds of knowledge are Tao. They are Tao of various subjects. For various subjects, Tao refers to all kinds of professional knowledge and technology.

As long as they are truth, they can be called Tao.

When heaven and earth took shape in the beginning, there was no life in the world except for inorganic substances. Life started to appear after the existence of Tao.

Regarding the origin of life, I think that biological evolutionism cannot be explained, and creationism is reasonable, scientific, and logical. Growing out of nothing, creatures are not an evolutionary process, but a very complicated biochemical process.

Inorganic substances are stones, water, air, sunshine, thunder and lightning, and wind. How these inorganic substances in nature form life naturally without the help of any intelligence of science and technology is a problem that any top technology cannot answer and simulate so far.

Any life, even the simplest life—virus—is a thing that is infinitely superior to, more advanced and complicated than our computers. It is impossible for a life to take shape spontaneously under natural conditions.

Therefore, Tao appears before any life. Similarly, technology and drawings appear before machines. With the existence of technology and drawings, there are machines that can operate. Those technology and drawings are Tao.

Technology and knowledge are intangible. Therefore, Tao is characterised by 'invisibility'.

However, all life has its objective law—Tao. Therefore, Tao exists in everything. Every life has Tao. As a result, Tao usually exists.

For people, knowledge is infinite. No scientist is sure about when people can master all knowledge in the universe. Therefore, Tao is very abstruse.

49. If all people know why beautiful things become beautiful, ugliness will be stopped

About 2007

Tao Te Ching: Chapter 2

Comment:

The people around the world, i.e., common people, have a very narrow dimension of consciousness, and they often consider things with a one-sided view that they consider is right.

1. For instance, a teacup can be round when observed from above but square when seen from the front. Moreover, it might present another shape when observed from the side face. However, a teacup will always be a teacup.

This can also be illustrated in the literary quotation of blind men and an elephant. Common people often consider things with extremely one-sided view. Therefore, they might be cheated easily.

However, wise men will consider problems from multiple and different angles in a comprehensive way.

2. Some Net friends do not understand my articles and viewpoints and have objections against my perspectives. In fact, they just consider things with one-sided view rather than look at the problems from other angles.

3. For another example, many democrats criticise Marx on the Internet.

However, they never censure that Marx never acted as capitalist and worker, Marx would never be a capitalist, or Marx did not write Das Kapital. Das Kapital is just a tale of a tub and fairy tale without practice.

Their thoughts are restricted to a certain range, quite stubborn, just like other people. Actually there is no right or wrong. It is just either comprehensive or one-sided.

All thoughts, belief in capitalism, belief in socialism, or even belief in feudalism, are comprehensive or one-sided, rather than right or wrong. The envoys of devils just utilise such narrow-mindedness of people's thoughts to trigger narrow-mindedness and to realise their own purposes.

All thoughts, belief in capitalism, belief in socialism, or even belief in feudalism, consider that they are beautiful and virtuous. In fact, they just do not know what true beauty is and what true virtuousness is. In order to judge whether a concrete object is beautiful and virtuous or ugly and evil, we must know this object in a comprehensive way and understand it from multiple angles and aspects.

Beauty and virtuousness mentioned by Lao-Tzu:

If a thing can benefit both parties, then it can be called beauty.

If a thing can benefit the opposite side but does not benefit you or even damages your interest slightly, it can be called virtuousness.

Lao Tzu considered that the world lacked beautiful and virtuous things, because people in the world just looked at problems by starting from their own perspectives and interests. They do not know how to do good and beautiful works.

The beauty and virtuousness mentioned by Lao Tzu do not mean minor beauty and minor virtuousness. When you give a beggar 10 yuan or 100 yuan, this is just minor virtuousness rather than virtuousness mentioned by Lao Tzu or true virtuousness.

What is minor beauty? When you sell a watermelon to passers-by who are thirsty, this is called beauty. You can earn money and passers-by can quench their thirst. But this is just minor beauty rather than virtuousness and beauty mentioned by Lao Tzu.

Common people around the world just don't know how to achieve and realise true beauty and virtuousness. True beauty and virtuousness are national policies, laws, regulations, and moral principles gained under comprehensive consideration and great wisdom in an authoritarian regime system.

Maybe common people around the world consider that this has nothing to do with them, and it is just the matter of the country. Therefore, they will not consider or care about it, unless their interests are affected. This is the reason why common people around the world don't know how to achieve and realise true beauty and virtuousness.

Democratic system aims to make the ignorant people that don't know how to achieve and realise true beauty and virtuousness control the national destiny. This is the fatal weakness of countries adopting democratic system.

Therefore, I consider that Lao Tzu's authoritarian regime system is a system more advanced than democratic system.

Experts guide common people and elites lead ignorant people. This is advanced productivity.

What does it mean to achieve and realise true beauty and virtuousness in the current situations of our country? When the state-owned capital of China can profit substantially and the money gained can be invested in places with underdeveloped economy requiring a large amount of input from the government, such as rural areas, education, social security, national defence, science and technology, etc., this means to achieve and realise true beauty and virtuousness.

How can state-owned capital profit? Isn't this the system of capitalism to create surplus value to the largest extent? Frankly speaking, it is state capitalism, law of the jungle, and economic rule.

To know true beauty and virtuousness means to know Tao. As for the fundamental reason why ugly things happen in the world, most people don't know true beauty and virtuousness or Tao.

The fundamental reason for all ugly problems in China, such as corruption, gap between the rich and the poor, urban-rural gap, etc., is that state-owned capital management goes out of control. Strictly speaking, ownership management of state-owned capital is out of control. Anyone that has power can occupy state-owned capital. Why? The ownership of state-owned capital is transferred to lower levels in China, and Chinese people are confused in this issue.

True beauty and virtuousness can be achieved when Chinese people realise this point and are able to flexibly use state-owned capital. Thus state-owned capital will become a treasure bowl benefiting the people.

If common people can absolutely master the methods and skills of applying state-owned capital, problems like corruption, gap between the rich and the poor, and urban-rural gap will be solved effectively. This is the true connotation of the sentence 'If all common people around the world know why beautiful things become beautiful, ugly things will be stopped; if all common people around the world know why virtuous things become virtuous, evil things will be stopped.'

50. During national governance, common people should be encouraged to pursue material benefits rather than ideology

About 2007

Tao Te Ching: Chapter 3

Explanation:

Common people should be encouraged to reduce desires and to care about whether they have enough to eat only. Common people should be made to care about their health only rather than realise lofty ideals. Common people should not intrigue against each other and possess great political ideals. Those demagogic schemers should be prevented from acting recklessly and occupying the market. If the above scenes can be realised, the sages will be able to govern all countries well without great political behaviour.

Comment:

This sentence is somewhat reasonable to some extent.

In Lao Tzu's country with authoritarian system, there is a social division of labour among people in the country. In any country of our practical life, there is a division of labour among people. People can be doctors, cops, teachers, workers, or self-employed labourers. There are numerous industries. In a micro sense, with a professional skill, people are able to make a living in the society.

However, a human being is not an isolated individual. In a macro sense, various industries are associated. The development level of scientists decides the productivity and consumption level of the whole society. The development level of medical science decides the average lifetime of people.

Politics has a direct and important relation with all other industries. Politics decides war or peace as well as the productive relation of the society. Besides, politics can decide laws, morality, principles, etc. Politics is actually a complex and professional job.

In Lao Tzu's authoritarian system, noble persons can adjust social relations between men as well as the social order through rational judgment, analysis, and political power after fully understanding true and comprehensive knowledge mastered by human beings, so as to realise social harmony and express the maximum potential of every person.

Noble persons mentioned by Lao Tzu are individual persons or leading groups mastering political power. They will always start from state interests, national interests, and people's interests. They come from common people, but they have better intelligence and political ability than common people. They are elites of common people but will always serve the people. They can represent people's interests, which are interests of people throughout the country, maximum interests, long-term interests, and fundamental interests.

Politics is professional and society is huge and complicated. In an optimal society, ideal society, calm society, stable society, and harmonious society, division of labour and trust must exist among people. All people are engaged in their own careers and interests, but they will not produce severe conflicts with other people. They are able to keep harmony with others. Such society is needed by us.

The basic condition for Lao Tzu's authoritarian system society is that people or groups called noble persons should come from common people, be superior to common people, and can absolutely represent people's fundamental interests. Three-representative thought is the basic condition of becoming people or groups called noble persons in the mind of Lao Tzu.

Without people or groups called noble persons, the basic condition of Lao Tzu's authoritarian system cannot be met. Therefore, the system will collapse soon.

If the authoritarian system managed by noble persons mentioned by Lao Tzu exists in the society, and the system is mastered by noble persons that can represent people's interests, then the following sentences of Lao Tzu will be tenable: 'Common people should be encouraged to reduce desires and to care about whether they have enough to eat only. Common people should be made to care about their health only, rather than realise lofty ideals. Common people should not intrigue against each other and possess great political ideals. Those demagogic schemers should be prevented from acting recklessly and occupying the market. If the above scenes can be realised, the sages will be able to govern all countries well without great political behaviour.'

In a country led by sages or noble persons, people do not need to care about politics or excessively participate in politics. Common people just need to worry about their houses, cars, money, children, and wives.

Actually, common people have two purposes to participate in politics.

1. Fun and curiosity
They want to confirm that they are safe. When common people go into politics, they just do for others, and they will never be elected. They have

no such ability. They tell themselves that they can master their fate, but this is no more than self-consolation. They just cheat themselves. Actually they can change nothing.

2. Helplessness

Because of the ugliness in human nature, no one can be trusted. Therefore, they have to go into politics by themselves and do for others. They just want to confirm that they are not betrayed and thrown into the garbage can.

Therefore, it will be a kind of happiness, beauty, and win-win result if people can elect or produce a collective and leader that will truly represent their interests and make them manage politics. Capable elites willing to make a contribution to the country should obtain the sovereign power of governing the country. It is also a sense of security and happiness if people have a person truly representing their interests to master administrative power and to maintain their interests.

Democratic politics means to let people acquire a tiny sense of security and vanity by spending a lot of time, energy, and money. This is a kind of pain and waste.

51. The universe is merciless and treats every living creature without dignity

About 2007

Tao Te Ching: Chapter 5

Explanation:

The universe is merciless and treats every living creatures like domestic animals; the deity is merciless, he treats the people like domestic animals. The space between heaven and earth is like a big bellows. There is empty between heaven and earth and couldn't force people to do anything. With the natural changes, everything happens naturally. People may feel days without changes if they talk too much, so please let people feel it themselves.

Comment:

These two sentences are the most extraordinary expression from Lao Tzu and the most worth thinking expression.

'Merciless' is the thought of governed by law of Lao Tzu. Mercy is the aim, and merciless is the way; only through mercilessness can we realise mercy. Heaven and earth is mercy, expresses it through tangible natural Tao; the deity is mercy, expresses it through perfect social rules.

The universe is merciless and treated every living creatures like domestic animals

Heaven and earth run by their own rules, the natural Tao, and nature won't pay preference to any creatures. Violating the rules of nature or ignoring it will definitely get punishment without any excuse to avoid.

What are the natural rules? Law of the jungle, survival of the fittest, the weak are doomed to die, and the winner takes all.

This is the real mercilessness. This is the truth. The Chinese learn from Lao Tzu, listen to Lao Tzu, but distorted it a lot and became a culture of sissiness. But the quintessential part of Lao Tzu is falsified by fools.

Even a word like 'chu dog' dare not to direct translation—a typical black sheep, a good-for-nothing.

The deity is merciless; he treated the people like domestic animals.

Netizens think this sentence is the thought of governed by law from Lao Tzu; it required the saint manage the country by law instead of emotion. I think it is partly correct.

People regulated the law and changed it day to day; a different law made by different people may have a different purpose in favour of a different person. Just like the laws of property, it aroused great discussion even before it comes out. Actually it isn't an argument, it is power-changing; every force tends to gain interest from it. So law may not govern the country successfully.

This book is the Tao Te Ching; the thoughts of Lao Tzu are not governed by law but by Tao. Only the law derived from Tao can govern the country. There is law if there isn't Tao, but the law without Tao can only exaggerate the social conflict, involving people in pains and injustice, and cannot accomplish the purpose of administering a country.

Tao is objectives, justice, overall, and proved by the practice. It can weigh the advantages and the disadvantages and fully consider every corner of the society. It is also considered the natural justice and human instinct, and after a deep consideration through elites' analysis, it can lead people to the right way.

Tao is the purest, absolute, without any affection, and only overall analysis and consideration. A result comes from reasonable sense. So Tao is merciless, unbothered by affection. It's all-or-none thinking. For everything that happens in a normal person, especially a big event, we need perfect analysis.

It's quite easy—those who refuse to admit that it's the state-owned enterprises that ruin the whole enterprises, those who refuse to admit that Karl Marx has no certification to write Das Kapital, and those who don't admit that the Islamic Wahhab is heresy, the people without Tao, they are blind, unable to see the essence of issues and they are incapable of managing the country's event and even don't have the ability to talk about our country.

The space between heaven and earth is like a big bellows. There is emptiness between heaven and earth and couldn't force people to do anything. With the yin-yang running, everything happens naturally.

Lao Tzu takes the heaven and earth like the bellows; it seems to have nothing between them, but once the time runs, everything is derived from it.

Heaven and earth can be taken as the social environment and social system in society, which contains law, ethical, moral, economic, and political relationships. The most outstanding social system never forces people to do this or that. It makes people naturally do things by their instinct. The country and the society never force people and bewilder people.

In nature, there is no stipulated rule between heaven and earth that the lion can only capture a special goat, but the lion will strive to catch it. Why? Because it's hungry. It responds to the call of nature. The fear of death drives the lion to chase the goat with great effort. This makes the yin-yang operate. The lion satisfies its need and accomplishes its mission as well.

It's the same thing in human society that superior social relation and social environment shall not be obliged to force people to work hard, for people pushed by their lusts would work hard naturally. Capital is just such an amazing thing that fully meets the requirements and natures of natural law, heavenly Tao.

According to the Marxist theory, capitalists use capital to set up businesses and plants, which are called investment. And then they entrust professional managers and workers to work for them, manufacture products that shall be sold at the market, exclude workers' salary, the spending of raw material, premises, management, power, etc., and the rest of the wealth is surplus value; also you can say capital income or capital gains.

When the business reaches at a certain level, capitalists can take all the investment back, reinvest in a new company, or spend the wealth at their own will. This is what we call natural circulation as in the problem of chicken and egg, also the circulation of heavenly Tao.

The function of the capitalist in the whole procedure is dominating, operating, planning, and bearing risks. Capitalists have no means to compel workers to work for them or not. Labour force is the goods that are equally exchanged by capitalists at the labour market—service commodity. This is a fair deal and exchange based on mutual willingness that if the worker feels the salary is low, then he can choose another job, and if capitalists think the worker is lazy, then they can dismiss him at any time. It's the same thing anyway buying labour force that can benefit more, and this is the rule.

However, in order to keep a secure job and wage, workers have to bust their asses to satisfy their bosses. No need to threaten them and induce them. Fair deal is natural law. It is not a threat but a legal right for capitalists to fire any worker in a legal scope; moreover, this is the most basic right and also heavenly Tao, for a large loss would occur if the occupations arranged by capitalists do not match the workers. The plant invested by capitalists is a machine that serves for capitalists, and it is a legal machine. Capitalists surely have the right to arrange men whom they think are proper to run their capital.

The main reason that the capitalist countries boost rapidly is that their production relations and social environment accord with heavenly Tao, endless heavenly Tao, and heavenly Tao of governing by non-interference.

All the capitalists have to do is to push their business onto the track and then naturally the wealth would flow into their pockets. No need to compel and threaten.

This is a system as well, namely, capitalists' business is a system. The management theory is just the system culture. The basic principle of a business is just the system management. The system turns harmony, and then the wealth comes in continually, while if the system breaks down, then it is the bankruptcy.

A capitalist country is a country comprised of small systems one by one. But at the macroscopic level, their country is disordered, scattered, and individually independent, which has no complete system; in other words, it has a loose system.

A socialist country is to fund a big and wholesome system. Whether it is big or small, one principle shall be conformed to—heavenly Tao.

The reason I think that our egalitarianism failed is no Tao and, completely on the contrary to heavenly Tao and humanity, taking the social rulemaking and social environment construction for granted.

Chairman Mao led campaigns like the Great Leap Forward, egalitarianism, smelting steel, cutting the tail of capitalism, abolitionist movement, and so forth. This old man's intention was that he hoped to dominate people's minds to control capital, holding the idea that the people would work for the country if their minds can be governed, and inspiring the people's labour enthusiasm if examples can be set.

The result was severe that complaints were everywhere, hens gone and the eggs cracked, and everything broke down. Non-Tao, humanity was killed and ignored, therefore this was the result.

Reach for success, then knowledge has to be studied and humanity is the largest knowledge and also the biggest environment. Meeting the humanity can profit from others' conflict, gain wealth continually, get anything fluently; otherwise, the moment that capital is gone is the time to die.

Some people always boast of the prosperity in Mao's period. What was the situation then? The revolution just succeeded with the largest collective capital, which included political capital, economic capital, and national capital.

It's just like someone picks up a hundred thousand RMB and plans to start a little noodle restaurant. He is astonished seeing his business runs hardly after a few months.

When our country has to restructure the enterprises, it is the time when only two thousand RMB remains out of the hundred thousand RMB. The capital is thoroughly eaten, spent by staff of the state-owned company, and still they are sleeping soundly. How hilarious.

For a nation system, the most effective management is capitalism, national capitalism. The capitalism principle is just on the contrary to Mao's theory.

Chairman Mao wants to control capital by dominating minds—bitterly beaten. Capitalism is dominating minds by using capital—truth.

National capitalism is dominating people's mind by using state-owned capital. This is the Tao of how a country is supposed to be ruled.

52. More and more people are engaged in the study of knowledge according to Tao; the things needing to be done are fewer and fewer

About 2007

Tao Te Ching: Chapter 48

Explanation:

More and more people are engaged in learning. According to Tao, daily things will be reduced day after day. Finally, there's nothing to do. It seems like there is nothing to do; however, it reaches the point that nothing can't be done. The one supported by the whole world is the one who never forced others to do something. If one forces the world to do something for him, he will not get the support of the world.

Comment:

In fact, the Tao Te Ching repeatedly talks about the truth throughout, which is the characteristic of Tao.

From the very beginning, there must be a very busy time for those rulers with the concept of Tao, who need to make a thorough analysis and study of the social problems and finally determine the direction of social development and the best social structure and mode. Then by changing the political relations and economic relations between people, the society will achieve a state of expectation, which is a long-term stability, from the internal, that is, a so-called harmonious state. Under this state, everyone is able to enjoy his greatest enthusiasm for production, to maximise the labour productivity, and all aspects of the interests can be fully protected.

In the future, after this state is fully achieved, there is no need for government to force people to do or not to do the certain things. Instead, all people know is what they can do, what they can't do, and how to do it to achieve their own ideals.

Everything is done in a natural situation. The police do what the police should do, the judge does what the judge should do, the workers do what the workers should do, and the capitalists make money from the capital. In fact, the reason for the contradiction between workers and capitalists, cops and robbers is that they have different moral standards, thinking, views, manners, and lifestyle, and they can't understand or communicate with each other.

If every worker once had been a capitalist and then declined, becoming an impoverished worker, he would never hate the exploitation from capitalists and no longer believe in the concept of exploitation; that is because the theory of exploitation is the biggest lie that Marx put forward to arouse the workers to seize political power. Just as I have said, most politicians have to lie to survive, and Marx is no exception.

In accordance with the view of Lao Tzu, the society with Tao is a harmonious society. Today, our country tries to build a harmonious society, in fact, that is to practice the concept of Tao. The harmonious society is indeed to be constructed, rather than relying on democracy, freedom, obscurantism to form spontaneously. Additionally, a harmonious society must be an autocratic society, because each ignorant person and every mortal are fighting to get the maximum interests for their own so that no one will have leisure time to care about other people's business. Therefore, democracy cannot build a harmonious society. The harmonious society is the patent product of the autocratic society.

Harmonious society is maintained by the power, also is in the power of deterrence. People have to sacrifice some of their own personal interests, making their behaviour not in conflict with the interests of other people and keeping it harmonious. Without the power of deterrence and in a lawless society, each person isn't a person; instead, each person is an animal.

If we can achieve the goal of a harmonious society under the premise of Tao, the autocratic society maintained by the power is what Lao Tzu called the inaction society.

The harmonious society is a social system that is customised for the autocratic society. Also, since the ugly side of human nature cannot be restrained without tyranny, it is the social state that can only be realised in the autocratic society.

However, human nature is the cradle of social creativity, which means when the society suppresses the ugly side of the human nature, it cannot dampen the productivity. So treating the ugly side of human nature should like treating farms not only to grow fast, but also it cannot blindly run and bite.

Capitalist society is the relations of animals in nature. Each American has a gun, and they protect their own interests and safety.

The feudal society of Confucius and Mencius is like a prison. Everyone is restrained by political and family relations layer upon layer; no one is able to move, which completely obliterates humanity. Now the relationship between men and women in a family still relies entirely on a feudal ideology and relations of Confucius and Mencius to maintain and turns humanity into restriction, constraint, distortion with the help of government.

Family relationship in the feudal society of Confucius and Mencius is completely based on male dominance and 'the father is the father, the son is the son'. Women are accessories of men, so women in feudal society have rights to manage family property and housekeeping; safeguarding heritage for women in feudal society is completely under the control of men, so it is perfectly reasonable.

But nowadays in society, men and women are equal and they have no subordinate relationship, so the women are not eligible for housekeeping. The woman is just a pretext today, which is a means of sex extortion to men for women and a social psychology and phenomenon of complete distortion.

Since the equality of the sexes, the subordinate relationship does not exist, and the property should go Dutch. The law should be explicitly supported that the default property of husband and wife is independent. Property relations during the marriage, rather than the default common property, should be consulted by couples.

At this point, the Western civilisation completely eliminates disputes and completely independent. It is the truth, but also the root cause of the development of productive forces.

A harmonious society should fundamentally eliminate the root that causes social contradictions first. Anything that can bring about social contradictions should be extinct before it happens. By elimination, rather than man-made contradictions, the government earns a profit without working for it. Charging lawyer fee and lawsuit fee is shameless.

A harmonious society is to create an authoritative environment, like a fence with a pasture and an artificial fish pond. In this environment, the relationship between the government and the people should be harmonious and smooth; so is the relationship between people. Law, morality, rule, and system are disharmonious relations, which make the society in conflict.

The default independence of marital property is a harmonious moral and legal relationship. Today, marital default property is the morality and law that cause trouble.

Abandoning children with congenital disability is a harmonious moral and law relationship. Treating them is the moral and law relationship which makes evil and trouble.

Unified management of state-owned assets by the state council is a harmonious moral and law relationship. Giving the ownership of state-owned assets to the local people's congress and even the factory director is a relationship of moral and law to make evil and trouble. It is the source of great disorder.

Of course, if the ownership of state-owned capital can really play the most efficiency role, used by the government standing for the most fundamental interests of the people, namely, for the people, then Chinese society is a real harmonious society.

The basic principle of the Marxist doctrine is to benefit the people with the state capital.

In view of the fact that Marx and Chairman Mao has never been a capitalist, and they do not understand the operation of the capital, they think it is the state-owned enterprise that benefits the people, or that it is the work of the people that benefits the people. This is the greatest tragedy of communism and is the reason for the biggest failure.

53. Paths and methods are variable

About 2007

'Tao' means the channel for people to move from one place to another, and people can go to place B from place A.

'Tao' in the Tao Te Ching means feasible methods and paths for people to transfer their current living state to another ideal and reasonable one efficiently, rapidly, and specifically, and it takes overall pattern and interests of all people into account with the least contradictions and least social resources consumed yet with maximum effects so that it conforms to human nature completely and it can be achieved by people.

'Tao' in the Tao Te Ching means the paths for countries and all humans to embark on.

However, Tao can mean healthcare of one person, known as a path of healthcare, and methods of healthcare. Development of one enterprise can be known as developing the path of the enterprise.

Business has business paths, kingdom has ruling paths, husband and wife have paths to follow; paths are existent in the world, and people have their own paths.

The author thought the Tao Te Ching means the path of ruling one country originally in content and its other meanings are extended ones.

Truth can be known, but it may not be the well-known truth. As mentioned above, the author thought human nature is the developing path of the society and country; and knowledge level of people, technology level, and social development are determined by people's cognition of themselves and nature as well as developing level of productivity. According to a specific situation of current stage, specific policies and methods can be made to adjust relations of people.

So paths will be changed with the changes of specific situation and paths are not constant. And paths cannot be described specifically with language and words. As policies and methods are under constant changes, the ones that can be expressed with language and words are not permanent ones. Perhaps, policies and methods can be completely abolished dozens of years later.

A path is just like our road filled with twists and turns. When people reach one stage, they will know the best scheme for the next stage. So path cannot be expressed with language, and path is not constant.

Tao just means methods that people think of so that Tao is invisible. As it is just a kind of method, thought, and concept but not a visible thing and it is changed with the changes of time, path is very subtle.

However, policies and legal regulations are visible as they can be put into practice and produce huge effects on the specific life of people. So path can be regarded to be existent under its specific implementation and people can sense the path of executors via policies and legal regulations of executors.

Policies and legal regulations, as concepts of execution, can be regarded as representatives of visibility and invisibility. They are just two different aspects of one thing: external reflection form of Tao and dominant thought of Tao.

So the two are from the same source, but they have their different names: one known as policies and the other known as concepts. The two are changed constantly according to different situations. This is the source of all beautiful things.

54. Further comment on ensuring people know what beauty is, to stop the hideous

About 2007

If all people of the world know the reasons, methods, principles, and sources for beautiful things to be beautiful, the hideous will be stopped.

If all people of the world know the reasons, excuses, methods, paths, and principles for kind things to be kind, unkind things of the world will be stopped.

The existence of the hideous and unkind things in the world is just attributed to the problem that people do not how to achieve kindness or beauty in the true sense.

The things for people to achieve supreme kindness and beauty are known as Tao. It means to find true and mutually beneficial best method for coexistence and co-development of things after comprehensively understanding human nature and all things of human occurrence.

In fact, all contradictions of human society are concerned with distribution of interests. Contradictions of any form, scale, and level are caused by conflicts of interest, from a world war to quarrel of a couple. If we analyse surface phenomena of things with psychoanalytic method, the thing left will be conflicts of interest.

The so-called kindness and beauty mean mutually beneficial and win-win effects and a pattern to maintain and admit interests of each aspect.

What is beauty? I thought beauty and kindness in true meaning are existent based on the following conditions:

1. When personal rights and property rights of the two parties are fully respected and protected

2. When the freedom of the two parties of contradictions are fully carried forward and satisfied, but not to be forced absolutely, and such freedom should be the one at the inner heart of people, without any unwilling or compromising parts in any meaning

3. When the two parties can achieve mutual benefits and win-win effects and the things that can be obtained by each other are known as beauty, including spiritual and material satisfaction

4. When one party does not obtain specific interests but creates

173

conditions for the other party to get interests, such a situation is known as kindness.

The things that can meet all above conditions are known as true kindness and beauty at the inner heart of people.

However, in actual life, kindness and beauty are instruments and measures taken for covering their own benefits under most circumstances, and such things are false kindness, social engagement, and the ones trying to satisfy one's vanity when one cannot really afford to do so. Essentially, they are real transactions and unclad business relations.

In addition, kindness and beauty also have a meaning of another level: the ones which take various measures to prevent occurrence of the hideous are also known as beauty, and removal and punishment of the hideous are known as kindness.

In actual life, if we give certain special power and high status for one person but do not effectively supervise or prevent power, a lot of things are caused in China like scandals, escapes of corrupt officials outside, gambling abroad, crash of BMW into people, etc. Systemically speaking, it means the failure of system control, or the system fails to effectively control its components.

Of course, the mentality of Chinese people to resist against monitoring and prevention originates from a tradition of Chinese feudal society: 'a man being used cannot be suspended while a suspected man cannot be used', a typical thought of rule by man.

55. Lying and the subconscious

About 2007

People can communicate using languages, but the main purpose of language is not expressing feelings, but lying.

Why do I say it? There are some implications.

It is the subconscious, not consciousness, that controls human behaviour and mind, and the consciousness is just a disguised form of the subconscious.

Some of the subconscious doesn't contradict rationality, and it can directly enter into the consciousness, but a lot of the subconscious conflicts with rationality, after processing and disguising, entering into the consciousness to provide impetus for human behaviour.

It's something Freud called libido, which can directly control the human endocrine systems, and it's subject to the subconscious rather than consciousness.

When people want to do something under consciousness but against the subconscious, the latter will hinder the supply of energy to undermine the thing.

There is a Chinese saying 'Lazy donkeys piss or shit frequently when driving the millstone' (the same meaning as 'Idle folks lack no excuses'). Donkeys do not want to work, but they are forced to do so. Under the control of the subconscious, the nervous system will make trouble for work, that is, to piss or shit. And this feeling really exists, no fake.

Freud used the subconscious to explain a slip of the tongue or pen and dreaming; in fact, all human behaviour can be explained by the subconscious. It's just like sort one thing out and you'll sort out all the rest, not complicated at all.

Knowing the relations of interaction among the human subconscious, control system, consciousness, nervous system, as well as the control system of humans, we can easily explain human behaviour and fully understand human behaviour and consciousness and the subconscious from the inside to the outside. Through observing people's outward manifestations, such as facial expression, tone of voice, behaviour or demeanour, mental outlook, and all kinds of emotions, we can make an actual and accurate speculation of people's inner world and true intentions and have an insight into human lives.

Language is just an expression of human consciousness, or is just a misleading tool full of lies. It can be no representative of the subconscious. And humans' true nature and real purpose lie in the subconscious. Only when the language is consistent with the subconscious, and other presentations on behalf of the subconscious are in line with each other can we believe that language is no lie for the time being.

Otherwise, there will be something that we don't know about but has a significant impact on the event. What we don't understand or grasp may blind us, and we are likely to misjudge others' real intentions. The polygraph training for agents, in fact, is a process of changing their subconscious by psychological suggestion.

Hitler had a famous saying, 'A lie repeated ten thousand times can be truth', which is consistent with the theory of psychoanalysis—because constantly repeating something to someone equals psychological suggestion.

56. All Chinese legal citizens should have the ownership of state-owned assets

About 2007

State-owned assets are also known as assets of ownership by the whole of the people.

What does 'the whole of the people' mean? That means all Chinese people are the 1.3 billion Chinese people.

State-owned assets should be the assets that 1.3 billion Chinese people jointly own, only then can these be called state-owned or wholly people-owned.

Whether the people working in foreign-funded enterprise belong to national people or not, whether people in retail belong to national people or not, whether people in private enterprise belong to national people or not, all of them are national people who should have ownership of all state-owned assets. This is socialism, legitimate truth, and justice.

Our ownership does not mean we have the ability to exercise this sacred power. Because the legal right we have is only 13 billionth of a $10 million factory, everyone should have the ownership of only 7 cents. That is, 1.3 billion people divide up $10 million; each person has a small part.

So individuals cannot exercise ownership of the factory. Similarly, all employees of the factory should have 7 cents of the ownership, so they can't be entitled to exercise ownership of the state-owned enterprises.

So who can be entitled to exercise ownership of the state-owned enterprises? The people who represent the interests of 1.3 billion Chinese people could be entitled to exercise ownership of state-owned enterprises. Only the central government led by Communist parties can represent the fundamental interests of the 1.3 billion Chinese people. Even local governments do not have this power. Local government can only represent the local people but cannot represent the 1.3 billion Chinese people. Therefore, the local government has no right to exercise ownership of state-owned enterprises.

Local governments have no ownership, and employees of state-owned enterprises should not have the ownership of state-owned enterprises. The people who are secretly against this power could plunder the fundamental interests of the country's 13 million people. Whether corrupt officials or employees want to carve up the state-owned enterprises is to plunder the property of all Chinese people.

But the Chinese people, from the common people to the government officials, could not understand the power they have and the role the central government should play. That is why state-owned enterprises have no owner. That is because the national consciousness is weak, neglected, and absurd.

Initial stages for reform and opening up, the majority of Chinese consider the staff in state-owned enterprise deserve to possess its ownership. The state-owned enterprises owned by the people who hold power not only harm the interests of the state, but also harm the interests of the 1.3 billion Chinese people. Minority people embezzle state-owned enterprises, which results in misappropriation of property of all Chinese people. It is absolutely intolerable. No matter if officials or employees, no one has the right to privately sell state-owned assets and turn public property into private property.

To sell state-owned assets privately without authorisation of the central government is illegal, infringement, and theft. State-owned assets can be managed by a central government, used for repair of bridges and roads, development of education, national defence, labour, and social security, and the ultimate beneficiaries are the 1.3 billion Chinese people. State-owned assets fall into the pockets of individuals, just good for a few spoiled people, but no advantage for 1.3 billion Chinese people.

Therefore, I appeal to the 1.3 billion Chinese people's conscience that protection of state-owned assets is to protect your own assets. Any people, for any reason, misappropriating state assets are criminals, including the employees of state-owned enterprises.

The fundamental rights of Chinese people have not been properly maintained at present, in the condition that these are trampled by others; this is not wrong, but on how to protect their most precious right, different people make out different prescriptions.

1. Mainstream economists believe that the state-owned enterprises need privatisation and to find a true master.

2. Among bourgeois democratic innovationists, they propose a multiparty rule as the best way to safeguard their fundamental rights.

3. Of course, there are conservatives to maintain the Communist Party. They think first of all to maintain the leadership of the Communist Party, on this basis, to make appropriate reforms to safeguard the people's interests and national interests.

China is in the most chaotic thinking period since its founding.

I believe that these theories of China are not all errors, and all of them take a part for the whole, just grabbing one aspect but not grasping the essence of the problem.

What is the fundamental reason for Chinese people's fundamental rights to have been violated?

Currently, communists cannot make good use of the communist theory. At first, they use false thought, thinking that communism is egalitarianism and commune populaire. After experiencing setbacks, instead of the capitalist economic theory to build the nation—MBO—they used the feudal separatist social resources management.

Communism is the advanced theory like a precious gharry, but communists don't know how to use it well, so they use it to carry dung. People with blood and life change to the socialist state system, a precious gharry. In China, use it to carry dung and bash it with a hammer, because no one really knows communism and the people who really understand communism haven't let it run.

What are the basic rights of the Chinese people? The socialist system is different from the capitalist system. The fundamental rights and concept are also different.

I think that the largest national ownership rights by people are holding all state-owned assets at present.

Currently, the typical capitalist roader is MBO; they take the reason of equalitarianism failure to crazily slander the state capital, wanting to completely transform it, dig out the final socialism building block for China to finally turn into capitalism so they can be satisfied.

On the other hand, the Communist Party conservatives holding national executive powers but knowing nothing about the economy let the capitalist roaders dig up the final block of socialism, the cornerstone of socialism. But they are helpless, even worse, in collusion with capitalist roaders' concerted efforts of digging socialist foundation and the sweat of the people.

These are the severe violations and disregard for the basic rights of the people. It is the truth of people becoming untouchables.

I have to wake the common people up, to keep the cornerstone of people's basic interests. Down with the capitalist roaders, clean up the scum of the party, and safeguard the people's interests. But now the central government has done it, MBO has been halted, and meanwhile, the garbage in the party has gradually been cleared. So the state is out of the morass.

Now if you ask all the Chinese people, 'Do the people who pick up litter and the street vendors of China have the ownership of state-owned enterprises?' I estimate that 90 per cent of the people would say no; there is another 10 per cent of the people who would think I was crazy. How serious is the ignorance of Chinese people? They are confused what their greatest rights are.

People often say that Chinese people are not united; in fact, every Chinese person has a certain capital at birth.

The problem is that because the Chinese people are not united, this right is infringed by power. State capital assigned to each person is actually a great fortune. Why do we not have any sense? Because the capital present with the form of national investment cannot be free to split. In principle, we can only get dividends but cannot be allowed to withdraw capital.

What is a dividend? That is in the case of all state-owned enterprises' profit; each of us has the right to benefit.

But the state-owned enterprises have been violated and lost money before, so there are no dividends for an unprofitable firm—not merely without dividends but also needing to repay a debt.

For these years, the state established the SASAC, improving efficiency of state-owned enterprises, to make state-owned enterprises have a certain profit. The central government took money contributions from Western development, exempting agricultural tax, which freed the tuition and books for farmers who have difficulties to go to school. This is the implementation of people's ownership. Although far from our goals, this is a good start.

State-owned enterprises and capitalist enterprise are essentially different; the most essential difference is that capitalists consume a large amount of surplus value. However, the residual value of state-owned enterprises is entirely back to the people.

Why did state-owned enterprises fail in early days of new China? That was because we did not have clear property rights. What is the proper ownership of state-owned enterprises? Look at the two types of errors of understanding on ownership.

1. State-owned enterprises belong to the nation, not me.

The idea is simple: literally understand 'state-owned'. State-owned, of course, belongs to the nation, not our home.

2. The state-owned enterprises belong to all workers of the factory.

This idea also has a theoretical basis. Workers are masters of the country. Right of the state belongs to the people, and the company's highest authority is the congress of workers and staff. As long as the employee congress passed, we can deal with the assets of state-owned enterprises.

The correct assets ownership is to get the average division of a factory into 13 million parts, with each Chinese person having an ownership. In this sense, unless the 1.3 billion people agree with a resolution at the same time, it would take effect. In practice, this is impossible.

Therefore, we need a special organisation that must be fully able to represent the common interests of the 1.3 billion Chinese people, 1.3 billion people to put their ownership entrusted to the organisation. This organisation will be able to exercise the legitimate ownership of the state-owned enterprises. Looking at the whole world, only the Chinese Communist Party has the qualification to take on this important mission.

57. Public capital constitutes the foundation of people's life

About 2007

Public ownership, co-ownership, ownership by the whole of the people, and state ownership, which appear different in names and concepts, highly resemble each other. However, I think public capital is most appropriate, compared to other terms.

1. Public ownership

As a concept of application, 'public' is relative to 'private', referring to public goods rather than private ownership. 'Foundation of people's life' relates to the use of public capital, and its user is also the beneficiary, but not everyone is required to use it. For instance, everyone has the right to take a bus, whereas a car owner will be probably reluctant to use it despite enjoying such a right, since they believe that taking a bus means lower social status, unable to meet their needs.

2. Co-ownership

As a concept of possession, co-ownership highlights joint ownership. 'Foundation of people's life' is not intended for possession but for use, and besides, possession of public capital is an illegal and corrupt behaviour that turns public property into private property.

3. Ownership by the whole of the people

Ownership by the whole of the people is also a concept of possession. In actual operations, however, ownership by the whole of the people tends to be transformed into local ownership, ownership by state-owned enterprises, or ownership by employees of state-owned enterprises. This is the fundamental reason for the collapse of the state-owned enterprises caused by employees. Employees of state-owned enterprises are so shameless to privatise the assets owned by the whole of the people, resulting in the collapse of state-owned enterprises.

4. State-owned ownership

There is a difference between public ownership and state ownership. In principle, since the state is only a principal, everyone who needs to make use of the assets owned by the whole people must seek approval from 1.3 billion Chinese people; otherwise, they will be deemed to have performed infringement behaviour or the behaviour of illegal possession. As a matter of fact, the whole of the people can neither manage nor operate such assets. From a macro perspective, the most realistic way is to empower the central government that can represent the fundamental interest of 1.3 billion Chinese people to exercise the right of ownership. In a strict sense, public ownership does not stand for state ownership. Only when the state can represent the fundamental interest of 1.3 billion Chinese people can public ownership be replaced by state ownership.

In other words, when the state cannot represent the fundamental interest of 1.3 billion Chinese on the condition of widespread corruption, unrestrained gambling, absconding, and unfair clauses, the state's disposal of public assets is illegal. The government, which causes the loss of its people's money for whatever reason, whether intentionally or unintentionally, is unqualified to manage the property for the people.

Undoubtedly, experience can be accumulated little by little. While learning something new at the beginning, all people need to pay some price, but it is worth noticing that different concepts should be clearly defined.

58. People's life is a capital operation

About 2007

Investment begins as soon as a child is born, or rather, before the child is born. Husband's request for wife's preparation for pregnancy can be seen as a kind of investment, since they are clear that they will spend a great deal in raising a child in the future. However, majority of parents are pleased to make such investment, and many couples feel anxious because they cannot make such investment (without a child) immediately.

The child, who is of vital importance to a normal family, is more than a kind of investment. The child can give rise to three benefits:

1. Retaining the affection between spouses—Many couples decide not to get divorced for children's sake.

2. Rearing children as a support in old age—Chinese moral and ethical views argue that rearing children as a support in old age is a most traditional and reliable approach to solving living problems in their twilight years.

3. Inheriting family property—For the poor, there may be little property to be inherited, whereas for the proprietary class and middle class, the child will be surely the only heir, or rather, the son is undoubtedly the only heir.

In addition, from the national and social perspective, childbearing is a process contributing not only to a larger population, but also to a higher number of social resources.

To a certain degree, social development has a need for population stability as well as workforce increase. Besides, population stability and workforce increase are the indispensable elements and assurances for the development of social productive forces.

No matter how developed a society is and how high the quality of life is, the continuous decrease in total population will be bound to result in a severe crisis or even national subjugation and genocide when reaching a certain degree.

Therefore, for a country, childbearing is a kind of necessary investment.

Children are supported by others from their birth to their growth into adults who can live independently. They need others' financial help in respect of basic necessities, education, skill trainings, medical treatment, and security assurance. Instead of making contributions or creating economic income, they require the investment from others.

In this stage, the state is responsible for environmental investment and the nine-year compulsory education, with parents for all other expenditures, mainly survival-oriented investment. As a matter of fact, in our life, environment is a kind of important investment as well. The environments described here refer to ecological and social environments.

1. Ecological environment is the natural living environment highlighting the indices like air pollution, noise, soil, and water quality.

2. Social environment is the manmade living environment emphasising the indices like social security, road traffic, social civilisation, public facilities, labour security, employment environment, and medical insurance.

Social environment investment is a concept completely different in socialist countries and capitalist countries.

In capitalist countries, tax revenue from the people is the only source of the government's income. Thus, investment and spending of the government is also the investment and spending of the people. It is understandable that the government short of money levies taxes to deal with official affairs.

In socialist countries, the government's income is not only constituted by tax revenue, but also by a large proportion of state-owned capital gains. Thus, governments of socialist countries can do many things that governments of capitalist countries cannot do, and for these governments, the major task is to make environmental investment.

Environmental investment is of crucial importance to the common people, because they live a life in social environment. Just like the fish living in water, people will have entirely different fates when living in different water. This point is easy to understand.

The social environment of the socialist country has been mentioned in 'How Socialist Countries Carry Forward Their Superiority in Socialist System'.

Public capital is required to build an environment essential to the common people from an overall perspective. Educational environment, employment environment, and secure environment have been described above.

I. Infrastructure Construction
Infrastructure construction cannot only transform our environment, including living environment, but also provide convenience for people living near the infrastructures. Land appreciation can create various benefits for

185

local people.

1. If the infrastructures near your houses such as subway, station, wharf, and road are put into practice, your house will be sure to appreciate immediately, i.e., your assets will appreciate immediately.

2. Large numbers of people become rich overnight because of demolition. If infrastructures are built in front of their houses, they will be allocated with several apartments when the country requisitions local land.

3. Because of national investment and construction, many places that were wastelands in the past have been turned into downtowns, which have attracted more visitors and travelling merchants. As a result of this, local people will be provided with more job opportunities and get a higher income.

Why do parents spend a great deal in rearing their children, providing a life of high quality for them, hiring a private teacher for them, and sending them abroad for further education? The reason is that they hope their children have a promising future and find an ideal job.

There will be more job opportunities and chances of earning money in a favourable environment, which is the environment resource that can never be bought. This is also a part of national investment benefits as well.

You will never find a satisfying job despite being well-educated and highly capable if the employment and business environments fail to be built in the absence of national investment. A significantly positive result will be achieved by national environmental investment, as opposed to the lack of national environment investment. It can be said that national environmental investment plays a crucial role. Ordinary people usually fail to discover this point.

Thus, in socialist countries, the investment in children is categorised into two types: (1) parents' investment, and (2) national and environmental investment.

Environmental and national investment plays a decisive role. Thus, investment is a most crucial element, which is the largest capital for the people.

II. Fundamental Science and Technology Studies
Many fundamental science and technology studies need tremendous investment, which will be unable to create economic returns for a long period of time. Nevertheless, such studies play a decisive role in national security, national economy, and people's livelihood. All these require not

only enormous investment to be made, but also national investment to play its role.

III. Safe Investment

Safety refers to national defence security, public security, etc. National defence security requires huge national investment, which represents national strength.

Public security is always of vital importance to the common people. People who have encountered public security problems can perceive its importance more deeply.

China performs well in respect of public security, which is closely associated with the socialist system. This is also an example for the public capital investment in a secure environment. The secure environment today is completely reliant on the infinite security assurance that public capital provides.

Mexico is an extreme example, spending $200 million on national defence every year, while the income of drug dealers is $2 billion every year. From the perspective of military expenses, Mexico's national army is overwhelmed by drug dealers' private army, as a result of which, Mexico is controlled by drug dealers on the whole.

Their presidents cannot find a way out, because the gap between $200 million and $2 billion results from their political system, ideology, values, and external environment. The United States, a bad neighbour and role model, has created a huge drug market for Mexico.

The fundamental reason is that Mexico lacks state-owned capital that can help to fight against the demon. This has reflected the hypocrisy, foulness, evilness, weakness, and ugliness of democracy.

The prerequisite for 'everyone is equal' is the equality in respect of public capital rather than in terms of human right. The most famous slogan of capitalism is 'All men are created equal.'

I have mentioned that men are not created equal, and 'All men are created equal' is only a capitalist slogan. Seemingly, people are spiritually equal. As a matter of fact, in the society with private ownership, equality cannot be achieved in a real sense because of the inequality in respect of means of production and means of livelihood, namely, capital inequality.

To achieve equality in a real sense, capital equality must be ensured. The whole of the people in possession of public capital will be granted corresponding dividends, which turn out to be the most fundamental assurance for equality. No matter whether you are poor or rich, healthy or sick, or tall or short, everyone competes against each other with the support of capital from their birth.

All the contents above have proved the importance and irreplaceable role of public capital, which proves to be the foundation of people's life.

59. The biggest problem for the poor in the world is that they don't know what their most fundamental interests are

5 April 2015

What are the most fundamental interests for the poor? And how can they be maintained? Human beings have not recognised the question yet.

The most fundamental interests are not only for the poor, but also for the rich, which is for all the people. While human beings have never realised it, this is the biggest problem for human beings.

This issue is the top-level design of the most fundamental interests and the most basic fairness and justice for mankind. There are some essential requirements for this top-level design.

1. Safe environment
No matter what race, what nationality, what faith, and no matter where we are at any time, the citizens should enjoy the government's security assurance not to be slaughtered, not to be murdered, not to be discriminated against, and not to be abused. Meanwhile, property rights and personal safety should be fully protected. And everyone is equal, and everyone should get the same and fair protection.

2. Material environment of living
No matter what race, what nationality, what faith, and no matter where we are at any time, the citizens should equally enjoy social public products offered by the state. No matter how much this protection is, it may be less in underdeveloped countries, while more in developed countries. However, in a country, such security is essential, and everyone is equal, which is the basic material insurance.

3. Development environment
No matter what race, what nationality, what faith, and no matter where we are, we are supposed to have the opportunity to equally get the social resources, make a contribution to the society, create wealth for ourselves and for society; moreover, we can show talents, realise our value as well as the ideal fairness.

If human beings can really practice the above things, then we are able to live in a country where we want to reside. But actually, an overwhelming majority of countries cannot achieve this, especially the poor countries, just because the whole world and human beings never realise the concept of top-level design. Perhaps the development of human society has not yet developed to such an advanced degree. But I think this is the idea and concept that should be owned from the beginning of civilisation, which is a fundamental concept. What's more, from ancient to modern times, many ideologists and philosophers have been struggling for such a favourable world.

What I am talking about is, what is a politician?

The purpose of politicians is to reconcile and balance the interest between various factions and groups by social management.

Politicians may have to reach a certain social management goal, but they determine the policy mainly based on acceptance level of people's existing ideology. And when most people's ideology cannot reach a certain level of cognition, a lot of things cannot be done, even cannot be said for fear that there would be political unrest. And the ideologists and philosophers should lead the society to engage in the social top-level design.

Some of the specific issues include

1. Security assurance

It contains personal safety and property safety.

2. Equality and justice

Without being discriminated against, being abused, being intimated, being threatened, being oppressed, and being persecuted, violation of justice or those who did things against others must be punished, without any escaping from the crime, as well as no evasion, compromising, and exception.

3. Education

Free compulsory education

4. Employment

The government should provide free vocational training and entrepreneurial environment, as well as supporting and occupational guidance.

5. Social security

To provide the minimum healthcare and ageing social security as much as possible for all the people

6. National defence security

7. Infrastructure construction

8. Fundamental scientific and technological research

9. And other projects

The above are the most fundamental matters that should be provided by a normal state and society. In fact, every country has and practices them, but restricted by the social system, not every country can achieve the idealised level and demands.

Every country has some of the above fundamental social public products and basically has legislated. But it is two aspects between what is legal and what the real is. For example, Mexico prohibits drugs, but the drug dealers dare to fight against government troops. Moreover, each country voices against corruption at a legal level, but corruption is rampant in almost every country. The above requirements that I said are not a verbal promise. The fundamental security that I required is what the ordinary people can see and get and should be better and better, which can be achieved perfectly.

For instance, in the Western society, some of the above things can be satisfied with education and social security. But the security assurance as well as fairness and justice, employment supporting, and other aspects is far from enough.

When talking about security and assurance, the lowest requirement is that one would not be robbed, raped, killed by shooting, abducted, and be in traffic at any road regardless of day and night. There are a few cities that can achieve such a requirement in the whole world, whether in developed countries or in underdeveloped countries. That is to say, Western countries are far from the requirements in terms of security.

To my point of view, if a country can try its best to achieve some of the above requirements, it can be seen as a society with a normal development; otherwise, it is a society with problems. I think that the satisfaction degree of the above conditions determines the state and society serving for whom.

If the above conditions are met with the lowest limit, it means meeting the minimum operational requirements, providing minimum security assurance, the compulsory fairness and justice, and the minimum educational level, and so on. Bluntly, I think it is like a country where people are treated as beasts, and it is enough to meet the minimum survival requirements or let people work. And if the society is in order, just don't trouble me. If it is in trouble, the authorities can also find a reason to make an excuse.

191

If only relying on taxes to raise money and then practicing the above matters, it will be regarded as a burden. The more you do, the more you spend. And the more you do, the less money you have, as well as the more you get tired.

While if you have the money firstly, then consider how to spend it, it will not be the burden, but a benefaction. Therefore, the key to the problem is that we should get the money at first.

With the money, the people to be served will not be disliked and avoided as beasts, or be regarded as a burden and debt. And the people are the real masters who have the dignity.

After the public ownership of land, the government collected not only the taxes, but also the land occupancy charge and rent. Moreover, with the appreciation of land, there is much more money. Therefore, ownership by the state is in the best interest of the people, which is the fundamental difference in whether you want to be a beast or a master.

What's more, the products from the land, such as oil, gold, diamond, mineral products, and so on, belong in the best interest of the people, which is also the fundamental difference in whether to be a beast or a master for people.

This is God's wealth, which should be shared by the people. However, it was robbed by the capitalists, landlords, and the kings. Therefore, people should take them back. Once being not regarded as a beast, you will be the master.

It is a simple truth, but people do not know what their best interest is and how to safeguard it, as well as how to use the love and wealth from God and how to increase the value of wealth. Marx's most basic theory is not wrong, only because they don't know how to use the state-owned assets and the state-owned wealth. It can be only said that human beings are ignorant, ridiculous, barbaric, and not civilised.

What are the beasts? It is spending the least money to maintain minimum survival requirement and ability to work. This is the beast.

What is the master? It is that I give you money, you should cope with the matters. If you do not do a good job, I will criticise you. This is the master.

Just think about it: does your country offer public products to meet the minimum requirements or to help people to deal with matters? This is the fundamental difference, as well as the key to the question.

Man is very stupid.

The fundamental logical error causing socialism's failure is that state-owned capital is not used to consume for the people, but to create a basic environment for people to work harder, more conveniently, and with more ability, as well as earn more money.

They tend to think that the money that can be put in their own pocket is their benefit, vice versa. That's what everyone thinks about, which is the reason and basic logic of the problems.

As for the poor, the most fundamental interest is not the limited money which can be in their own pocket, but the social and living environment. It is the perfect social system that brings living environment to people. Just like a fish if it lives in a polluted environment—it will be of no use, no matter how hard it is, and it is a tragedy. However, if living in a perfect environment, you also can get whatever you want and be satisfied with everything even if you are going with the stream.

Why the poor are poor is that they are insufficient in all aspects, being unable to compete with the elites and get something with their capability. Therefore, it is necessary for us to gather the strength to create and share something together. This is the living environment where we live; of course, the rich need such an environment. Thus, such a perfect environment is the greatest wealth of mankind.

The fundamental reason why the poor are poor is that there is no top-level design. From their birth, some people are supposed to be poor, because they live in a poor country, or they cannot be educated by their poor family, or because they don't have the capital to compete with others. The social environment and law are not for you, so you are poor. No matter how hard you are, it is of no use.

Decades ago, with billions of population, China was the poorest country. But now it's not. Those Chinese who have a very low quality also go shopping around the world, while others should be polite. These Chinese were the so-called poor decades ago, who were looked down upon by others; they go abroad to go shopping maybe because they just want to make up the heart. People are the people, but after a few decades, they have become rich now.

If your country can also do a good job in the top-level design, it also can become rich quickly. Creating wealth is not complicated; so is living a happy life. As long as there is a right way, all people can live a better life.

Like those countries in the Middle East, the oil and wealth from God has been plundered by the king, chief of tribe, landlord, minister, and nobility. So how can you, the poor, have money? And who will take charge of you? Thus, you must be poor. This is the top-level design.

60. China's socialism is the improvement and progress of Marxism

About 2007

The reason why Western countries are hostile to socialist countries is that the theories Marx created have brought so much mental and material damage to mankind that they shrink away, from fear. As the Bible puts it, the original sin humans possess will make us pay with blood for all progress we make.

In a general way, a uniformly administrated social system is superior to fragmented administrated social system. How could humans realise uniform administration? How could a well-ordered society be built? To address these questions, public ownership system can be a rational choice.

But the realisation of a public ownership system and well-ordered system cannot do without the cost of blood. Now with bloodshed all over, we might as well calm down and contemplate some issues.

Everyone has learnt about Marx's profile. Without any significant setbacks in his life, he received college education and married his wife, a beautiful and cultured woman. He had never served as a capitalist nor did he have to work as a labourer because he was subsidised by a helpful person, Engels. As Mao Zedong put it, he who makes no investigation and study has no right to speak.

Because of the fact that Marx had never been a capitalist, he had no idea how much risk and painstaking effort a capitalist must take to make profit. Nor did he serve as a labourer even for one day; thus he could not imagine how impoverished an unemployed labourer would be and how suffering was without any money. Neither did he know why some capitalists made suicidal jumps from buildings, nor would he learn about why some poor people stole, robbed, swindled, and jumped into rivers, compelled by life. In spite of every cruelty outside, he was living like a parasite with a beautiful wife and children accompanying him. In such a case, he seldom experienced what bitterness and misery the common people suffered.

In order to graduate, every student had to attend internship and accomplish graduation thesis, and it would even take years for medical college students to finish interning. All of these weren't Marx's concern as he did not intern for even one day, make even one penny by capital operation, or work for a capitalist to make a living. No one would doubt such a man like him can become a writer of science fiction, but unfortunately, he represented himself as a capital expert and wrote Das Kapital. How confusing it would be since the publication produced by such a man should convince some people and was taken as the only foundation for massacre—violent revolution. What a tragedy for mankind! Maybe it is inexorable doom of God working. Humans step on their own blood to progress, and they won't ponder or advance without bloodshed.

The most ridiculous statements Marx made were 'Labour is man's primary need' and 'Capitalists don't work, they make profits by exploiting workers for surplus value.'

The author holds that the only correct saying made by Marx was 'Public ownership system is superior to private ownership system.' The rest of his viewpoints, apart from this one, are all nonsense. But at least this is humans' orientation of efforts.

To realise the objective of public ownership system, the Communist Party used to apply wrong directions; even the name Communist Party itself is also a misnomer.

The author believes that the only way to realising public ownership system is as follows:

Universally owned assets—the whole of the people jointly possess national assets and preserve or increase the value of national assets with rational operation to provide material insurance for the realisation of fairness and justice.

Not universally owned means of production—previous communists all believed that communism meant the whole of the people jointly owned means of production and worked together.

Universally owned assets refer to state capitalism, which is also the policy and direction China is applying currently.

But we shall not realise a complete state capitalism, for state-owned capital doesn't generate profit with voluntary labour; therefore, it won't work without the combination of private capitalism. Current communism China is applying does not differ from Western capitalism in nature; in contrast, China's state-owned capital takes a little more proportion than that in capitalist countries.

In addition, we are developing state-owned capital with certain targets, reasonable methods, and scientific concepts. In a communist country, state-owned capital development is certainly taken as priority.

To sum up, the author holds that China's model is the progress of Marxism as well as the scientific socialism. It is absolutely feasible that Western developed countries and other less-developed countries develop some state

195

capitalism based on their own conditions. The author believes that these countries will do even better than China, so all countries will develop and make profits jointly.

61. Communism should be understood as a common capitalism

About 2007

Communist ideology has been practiced for so many years in our country, but in fact, the core concept has been changed a lot.

The governing idea of high level has been transformed from the state-owned enterprise to the state-owned capital.

In today's news economic reports, there are no state-owned enterprises, which has been replaced by the state-owned capital.

In fact, the word 'communism' should be abolished, and changing it to 'common capitalism' is the most appropriate.

What is communism? It literally means a doctrine of common labour and co-production.

What is common capitalism? It literally means a doctrine of jointly owning capital, commonly being the capitalist, and sharing out bonus.

Whether it is the workers or the government, do you like to work? Or do you like to share out bonus and be the capitalist?

No one likes to work. From the government to the workers, everyone wants to share out bonus and be the capitalist.

Because of labour, there still exists a problem that production can be divided into valid labour and invalid labour. Labour and production cannot represent the improvement of social wealth and personal income.

As for the capital, it can use money to earn more money, which is an endless matter.

Temporarily controlling the property is not necessarily able to preserve or increase the value. However, if the capital can be rationally operated and managed by a suitable person controlling it, it can preserve or increase its value.

Previously, the reason why communism failed is that there was no common capital. They believed that capital is a dirty thing without work; thus, they made the utmost effort to reject and avoid it. Or to say that communists were disgusted with being capitalists and operating capital.

However, after several years of the operation of common capitalism, they felt good. The country's leaders were speaking harder. Once with a hard spine, their tone would be hard; once they owned enough money, their spine would be hard.

Owning capital means owning money. And after owning the money, they would be unscrupulous.

I think it's time for capitalism and communism to be reconciled. In fact, each of them belongs to capitalism. And the only difference is that one is state capitalism; the other one is individual capitalism.

The sole distinction between state capitalism and individual capitalism is that the state-owned capital of state capitalism accounted for a little more, while that of individual capitalism accounted for a little less. However, by the little bit of state-owned capital, state capitalism could play a more dominant role than individual capitalism.

The government of common capitalism is independent, and so is the regime, without any inference or restriction.

The government of an individual capitalist country is a puppet government, and they are the spokesperson as well as puppet of a monopoly capitalist, whose every movement is totally restricted by others.

However, the government of common capitalism can administrate the country according to just, fair, rational, advanced, and independent principle, offering services and public products for the society.

As long as a little changes in the capitalist countries, adding a little bit of state-owned capital, they can reach common capitalism. But the law-of-the-jungle culture is the best folk culture that can match up with common capitalism.

Chinese Lao Tzu's moral culture is a deadly poison in a common capitalist country.

62. Harmony is big love

About 2007

The current society of China is a completely human civilisation society with public ownership and state capitalism as the political and material guarantee and for the purpose of solving the deep-seated problem of the society and building harmonious society under the construction of powerful guarantee.

Harmonious society is to ensure the harmonious coexistence between man and man, man and society, man and nature. The purpose of harmony is to require the co-prosperity and coexistence between man and man, man and society, man and nature without essential contradiction to achieve a state of unity of nature and man.

What is essential contradiction? The contradiction between America and bin Laden is essential contradiction. The absolute irreconcilableness between two is essential contradiction. The conduct of Khmer Rouge in Cambodia in the past years was essential contradiction.

The root reason for essential contradiction between man and man is being unable to understand and communicate between man and man, causing mutual non-recognition of the other's interest, each restricting the other, and the contradiction cannot be reconcilable. Essential contradiction is represented in the form of absolute irreconcilableness and that one side must die.

The way to avoid essential contradiction between man and man is mutual respect, understanding, and communication really.

To achieve mutual respect, understanding communication really, one must achieve mutual unlimited respect, understanding, and communication.

Unfortunately, this is just a theory. As an individual, man can only communicate with the surrounding persons limitedly, but it is impossible to achieve unlimited communication.

Men are different; no one can really understand the other's thought.

Having no alternative but to give up our preference can only achieve no conflict of fundamental interests between man and man, man and society, man and nature as far as possible. As long as there is no conflict of fundamental interest, there will be no absolute irreconcilableness between man and man.

What is 'mutual unlimited respect, understanding, and communication between man and man, man and society, man and nature'? It is love.

As man cannot communicate with others unlimitedly but limitedly and even is unable to communicate and understand, man always damages the fundamental interest of other persons and other groups inadvertently, intentionally and unintentionally, or deliberately.

How to avoid this? We need people of the whole society and even the world to adjust the political and economic relations between man and man, man and society, man and nature systematically, that is, to adjust the fundamental interest between man and man, man and society, man and nature systematically.

This can only be guaranteed in a completely human civilised society with public ownership and state capitalism as the political and material guarantee and for the purpose of solving the deep-seated problem of the society and building harmonious society under the construction of powerful guarantee.

Only public ownership societies can have maximum equal and fair distribution of social resources and interests. Of course, such equality and fairness are not absolute; there should be a process.

State capitalism is the only correct material guarantee of public ownership. Without state capitalism, the state-owned enterprises and assets will be melted like ice cream in summer. The fact we see is that it is the state capitalism that saves the socialism of China and saves public ownership. Because a harmonious society is for the purpose of solving the deep-seated problem of the society by adjusting the political and economic relations between man and man, man and society, man and nature.

With people living in the harmonious society and no need to adjust their behaviour painstakingly, the system will adjust the fundamental interest between man and man, man and society, man and nature naturally. Men only need to live according to their own habit.

Whether you are poor or rich, illustrious or ordinary, the family harmony, social stability, and favourable weather are the basic demands for men. Nobody wants to live in a horrific family or wants to be pursued and captured by the government, let alone to live in nuclear radiation.

Harmony is to love the surrounding persons, love society, and love nature. It is also to be loved by the surrounding persons, by society, and by nature.

Harmony is big love.

The current human beings are pursuing material civilisation extremely, but ignore spiritual civilisation completely. Because private ownership and capitalist system are the Darwinist law of the jungle, where the fit survive, while those not fit will perish, and the weak are the prey of the strong, and interest of the weak has never been considered.

Do you want to be loved by the surrounding persons, by your country, and the whole earth? Only a harmonious society, public ownership, and state capitalism can achieve this—harmony is big love.

Why do human beings need a harmonious society now?

Because all our past cultures and civilisations and all rules of the game were established under the premise of low productivity. People worked day and night but could only afford the food and clothing for themselves or the surrounding persons. In this condition, the fighting of human beings was of small scale and partial and did not have a large influence on the natural environment. Even if hundreds or thousands or millions of people died, it was just knife and axe chopping, and the previous civilisation could be restored after several decades.

However, with the improving of human productivity, the destructive power of human beings has also rapidly improved. The nuclear weapons owned by human beings now can destroy the earth for many times. Much destruction is irrevocable or can only be restored after many years, and all the destruction is large-scale and transient.

In this condition, human beings must set up a new rule of the game. There must be a higher requirement for the spiritual civilisation of human beings; the spiritual civilisation of human beings must be improved. Just as a monkey cannot drive a car, people with weak intelligence, mental disorder, weak sight, or achromatopsia and those not trained are also disqualified to drive a car.

God would not let a group of monkeys drive a car; if they insist on doing so without listening to the advice, God will make them all die, unless they become qualified men within the specified time. I don't want to see this day, but it will come irrevocably, because it is the time to make a choice for the technical advancement of human beings, that is, harmonious or perishing.

63. The world can be great unity

About 2007

The world great unity refers to the people of the world, no war, no pressure, no discrimination, no suspicion.

Many prophecies said the world will be great unity in the end. I think the world can be great unity, but it requires hard work and efforts around the world.

At the beginning of the Bible, it has mentioned the contradictions at the root of the world.

Genesis chapter 11

11:1   And the whole earth was of one language, and of one speech.

11:2   And it came to pass, as they journeyed from the east, that they found a plain in the land of Shinar; and they dwelt there.

11:3 And they said one to another, Go to, let us make brick, and burn them thoroughly. And they had brick for stone, and slime had they for mortar.

11:4   And they said, Go to, let us build us a city and a tower, whose top may reach unto heaven; and let us make us a name, lest we be scattered abroad upon the face of the whole earth.

11:5   And the Lord came down to see the city and the tower, which the children of men built.

11:6   And the Lord said, Behold, the people is one, and they have all one language; and this they begin to do: and now nothing will be restrained from them, which they have imagined to do.

11:7 Go to, let us go down, and there confound their language, that they may not understand one another's speech.

11:8   So the Lord scattered them abroad from thence upon the face of all the earth; and they left off to build the city.

11:9   Therefore is the name of it called Babel; because the Lord did there confound the language of all the earth: and from thence did the Lord scatter them abroad upon the face of all the earth.

God thinks that life on earth is better than too much, they need to get original sin of punishment, so he deliberately confounded the language of people, made people unable to communicate and understand, have mutual suspicion, hate each other.

Whether there is this kind of history, and frankly, ancient Rome, one thing is true, because people can't communicate normally, leading to them not understanding each other, having mutual suspicion, and hating each other.

The conspirators use the weakness of human nature, making people hate each other and kill each other. In other words, whoever spread hatred and suspicion, thought the slayer, are all conspirators. They are the envoys of the devil! This kind of person is at all times and all over the world everywhere.

Actually, if the abnormal communication between people, abnormal understanding, mutual suspicion, and hating each other are eliminated, then the world can be great unity. But abnormal understanding between people, mutual suspicion, and mutual hatred cannot be eliminated if we just rely on the language of unity.

The abnormal understanding between people, mutual suspicion, and mutual hatred—how do these come about?

It's human nature. Human nature is always selfish, greedy, mercenary, bullying, and ugly. But humanity is the nature of people; since people are born, that cannot change.

Both in religion and saints, they thought a lot, such as using sweet words to cajole or using harsh punishment to bully. But they can only succeed temporarily; they cannot change anything, apart from the numbered, as the white terror, nothing has been changed.

Of course there is another side of human nature—weakness, death, and a little bit of reason.

I think that there is a channel in human nature that would make people get rid of abnormal understanding, mutual suspicion, and hating each other.

That is, the artificial, wide-range, purposeful, planned, organised interracial marriage! Foreign marriage! Marriage is just a tool, not at all, what is madly in love!

Regard the large-scale intermarriage as historic, sacred mission, work to do, then it can achieve great unity.

Simply, nearly half of the people have blood relationship with neighbouring countries in the region. The existence of the country will be regarded as a stumbling block, be kicked by voters. And wars are not needed to achieve national merger and extinction, but through democratic means.

But in the meantime, there will be the envoys of the devil, like Nazis, to destroy ethnic integration. Deliberately highlight the diversity of ethnic groups. And deliberately stir up ethnic hatred and conflict. Then you may need wars to solve the problems.

But the idea can be widely spread and identified. Then wars can be avoided, and the devil can also come in a bottle.

Interracial marriage is one of the most ancient, effective, thorough ways of human nature.

64. I Do Not Think That I Am So Wise

9 October 2013

Sometimes I think I'm smart. I want to know why I think something is simple, normal, and ordinary, but others don't think so; however, the facts proved that I was always right.

I think my idea is that normal people should have, but I don't have anything special. The reason why people look so stubborn and stupid is that there are a lot of problems they never think of or never think about in a right direction. And they never think from good intentions towards others but are busy with calculating gains and losses, the pros and cons as well as fame and wealth, etc.

I don't think I'm smart. To be honest, I have only a college degree. I majored in science, but I have still not fully understood higher mathematics. The difference between me and others is that our ways of thinking are not the same. I think the world should be beautiful, but why is the world is so cruel, troubled, and unsatisfied? And the reason for this question is what I am interested in studying on. I dislike ugly, unkind, wrong, and vicious things, hoping to rectify them.

While as average people, you are just considering temporary fame and wealth as well as some ordinary things, instead of caring about or pondering over those problems of human society, because you may think that it is none of your business, and it cannot help you to make money, though it may seriously affect you to earn money.

I write down these things just in order to urge you to think about some problems and some simple questions in human society. The idea that I have raised is neither complicated nor abstract. I believe that everyone can understand it, as long as you don't consider it as a joke.

Many of my ideas are published on the Web or on the website of the government and sent to my friends in Taiwan through some other channels. In fact, they all seriously considered my suggestions and ideas; moreover, most of them adopted and listened to some of my suggestions.

Many ideas and practices have been put into trial use in China for more than ten years. Though there are a lot of restrictions as well as twists and turns, I think that it was achieved successfully as a whole.

China's model is not a patent in China, which is also suitable for other countries. It is suitable not only for the socialist countries, but also for the capitalist countries.

This book is for our ordinary people, and I hope that there exists a social system or social order that can really protect their interests. At the same time, the role of social elites in the country must be recognised and protected. In short, everyone's rights should be respected and protected effectively.

To be honest, what is the human society doing in modern times and the contemporary age? Don't you think it is ridiculous and funny? Or shameless and lamentable? The war and political battles will result in too much death. Is this action what has been done by man, the wisest of all creatures? It is a garbage action, which is worse than the animals.

I don't think I'm so clever. I just hope the human society can live a normal life. In my view, the life that I have described is the lifestyle which is supposed to had by an average person, while all of you are living in an abnormal way of life at present.

I think that you are abnormal, instead of me. I am a common as well as sober person. Those who do not recognise my ideas or the book that I wrote are abnormal, and it is the ignorance and barbarism and selfishness blinding your hearts and minds. Even the thought of normal people has gone.

But back to where we were, you cannot be blamed. It should be said that our human beings' science and technology level has been developed too fast, or that the level of science and technology in China has been developed too fast. Chinese way of life and the level of consciousness have been changed a lot. Never having been abroad, I do not know whether the foreigners' thought is as rapid as China's. Maybe you develop slowly.

But in my own experience, when I am watching the old movies in China, especially from the 1970s or 1980s, or the old movies when I was a child, I don't think the people in the movies are normal. Because their way of thinking is too strange, too stupid, and too outdated.

I don't know if you have such feelings. If not, you do not have the progress with the times, and you would be abnormal.

65. It's None of My Business

16 August 2014

I'm not a troublemaker, and I don't care about anything that has nothing to do with me. I never give money to those beggars on the street, not only because I have no money, but also it's none of my business.

I'm only a person who is interested in exploring, and I always want to make clear those things in the world. I remember that I have argued on physics problems with my physics teacher for two times. And both in the end, I achieved the academic success, and the whole grade corrected the problem that I supposed. Those physics problems are simple but a little bit rare.

I will stick to things that are right in my mind, and I'll prove it to the entire world.

With more and more things I studied, I think I was further and further away from this world. An increasing number of things have proved that only my opinion is right, and others are wrong. But in my mind, those things are simple and basic; they are basic requirements and basic knowledge to be a man. Why are people in this world so strange? Why are they so stubborn? And why are they even so evil?

One day, I suddenly discovered that something would never be come up with or done if I didn't.

I really don't know whether I should be pleased with my intelligence, or I should be afraid with the world's evil, backwardness, and ignorance.

I don't think I'm smart. It takes a long time to learn something, and I even cannot get it. I'm only a normal person. Others are just too smart or born evil.

I only want to go through my life happily and peacefully. But one day I suddenly discovered that those who used to have no relationship with me are all my business. No one would get it done if I didn't. I'm a part of the earth, and I can't be the witness of its decay without doing anything. But what I can do is just make some complaints and put forward some suggestions. Other things are not my business.

I think I'm just the boy who reveals the emperor's nakedness in 'The Emperor's New Clothes'.

This world is too dirty, too ignorant, and too deceptive to see the true world clearly. Everybody lives in a dream filled with dirt and hypocrisy. But I will say some true words to you.

It can be proved what I said are all truth whether you believe or not. But I gradually became embarrassed to say anything. I feel it's funny. But it is the fact. It's too cruel and too funny.

66. Reflection on inequality among people, based on 80-20 rule

About 2007

80-20 Rule

In 10 persons: 2 persons are wealthy and 8 persons are poor.

In 10 persons: 2 persons are in command of 80 per cent of the wealth in the world while the remaining 8 persons have only 20 per cent.

In 10 persons: 2 persons make money with their brain, while 8 persons make money with their body.

In 10 persons: 2 persons think positively while 8 persons think negatively.

In 10 persons: 2 persons purchase time while the rest sell their time.

In 10 persons: 2 persons seek an excellent employee while 8 persons are hunting for a good job.

In 10 persons: 2 persons are in charge of others while 8 persons are in the charge of others.

In 10 persons: 2 persons have their own business while 8 persons are working for other persons' business.

In 10 persons: 2 persons prefer work experience while 8 persons prefer a diploma.

In 10 persons: 2 persons believe that action prevails over results while 8 persons believe that knowledge is power.

In 10 persons: 2 persons are clear about what qualities and actions they should have to be wealthy, while 8 persons picture what they can be if they are wealthy.

In 10 persons: 2 persons prefer to invest while 8 persons prefer to buy.

In 10 persons: 2 persons are target-oriented while 8 persons are daydreaming.

In 10 persons: 2 persons seek answers to questions while 8 persons seek questions from answers.

In 10 persons: 2 persons look afar while the rest only care about short-term profits.

In 10 persons: 2 persons seize the opportunity while the rest miss the opportunity.

In 10 persons: 2 persons plan for the future while 8 persons consider what to do today only in the morning.

In 10 persons: 2 persons take actions based on successful experience while 8 persons take actions based on their own wills.

In 10 persons: 2 persons repeat simple things while 8 persons hate simple things.

In 10 persons: 2 persons finish tasks in advance, while 8 persons procrastinate on tasks.

In 10 persons: 2 persons can achieve targets while 8 persons fail.

In 10 persons: 2 persons are influenced by successes while 8 persons are impacted by failures.

In 10 persons: 2 persons are in a good state while 8 persons are in a negative state.

In 10 persons: 2 persons believe dreams will come true while 8 persons are affected by previous failures.

In 10 persons: 2 persons live with success while 8 persons do not want to change the current situation.

In 10 persons: 2 persons change themselves while 8 persons change others.

In 10 persons: 2 persons encourage and praise while 8 persons criticise and scold.

In 10 persons: 2 persons persist while 8 persons give up.

Reflection on inequality among people, based on 80-20 rule

Indeed, each one in this society looks similar, with one head, four limbs, and a body; they all can talk and think. However, everyone is different.

From the 80-20 rule, we can see that people are divided into two classes in which people in the respective classes think from different respects. We divide them into smart people and ordinary people. Wealth and resources are assets of smart people, who can start their own business from nothing, but they are able to accumulate wealth. Gradually, small profits grow bigger and they become wealthy.

However, when the remaining 8 persons (80 per cent) have those assets in their hands, they end up abusing and wasting it. Finally, they have to be homeless and even have nothing to lose.

People who appeal to equality have no idea, and they only think by killing the 20 per cent people they can achieve everything.

Eventually, God disposes and men only propose. Regardless of any struggles, dumb people remain dumb and they will never be rich. Without the talent to be rich, though a dumb person is appointed to be the president, he will lose everything and be laid off. That is called destiny.

Men are born unequal. If one wants to pursue equality, he should suppose it is true and not take it seriously, or try some self-comforting and cheating himself.

All can be seen as daydreaming.

67. Scholars should defend truth, rather than blindly protect certain people's interests

About 2007

Scholars have knowledge from both learning and thinking, which make them more visionary than ordinary people.

Because scholars are more literate than ordinary people, they are easier to earn certain people's trust. But scholars are neither beaters nor executioners.

Scholars should have independence, objectivity, and justice.

Because scholars are more informed than ordinary people, they are liable to let people learn the truth, rather than fooling people to win the favour of somebody.

Scholars only discuss the good and evil, beauty and ugliness, right and wrong, advantages and disadvantages on the basis of truth.

Another task of scholars is, on the basis of facts, to resolve disputes between common people, rather than taking a more foolish method to defend the interests of certain people.

That's what we call Tao.

Because there are weaknesses and shortcomings in human nature, humanity still has vortex and trap. Once people fall into a trap or are involved in a whirlpool, they can't help themselves, such as those into drugs, love, cults, religious extremism, etc.

Sometimes they completely lost control of themselves, and they have no ability to tell right from wrong. They just blindly do some repeated and foolish things.

Sometimes they brought serious trouble to the government and the world, so they had to be defeated.

People once involved into a whirlpool, only when they use their will, refuse to blindly pursue the truth, can they slowly break through the dilemma and return to reason? Otherwise they are just walking dead.

The biggest characteristic of these people is blindly, wildly, and irrationally worship someone or something, such as blind worship for God, Allah, and Buddha.

Scholars should rationally analyse problems and scientifically research knowledge, rather than blindly believe, obey, and worship.

68. Politicians almost tell lies while philosophers must tell the truth

About 2007

Often, politicians say what they should say and do what they should do, rather than consider objectively and impartially. It is the great difference between them.

Only when philosophers tell the truth can they be convinced.

However, the politicians tell lies almost to cater to the psychology of the public and consolidate their status.

Therefore, politicians are good at telling lies. If a person who is not good at telling lies politicises, he will fail totally.

Politicians need to tell lies, while theorists should tell the truth.

Lin Biao said, 'You cannot succeed without telling lies.'

Hitler said, 'Ten thousand of the same lies will be the truth.'

But I am not a politician, so I must reveal the truth no matter if you like it or not.

The truth is the truth, and the fact is the fact.

Politicians will maintain their status through neutralising and balancing the opinions of most people. Philosophers must tell the truth to win the trust of the public and bring humans to another direction, a real world.

This world should not be filled with lies, and people should not live in lies.

I never tell lies and say the real fact and truth.

What I see is that the politicians in the world always tell lies about religion, especially Islam. They know clearly that Islam is a heresy and the root of all evil, the source of the devil, the axis of evil, and the nature of hooliganism. But they still advocate that Islam is a peaceful religion. This is because Islam is cruel and evil and commits all manners of crimes and they are frightened. The people believing in Islam are numerous and spread all over the world. They may be just passers-by. They are scared of revenge and are afraid of losing votes and job title and implicating families, so they say nonsense unconscionably, mislead the public and people, as well as harm themselves and others. So politicians like telling lies.

69. Women Only Have Consciousness, No Thoughts

About 2007

The Bible says the first woman was made from a man's rib, so she is the man's bone of bone, flesh of flesh.

I'm not sure whether the story is true, but I do believe that men and women are different.

According to the theory of yin and yang, the male is yang, the female is yin, so women have to obey the men.

All classical theory in our world is the same, namely, women must obey men.

An astronomer once said you only need a whip to talk with a woman. To a certain extent, I think he's right.

It occurs to me that neither a philosopher nor thinker was a woman in human history. No woman can become a philosopher or a thinker.

Why?

That's because women have no thought; they don't have the function. Just like men have no uterus.

Men can't give birth to a child; woman can't think. Women only have consciousness, no thoughts.

Consciousness is just a reaction and judgment towards the things around.

Being a philosopher and thinker is to judge, analyse, design, and guide human behaviour. It is a study of extremely abstract concept.

I know a lot of women; certainly some of them are very smart and capable of making money. I always had the feeling that their mode of thinking is different from men's, though it is hard to tell the difference. Maybe the aspects of psychoanalysis can find some answers.

I've pointed out that women's and men's subconscious are different.

Women's function of design of genitals is different from men's. Men are positive while women can only passively accept. Men can force women to do anything; women can't.

So in terms of sexual satisfaction, only the men can make the first move. Women can only attract men, seduce men, recall the men's sexual drive, but they can't make men have sex with them.

According to the subconscious theory of Freud, men and women have different starting points when it comes to thinking.

The subconscious of men is masculine, aggressive, compulsive, and progressive. Women's subconscious is defensive, sustainable, receptive, and acceptable.

Philosophers, thinkers, and politicians are completely different concepts. The politicians balance relation of various powers to achieve a political purpose. So in most cases, politicians need to consider most people's ideas and acceptance, from the political point of view, by weighing different benefits to determine what to say and what to do, rather than consider things from the perspective of objectivity and justice. So in many cases, politicians are lying. They need lies to do big things, by catering to the public's psychology to consolidate their status.

But philosophers and thinkers study nations, the world, universal truth by studying the truth and facts to lead the human society to a new civilisation. They need to tell the truth to make people believe. Because the thought of philosophers and thinkers is always out of ordinary people's reach, even contradicting the public's existing ideology, they always find themselves in the position to fight against the whole society, against the entire mainstream society, which might lead to their tragic fate.

There was a joke, 'If you want to be a philosopher, you need to marry a bitch first.'

But I think the sequence should be reversed, that is, marrying a philosopher will make a good woman a bitch.

Women have to give birth to children and take care of the next generation. That's why they need a lot of material to guarantee family security and children's needs of life. This is the starting point of how women deal with general issues. The first thing is conservation, assurance, and security.

Philosophers' thinking is giving correct guidance to the social problems and studying the theory of truth. These are all vain and impractical things, which can't bring with instant benefits. And investment is never-ending. Sometimes they even have to directly fight against the government, the mainstream society, or the mainstream thoughts. And they will get themselves in trouble, even get themselves killed, which is incompatible with women's starting point of family security. Something men may take as glory or with enthusiasm, women may see as a scourge and avoid it like the plague. So women are subconsciously different from the philosophers. That's why they can't be philosophers or thinkers.

Therefore, women should obey the supervision of men, and men should take care of women.

70. The otherness of people's understanding

About 2007

We meet and come in contact with a lot of people every day. However, the degrees of awareness of people on an object have nothing in common with each other.

Take driving as an example; more and more people are learning how to drive, and when we go to the driving school, we shall understand the coordination operation of the steering wheel, the throttle, and the brakes. Knowing this can help us to drive in accordance with our desires. It can be regarded as applying and using the car by us. We call this driving skill and cognitive level on handling the car as application-grade level.

If the car broke down on the road and I just can't fix it by myself, I would call the maintainer for help. The cognitive level of the maintainer on the car is much better than most of us. At least they know the function and principle of each part of the car. Also, they know the way how all the parts work together in a car system. When a certain part of the car breaks down, or in other words, the system won't work, the maintainer can check out the faulty part and test and replace it based on the fault phenomenon and by testing method. Then the car system can run normally. And it can be handed to the customer. We call the cognitive level of the maintainer on the car as maintenance-grade level.

We know that the cars are manufactured by the car factory. And the cars are designed by the designers in the car factory. They could design and produce the cars based on existing technology and market demand and in accordance with their designing level and desires. The degree of cognition of them is the highest in the world. We call the cognitive level of the car engineer on car as design-grade level.

In fact, everything in the world has a process of cognition similar to that of cars. We have more than three levels of cognition on cars: use-degree, maintenance-grade, and design-grade. Almost all the things in the world have a three-degree level of cognition like that. Of course, the division of level of cognition on an object is a simple method. There could be a more exquisite division method or a simple method. I just want to show that the level of cognition of everyone on an object differs one from another, like that of this case.

Besides, even the cognition of the same type of people on the same object differs from each other. Take the car as an example; for the drivers, some may be dedicated in driving and some others just learned it not long ago, and the others can drive and solve some small faults. Those who can fix problems are the ones close to maintenance-grade. And there are also some car fans that can both drive and even modify a car by themselves. So all the drivers, the beginners, regular drivers, and car fans have different understanding and cognition on cars.

Everyone has different levels of cognition on the same object. And the cognition of different people on the same object is different from one another as well. There are numerous types of objects in our daily life. Although we live in the same world, our cognition on all the things in the universe has a great deal of diversity.

The statement above shows that when we look upon all the things around us, we should keep one concept in mind—the conclusions made by all the people in the world for a single matter might be different from your understanding. Your understanding on things can only stand for no one else but yourself. You shouldn't wish that everyone could follow you. This is absolutely not possible. Making the Procrustean bed is a sign of obstinacy.

71. Let's make up

A Letter to Taiwan Compatriots

October 2004

Hello, Taiwan compatriots, I am a commoner from China mainland. I do not belong to any party or any organisation, and thus represent nobody but only myself. I have something to say to you because I think it must be said now for your careful consideration.

From ancient history, Taiwan has been part of Chinese dominion. For the Chinese people, it is just a small island, but the respect of the nation. Not handling the matter well would put disgrace to all of us. As a result, the world would find another ground for the labels for China being called 'inferior nation' and Sick Man of East Asia, if it cannot find a way to handle its own domestic affair. That would lead China to an absolute disadvantageous position in any international negotiation.

Let me talk about it in the manner of a common person, not on behalf of anybody but only of myself.

I think one must have some problems in his mind if he still fights for a certain ideology in the era of new century, and the one who still deceives others under the banner of ideology must suffer retardation.

The truly smart one holds the goal that is the most practical only for himself, not for anyone else. There is no sage in the world that lives only for anyone else; either it is communism, capitalism, human rights, or democracy. There is no real hero but only the instrument under the control of someone else. Each of us would become others' pawn only if we believe in others' lie and rumour; at the final analysis, I do not believe anyone but only myself.

I will not fight for anyone and only for myself.

If Taiwan gets independence, it would mean the Chinese people are incapable, weak, not solid, and any other country can come to gain some interests from here; in that case, all our future generations will be at others' mercy. For the interests of our future generations and the whole Chinese nation, CCP has really got a point to equate Taiwan independence to a war. To curb national separation, we must be prepared for a war. The view represents not only CCP, but also the whole of the Chinese people on China mainland. The announcement of independence is just the announcement of a war—there must be an equal sign between them.

For my personal intention, I do not want to fight. Nobody is born inclined

219

for a war. But I will never be afraid in the face of a war. Anybody may go to die, but there must be a point in it. Anyone who breaks peace, destroys my home, and leads me and my offspring into disaster would be paid with his life. I hate them and I will cut their head off.

If we have to go to a war for Taiwan, I will be the first to join the army and fight to the end. I have no alternative for my wife and children when you break the peace and destroy my home.

There is one other thing I need to tell you. Since CCP came to lead us, we have never been defeated in a fight. I believe it can be a small case to win the fight with 13 billion against only 20 million.

Anyway, why don't you want to unify with China mainland? I understand you perhaps think we are living a poor life. But we all wish to get rich, and perhaps even a fool does not want to return to China mainland before we get rich. We are all Chinese and we can understand each other.

We are all so smart. Only price is the topic between the smart, and only fools come to talk about ideology.

What is democracy and human right? They are all just the gimmick and camouflage. How can they explode Chinese embassy when they are talking about human right, and how can they invade another country if they hold a strong view on democracy? I have seen so much of the gimmick that can be seen everywhere in history books. I do not believe anything except myself. Everything is false in my eyes except the thing that I can see and touch, such as my house, my wife, and my children. I only fight and live for them, and there is no way letting me to be a pawn.

Taiwan compatriots, let's make it up. Don't listen to the bullshit of the deceiving politics anymore. Both sides across the strait are calling to be the most democratic, aren't they? Let's draw an agreement and see who dares object to it. No matter what is said and what excuse is used, objection to the agreement is an objection to democracy and human right. It is a deception for the whole public, and it is a totally false democracy. Our fate is in our own hands. I want to see which side holds the real sense of democracy, China mainland or Taiwan authority, socialism or capitalism.

Think of your house, your wife, and your children. Let's reach an agreement, only if we both have the sincerity.

Nothing can be reached without reconciliation between brothers. Let's compromise and bury the hatchet, since we're all one family.

I know why you do not return to China mainland—just because China mainland is in a poor situation. This is the most practical and fundamental reason. Anything else, like democracy, human right, ideology, and thought are nothing but blind excuses. You always talk about these stupid things until you yourself don't even believe; as a result, only one thing is left that you are so implicit about—money.

If China was as rich as West Germany with gold seen everywhere, and even if you guys could get some even by swimming across the strait, you would never come to deceive us with the so-called ideology and thought. I know you too well; to be more precise, I know the entire human. Never deceive yourselves anymore, be practical and economic, and set a price where, when and under what conditions do you want to return to China mainland peacefully. We are all brothers. Never say those things hurting feelings, such as fight, killing, win, or defeat. There is no point talking about it too frankly.

I even worked in Taiwan as a top salesman for Mr Chan Yongtai. Taiwan people like bargaining and giving the run-around. Let's come straight to the point—think of your house, wife, and children and set a minimum price that you can bear in mind.

Let me set a reasonable price.

Before that, I want to emphasise again I belong to no party and do not represent anybody, any organisation, and only the conscience of a Chinese person. Please consider it carefully; I believe the whole public in China mainland can reach an agreement with you, if the agreement between you and me can be possible. We are all Chinese. No matter how the strong power wishes to separate us, we share the same ancestors and cultural relics; we are all under the deep influence of Confucianism, and the blessing of Mercy Buddha and the god of wealth. We all know how Yue Fei and Qu Yuan died, so we also know what duty we shall take for our parents, wives, and children. Although we are in the disadvantageous and powerless situation, we must hold our own fate and refuse to be the puppet of the politicians and adventurists. We are not fools, and the smart only talks about business. Anybody who wants you to be the fool and cannon fodder, fight and kill him. Now I have finished all that I want to say, and let's sit to talk about business.

I think the conditions are reasonable and fair, and acceptable to us.

Taiwan will return to China mainland only when at least three big cities in China mainland have the GDP per capita reaching the average level of the island. Or else, we will never get a result in the issue; when the condition above is not satisfied, China mainland government shall promise not to use force against Taiwan.

221

In any circumstances, Taiwan shall never announce independence in a form, or else it can be deemed a war declaration against China mainland.

When the economic construction and revenue of China mainland reaches the level as stipulated in the first article, Taiwan must hand over power to the mainland, or else it shall be deemed as breach of agreement on Taiwan side. According to the agreement, the people in both Taiwan and mainland have the right and obligation in any approach to kill those who oppose unification in the island and put in joint efforts to achieve national unification.

The Chinese government must promise to retain the current political and economic systems after receiving Taiwan power (except if the local agree) and promise not to persecute the authority's military and political staff of Taiwan.

I am offering a peaceful settlement for Taiwan compatriots on my own conscience. I beg your careful consideration for the following merits to you:

Turn cross-strait military competition to economic competition.

Taiwan authority can always find a way to get rid of the bother from the mainland. It just needs to keep its economy in the lead and leave the Taiwan issue aside. Those political shams under the banner 'For the interest of Taiwan people' shall turn the money that is designated to purchase weapons to economic construction. Even a fool can do well in buying things to destroy the world, but taking up economic construction and leading the people to rich life are really a technology. People are concerned only about money, not about the independence. If the authority cannot get people rich, they may as well hand over the power.

The mainland government has to push up the economy to recapture Taiwan. We cannot drag someone else down when we can in a messy economic situation. We need to solve the Taiwan problem with money and economic power, instead of pushing others down by overwhelming manpower.

Therefore, the proposal can bring the most favourable benefits to the commoners. The commoners can receive the most benefits no matter which side finally wins. For the officials, it is the real test for their ability.

It is a really stale practice to convert people's attention from the messy economy by stirring up a war. We do not need that old practice; instead, we need to put in more efforts to develop our economy and avoid the commoners as the cannon fodder.

There is another side who only knows how to pay lip service to the mainland or Taiwan, but what has it really done? We all know I am referring to

America, who is only crazy about wars. It did that during the Second World War and is still doing it now. It has gained so many benefits from the issue of cross-strait relation, and what's worse, it remains greedy for more against the conscience. An old-fashioned warship piled just with waste metals was sold even for over 600 billion. How much commission has the authority gained? Now that you have so much money, you have to cheat the whole Chinese. Are you taking us for fools, trying to fight with the 1.3 billion people with those old and stale warships?

Use money to maintain monopoly and world hegemony, and help Taiwan with economic construction. As long as you can make investment to revive Taiwan economy and keep it in the lead, your ideology and thought will take root forever.

Since CCP led the mainland, China has never suffered any humiliation in wars or defeat to any invaders or separatist plotters. Each inch of the territory represents the respect of the Chinese, with no exception of Taiwan. The announcement of independence shall be seen as the war action. We must win the war of protecting national territory. Chinese commoners have long hated the few corrupt officials and have accumulated enough strength for a fight with all of the anger vented on to the Taiwan separatists.

Never take any hope for independence, and instead, take your time making some money and supporting your family. Never get involved in politics to be used as cannon folder. Remember the principle of being commoners—elect those who give you more money and kill those who want you to fight in a war. It is never wrong to hold such a principle (except the war against the national traitors and foreign invaders).

The third article is of course easy to comprehend.

Once the agreement is reached, we must keep it. Anyone has the right to punish those who breach the agreement and fool the public on both sides and even the whole Chinese nation. We are all businessmen who put honesty above all and bear top hatred for the dishonest. But I think only idiots can take the risk of breaking the public wish; of course, I don't hope there are any idiots who make that happen.

The fourth article is the consistent practice of the Chinese government to solve regional dispute. As it is implemented nationwide, I will not say much about it here. It is just that some Taiwan separatists are trying every means to even the old scores against CCP and blacken the image of CCP. Here I'd like to say something fair. Anyone who breaks the agreement is turning the people into the enemy. Agreement holds a position above all in business; the Chinese government also needs to maintain its international image, refuse to break promises, and make enemies with some small potatoes who damage its own image. I incorporate it into the agreement just to avoid others making irresponsible remarks.

I have finished all that I want to say. Now let's sit down for a talk to make the agreement more complete and implemented as soon as possible. Let's not prepare for wars any more, and just think how to make money. Just let the warmongers fight themselves and keep a clear mind to do the things that can bring us more benefits.

72. Whether the petition letter should be abolished depends on its function

About 2007

The petition letter is one form of rule by people. So why are officials afraid of petition letters? Why do they try to prevent petition letters? That's because a petition letter causes the pressure of public opinion and leads to promotion trouble for the greedy officials. Therefore they are afraid of petition letters and spare no efforts to prevent the petition letters.

The key to the petition letter system is public-opinion supervision of authority. The key lies in whether the supreme decision-making layer of the country wants the public-opinion supervision of officials.

If the supreme decision-making layer really wants to make things in order, there are lots of effective and money-saving methods for them to adopt. If the supreme decision-making layer just wants to do some superficial work and does not aim to solve the realistic problems, they can say and do anything they want. As long as everybody knows the fact, it is enough; it is of no use to say more. No one is foolish, and everyone is clear about the truth.

I just propose an effective method.

The country sets up a central petition letter network in Beijing.

2. The petition letter network is made in the form of a forum. But the forum has authority. Only the party and the administrator can make statements; others can do nothing but read.

3. The forum divides the column and the theme zone according to the provinces and cities in China. The events are written in the column of locality. It is clear to know which place has the largest number of petition letters, through looking at the quantity.

4. The column displays subgrade administration. For example, if petitioners begin to propose petition, display the petition title, but the party can see the whole contents. After petitioners propose the petition letter, the central petition letter network displays the petition contents to the local place. After the local government sees it, it can investigate and reply at once. After petitioners see the reply, they can end the petition or propose new evidence to make pleas on the Internet. It is all done in secret. The central government can make adjudication according to the reply and evidence of both parties and order the local government to finish it. In addition, the local government should reply to the handling results in forum. In this way can the

petitioners make a reply concerning whether the local government executes the judgment. If the local government refuses to execute the judgment within the stipulated time, make the reply contents public, including the whole process of adjudication and petition of both parties. People in the world can see the dispute and adjudication results of both parties.

5. The reply contents continue to be concealed to the public after the local government finishes ruling and petitioners recognise it. Only petition introductions and handling results are left there.

It is the most effective and easiest method. It is a matter of whether they want to do it rather than a matter of whether they can do it.

73. Ethnic integration policy

About 2007

The reason is simple why there have been wars and strife on earth since the ancient times. It lies behind the conflicts of interest between regions, ethnicities, and parties. And ethnicities and races have largely a negative impact as the main cause of the conflicts.

Why there is strife between ethnicities and races? The main reason is the huge discrepancy between them in language, faith, lifestyle, custom, economy, region, with language the most important one.

Communication can't be achieved because of the language barrier. Even though the promotion of Mandarin Chinese gained some effect, as long as there is the language difference, there is always an intangible barrier between people with different languages, which is difficult to bridge. It is an intangible barrier in people's heart.

There is a good explanation in the Bible of how the barrier came to exist. The Bible says God was afraid that people would be overly successful with the same language, so he made them speak different languages overnight, thus driving them apart, and wars arose.

It's a legend, almost a myth, which cannot be verified. But the reason in it is true—it is the discrepancy and barrier between people that generates conflicts and strife, resulting in human disasters. Human disasters are rooted in discrepancy.

Smart-aleck and always arrogant humans take it for granted that they are masters of the earth only because they have mastered advanced technologies, which is ridiculous in that advanced technologies can only take them into more dangerous situations. Conflicts were only swords when there was no nuclear power before, with the result of lower loss of lives, while now the society is so advanced and things have got so out of control that a city, even a country, can be razed to the ground all at once.

It can't be said that people are not improved, but their smart heads are always full of tricks for how to be stronger, tougher, and more powerful than the others. Only then can they get a good sleep. They are only thinking about how to escalate the conflict, instead of settling it radically, to conciliate the conflict and hatred.

Since the root of human conflict is the discrepancy between ethnicities and races, to solve the conflict is to eliminate it.

How to achieve it? It's very simple—interracial marriage, which simply means marriage between men and women who belong to different races, then giving birth to children.

First of all, to give birth to a child or not is one of the basic human rights, which the modern society, a civilised society, should respect and protect. And of course the nation can't force somebody to bear a baby with someone else.

Secondly, humans are higher animals with their own thoughts. Marriage and childbirth, the biggest thing in one's life, can't be manipulated by others.

What's considered crazy in capitalist countries is an achievable goal in a socialist country. Why? By what? Government capital.

A real socialist country should be one that represents the interest of the whole nation, holding most of the capital of the nation—government capital. There is a saying, 'Money makes the mare go', which may be vulgar, but the reason in it is the truth that money is too powerful to be neglected, and there are even situations where guns are useless while money can easily get things done.

For example, the problem of ethnic integration by large-scale interracial marriage mentioned above can be solved by government capital if used properly. It is illegal and infringes on human rights to force a person to marry one of different race with guns, but it is legal and reasonable to induce people to do it with money.

How to induce? Here are some of my ideas for reference:

> 1. China can adjust its one-child policy, like one child for spouse from the same ethnicity, whether they are Han people or minorities. And there is no limitation for spouses from different ethnicities, and the more, the better with national support of fiscal subsidies and special care.
>
> 2. Propaganda of interracial marriage to form the consensus of the glory of it
>
> 3. Interracial marriage as political duty to exam cadres
>
> 4. There should be some positions reserved for ethnic minorities in state-owned enterprises, with the house allocated and requirement for them to leave their home to live in the city and marry Han people.

5. Free board and lodging is provided in other cities for students of minorities, with arrangement of work and requirement of leaving their home to marry Han people.

Ethnic integration can combine the nation into a monolith, with no ethnic discrepancy existing within the nation and thus no ethnic conflict at all, leading to a harmonious and perfect country and society.

Especially in unstable districts, the government can introduce policies to award interracial marriage to lead the population structure of these districts into ethnic integration step by step. As long as there are offspring from one of local ethnic minorities and the other of Han, it will enjoy a lasting peace with no worries. It is a contribution that could benefit generations, which deserves efforts.

Promotion of Mandarin Chinese is just a necessity for communication, which can't solve the fundamental conflict of ethnic discrepancy at all. Ethnic discrepancy is regional discrepancy. People take it for granted that the land is theirs because they have stayed there for a long time, such as Tibet and Taiwan, where the local people won't acknowledge those lands belong to Han or China. This idea can only be changed when they've left there and are distributed all over the country.

The increase of interracial marriage is a long-term investment, which is highly profitable, and it turns the national consumer behaviour into a national population investment behaviour. The difference between consumption and investment is that consumption is the behaviour of spending money with no big benefit for the future, while investment will bring a ten-thousandfold profit.

In government capital-holding enterprises, government, the capital investor, has the right to arrange children from interracial marriage to work there, which is proper and right. State-owned enterprises have to hire someone and pay him salary. Who would not take full advantage of the rights of a boss?

State-owned enterprises are a part of the national machine, which is quite suitable for solving ethnic problems, otherwise a waste of resources.

The cadres want promotion, so assign them something to do to show themselves, by setting target of interracial marriage. It's a perfect chance to weigh their working ability by interracial marriage.

Interracial marriage can greatly promote business and trade, leading to reasonable flow of social goods and materials, remarkable increase of job opportunities, and effective decrease of region gap and wealth gap.

74. 1.3 Billion Chinese People, 1.3 Billion Minds

About 2007

China has a population of 1.3 billion, each of whom has his/her own mind.

South Korean would commit happy dispatch, conduct self-burning protest, and cut-finger protest against Japan's declaration of sovereignty for Dokdo. Chinese will never do this.

China is in a state of disunity, which is objective fact.

Apart from centralisation of power, Chinese people will not buy into any story. China needs centralisation of power, which means Chinese people need an emperor.

Democracy, human rights, and liberty are rubbish and poison in China.

Chinese peasants are the best-behaved people in the world. As long as not being driven to the wall, they will not ask for anything. Democracy, liberty, and human rights are nonsense to Chinese civilians; what they need is just a little bit of money to live on and work in peace. The government that drives Chinese peasants desperate is the most incapable government.

Intending to call on Chinese people to do something with democracy, liberty, and human rights is in vain since nobody will take notice of it. Except for being punished by the people's government, no good outcome will be generated.

For progressives who sincerely want to do something good to Chinese people, making a fuss about centralisation of power and despotism is what they really should do. Otherwise, they will get no agreeable face from the Chinese government or the Chinese people and bring contempt upon themselves.

I'm not intending to strike anyone, just saying the truth.

Studying theories about Chinese people without knowing them is just like building a palace in the desert; you will get nothing apart from experiencing what is bitter.

75. It's suggested that China announce all corrupt officials fleeing to other countries and post a reward on chasing and killing them

About 2007

It's just ridiculous that the country cannot do anything to punish so many corrupt officials fleeing to other countries.

Corrupt officials fleeing to other countries should be sentenced to death for treason. Anyone can enforce the law. Since the authority finds it inconvenient, there are many who can do it. Just as the saying goes, generous rewards rouse one to heroism. No-cost deal will bring about more heroes.

While the authority cannot handle corrupt officials, they are extraordinarily brave and smart against their people.

It is said that Chinese people always have infighting. It's true.

It's not that they cannot do it; it's that they don't want to do it.

The Communist Party of China promises to represent the interests of the people, so it's entitled to manage money matters for the people. Now the money is stolen by your people. Therefore, you owe people an explanation.

Kill them.

Why are officials so unscrupulous? Because they know if they steal the money of private bosses, they will be hunted down; if they steal the country's money and the people's money, nobody will question them and nobody will feel distressed.

Just because they know so well the national nature of Chinese people, they are so full of guts.

All in all, it's the fault of Chinese people, and they deserve being bullied. Before liberation, they were bullied by foreign imperialist powers and now they are bullied by traitors.

All people mind their own business and play it safe. Ultimately, Chinese people are tied up by varied feudal ethical codes and ideologies, and don't have any courage and uprightness at all. They don't know what justice is and how to uphold justice.

A man has a clear-cut stand on what to love and what to hate. He extends gratitude to those who help them and revenges on enemies.

Those who steal people's money and are beheaded no matter how far they are chased are real men.

It is agreed that the Communist Party will be the boss if it is able to deal with any trouble that happens.

Domestic corruption and officials fleeing with money are completely two issues of different nature. Domestic corruption is a vulnerability of domestic finance management and a problem of financial distribution. No matter how greedy corrupt officials are, they spend money in China, and the difference is that the money finally belongs to whom.

For instance, a corrupt official takes a bribe of RMB 20 million, buys one house and one car, and has three mistresses. The money will be owned by automobile dealers, real estate developers, and Chinese people. Their consumption drives domestic demand. The masses cannot get any benefit, and they are unsatisfied.

Yet, fleeing with money is totally different with domestic corruption. It's the updated version of bribery and corruption. They know sooner or later they will come to light, so they take a drastic measure to end it and flee to foreign countries. By doing so, they evade the law.

At the moment when they transfer money to foreign countries, the money no longer belongs to Chinese people. No matter how they spend it abroad, Chinese people won't benefit at all. It will only increase national income of other countries who are competitors of China. Contributing to China's competitors will do no good to any Chinese person.

Hence, fleeing with money and domestic corruption are totally different contradictions. Fleeing with money is the most severe corruption and the most serious loophole of China.

To put it simply, if a husband snatches the meat in his wife's bowl, it's called domestic corruption. If a husband takes his wife's money and elopes with another woman, it's fleeing with money.

The two are completely different. Hence, fleeing with money is treason and betrayal of family.

When corrupt officials flee to other countries, they collude with family members to transfer national property. Their families are accomplices and should be sentenced to death as well. Accordingly, only when all their families are killed, justice is upheld and the interests of the people are safeguarded.

If the authority feels it's not suitable to send agents to enforce law abroad, they can sentence them to death in domestic trial and then post a reward on their death—anyone can kill them and immediately get the immense reward. The reward can be one tenth of the money which they took with them. Therefore, the more bribe they take, the sooner they will die.

However, if they can surrender right away and return money to people, they can be exempted from death and even won't be held accountable. What people want is still money, not their lives.

Generous rewards rouse one to heroism. They will be hunted down by gangsters of the whole world, and they are bound to die.

In order to safeguard the interests of its capitalists, the US can randomly dispatch troops to sovereign countries. Even Hitler had a reason to extinguish a race.

Chinese people just want to kill two traitors but cannot have any reason, which is so ridiculous.

It's not that the authority cannot put their hands on it; instead, it's because the masses don't have the concept of safeguarding their legal rights. If China can get such amount of money back, how many children can go to school for free? What's the greatest interest of the masses? They themselves don't understand it. What a pity!

As long as several traitors are killed, the rest will undoubtedly return with their remaining money. More importantly, nobody will dare flee again. This is the greatest interest of people and the country's as well.

76. The Chinese wisdom: no fish can survive if the water is too clean—one should not demand absolute purity

About 2007

No fish can survive if the water is too clean. For the same reason, no company can bear one whose requirements are too critical. This is an old maxim.

But this is not just an old maxim. Instead, I think it is the truth which has gone through tests many times.

The words of wisdom are not obtained by me from official circles but from business circles. It is my personal experience after countless communication with the public masses.

For people who hate this saying like poison, I can be 100 per cent sure that they have not done business by starting from scratch. They don't know how to do business at all, or they have never done any small business.

The way of doing business is also the way of being a person. Doing business is being a person—this is the first rudimental lesson I have learned, and it is also the classic saying of my predecessors and countless successful marketing people.

What is called being a person? Or what is called being a businessman?

1. To study the nature of human beings and understand real people, especially the clients you need to deal with every day

2. To try to overcome the undesirable part of our nature

3. To take advantage of the weak part of other people's nature.

Thus, successful businessmen know people, the good and evil of human nature, and human weaknesses best. Because they have to deal with people every day and must deal with people successfully to make a living.

This aspect is most lacking in men of letters and all the Internet users.

In the conclusion of my experience in business circles, no fish can survive if the water is too clean. Such is human nature. Thus, I say that human nature is ugly. Human greed is a kind of natural instinct that cannot be changed by whoever who wants to change it.

Chairman Mao launched the Cultural Revolution to change humanity, but what was the result? Crushing defeat that left people plunged into an abyss

234

of misery.

Whoever wants to change anything must pay cost, and this is a bottomless pit that can never be filled to the full by human nature. It can only be bypassed and made use of. The defiant can only bring about one's own construction.

Nobody is perfect. There are both goodness and evil in everyone's human nature. Wise leaders should make use of the goodness in the human nature and try to overcome the evil.

Good systems can make use of the goodness of human nature and overcome the evil.

One of the essential measures of whether a system is good or bad is 'make good people do more good things, and bad people find it difficult to do bad things'.

Good systems can make use of and ease human nature. It is conducive to make everyone serve for socialism voluntarily and involuntarily. This is the truth and right way.

Do not consider corruption as a great scourge.

People's hearts are the same. In the social system full of loopholes, anyone can be as corrupt and seek money. It is only because these people are not bold enough or intelligent enough. There are no essential differences between them.

Evil people are as bad all over the world. This is also true of the human heart.

Therefore, to carry out anti-corruption from both origin and system when problems arise is to truly take care of the cadres, which is only the truth and right way.

Only hatred towards corruption cannot solve any problem.

77. The most disgusting words in state-owned enterprise

About 2007

Sacrifice—'I shall sacrifice my youth, I shall sacrifice my descendants, I shall sacrifice my whole life to my great homeland.'

This is the most shameless lie, which calls white black.

Everyone knows the state-owned enterprise is a sinister gang. There is only promotion without demotion, only entry without discharge.

It is obviously the workers want to stay and coast along in state-owned enterprise for their whole life. But they make up such a beautiful lie to deceive the public and win reputation.

Free men seek jobs on their own and are self-reliant. Workers of state-owned enterprise rely on government capital. This is the only difference between them.

While the staff of state-owned enterprise are lazy, parasitic, and indolent, they drag down the business. They are sinners through the ages.

On the other hand, free men didn't participate in the contemptible dragging-down progress. So they are the master of state and are the most innocent.

Master

The master of state is also one of the most contemptible lies. They thought they were the master, so they found a perfect excuse for many awful things such as

Because they are masters, they have the right to show up for work but do nothing.

Because they are masters, they can only be promoted, can't be demoted.

Because they are masters, they can only be employed, can't be discharged.

Because they are masters, they can pretend sickness and leave the office.

Because they are masters, they can sneak away and do personal things.

Because they are masters, they can malinger with salary.

Because they are masters, they share the welfare and get each penny.

Because they are masters, they can be allotted house without blush.

Because they are masters, their bonus can only be raised.

Are they the masters of state-owned enterprise?

Does the state-owned enterprise belong to them?

How can they exploit national people?

Please remember, the state-owned enterprise belongs to 1.3 billion national people. Everyone should have the profit, and no one can be ignored. As for the one who drags down the enterprise, they should compensate for our people.

The staff of state-owned enterprise are corrupt and exploit our national people. Therefore, they should be dismissed, and hire our free men instead.

Only the labourer makes the fortune. The capitalists squeeze labourers and do nothing. This is the most ridiculous lie by Marx. There are many elements to create a fortune:

1. Funds

2. Technology

3. Market

4. Management

5. Labour

We can see labour is only one factor to make a fortune. Moreover, the capitalist bought the labour from the labour market by equal-value exchange.

It is the capitalists that give value to labourers.

The work value of a labourer can only be recognised by capitalists. Otherwise, he is producing rubbish, not creating a fortune.

To call a revolution, Marx told the biggest whopper that the labourer makes the fortune. He called white black.

78. Distribution according to work is equalitarian, and distribution according to price is reasonable

About 2007

China broke down the equalitarianism in which people received the same treatment regardless of their performance, and then proposed the work-based distribution, i.e. the distribution according to the amount of work.

Work can be interpreted as labour directly. It is an unscientific proposal not much different from the equalitarianism. Work is divided into effective work and ineffective work.

For example, a transnational group CEO works for one hour, and a toilet cleaner also works for one hour. A worker in a top-100 enterprise works for one hour, and a worker in unprofitable enterprise also works for one hour.

They all work but show totally different work value. Workers create totally different labour value, so their income earned from work should be completely different.

The work of a transnational group CEO may produce a difference of tens of millions, hundreds of millions, and even billions of RMB. In a good case, the enterprise will be prospering with each passing day, while in a bad case, the enterprise may fail and go bankrupt, and tens of thousands of people may lose their jobs.

The work of people like CEOs creates labour value of hundreds of billions, billions, or tens of millions of RMB, so they should get the income of hundreds of thousands, millions, or tens of millions of RMB.

Not to mention the workers in unprofitable enterprises, their labour creates no value at all; instead, they are wasting social resources. Some state-owned enterprises make loans for payoff to prevent workers from unemployment although the enterprises are suffering losses.

These workers are sheer parasites, and they are creating negative value—social pay for the keeping of unprofitable businesses.

Therefore, the distribution according to work is a plot. The distribution according to price is the right choice. The distribution according to the value created by labours and the market value of labour force is the most reasonable. The labour of workers should have a market price in the labour market, such as the price per hour or the price per month. So after enterprise bosses and all these people pay workers according to the market price, the workers have no relationship with the enterprises.

Workers have traded their labour force with bosses and enterprises fairly—workers have received the payment.

79. Property law signifies that all wealth in China will be subjected to the state council

About 2007

Property law signifies that all wealth in China will be subjected to the governance of the state council. Since then, any related misconduct is blamed on one unit. Thus there will be fewer disputes.

The Chinese are always fond of disputing over trifles. It means buck-passing, irresponsibility, and lack of responsibility.

Who should be responsible for the collapse of state-owned enterprises? Who will be to blame for the fleeing of greedy officials? Who should be held accountable for overseas unrestricted gambling? And who should condemned for the sacrifice of state-owned enterprises?

One or two formalistic measures won't deceive the public.

Everyone knows the rule of Chinese government in all ages: bureaucrats shield one another. Once something happens, certainly various departments will be involved. This is the case.

Anything occurring in future, the state council should be the first to be blamed for the primary responsibility and then the party concerned. Ownership means power, but is more about responsibility.

The almighty money has extended its omnipotent hand everywhere, regardless of justice, while it is only a matter of application.

80. The rationality of unequal social status

16 February 2016

As far as I am concerned, there should be two kinds of concepts. One is for the ignorant masses who are fit for Confucianism since they cannot understand sophisticated theories. The other is for the wise who can adapt to the law of the jungle, which they have innately understood.

As long as their thought is free, people can make independent choice.

This is just like a sheep for the grass and a wolf for the sheep. Each knows his needs. Confucianism completely reverses the law of the jungle, just like the state of feminine tenderness and masculine features. From my point of view, people can bear two thoughts in mind with different handling ways. In this case, they can judge for themselves which one is optimal.

Those who favour one thought while neglecting the other will be defective in personality. Therefore, cowardice and foolhardiness are not perfect.

It is traditional Chinese aesthetics that one should be courageous and prudent. Courage means masculinity and the law of the jungle, while prudence refers to delicacy, convincing others by reasoning, and winning the game by strategies. Thus Chinese people should integrate both of them.

The Indian caste system represents two cultures and the combination of two thoughts. Those with low-grade caste are contented in poverty and devoted to things spiritually while the people of higher caste master the law of the jungle. Anyway, they coexist peacefully.

The caste system may be not scientific in all cases since intelligence, morale, and social status are not completely related to it even though there are some links. There should be other factors.

What's reasonable is that a society should tolerate the existence of different classes. Some people are wise and noble, while some are humble. Those lofty people may be smart, virtuous, and thoughtful, so they enjoy higher social status with strong capabilities to a supreme degree. However, some are degrading with demoralisation, low intelligence, and weak abilities as well as logical judgment, so they cannot perceive objects correctly. They are less skilful and vulnerable in the society, with hostility to the public and God to a hellish degree.

It is preposterous to grant two kinds of people with equal rights.

Democracy can protect the evil and heresy to some extent.

Skilful people learn how to be merciful while the less incapable know their distance to obey the rule. This is the scientific, sensible, and just social management and social relations.

If those highly competent do not cherish others, they should be blamed. Those with poor capabilities being hostile to the society should be blown ruthlessly.

Human beings are filthy, especially those inferior groups with low intelligence or skills, who will by all means make troubles and niggle to vainly attempt to get what they don't deserve.

I have profoundly understood that some people will absurdly try to change the will of God by creating disturbances.

Palestinians

God promised Palestine to the Jews thousands of years ago and wrote it in the Bible, while some confused inferior people are fanatically throwing stones, stinging the civilians with knives, and pretending hunger strike to threaten and challenge God for compromise. Those foolish animals!

God creates the land, so he has the right and will to divide it. It is not Palestinians that bring the wealth, thus you have to follow God, with no right to express discontent.

What you have created by yourselves can be on your hands. What God has created belongs to him forever, thus he has the full right to grant it to anyone. It is the gift and authority of God.

It is evil to blaspheme the Bible and revolt against God. Why haven't those merciful Jewish killed you?

Troublemakers in Hong Kong

Hong Kong is one part of China rather than an independent unit. God has vested the land for Chinese, not several Hong Kong people. If you deny this, you will end as Palestinians.

81. The corruption in China is mainly caused by the left

About 2007

The Left mostly possesses these characteristics—simple mind and developed limbs.

They mostly boast their excellence in class origin—the poorer, the more revolutionary; the poorer, the more glory; the poorer, the more reasonable. Therefore, the Left sympathises with workers and peasants, especially the laid-off workers and migrant workers.

In addition, their political level basically doesn't have much difference from laid-off workers and migrant workers—this is called having mass base.

Why say that the Left is simple-minded? There is a most basic standard— views on humanity.

Most children with Down's syndrome laugh foolishly all day; they inexplicably treat all people with friendliness and extreme trust, whether they know them or not. They always giggle no matter if they're treated well or badly.

Why do we say that the fox and the cat family animals are intelligent? Because they particularly guard against all others, even keep a distance from very familiar ones. They think all others may attack them.

All that admit the theory of original goodness of human nature are all simple-minded, only slightly better than weak intelligence.

All that identify with the theory of original evil of human nature are thinking normally; they have at least judging ability.

What most makes the Left's blood boil is 'You work, I rest assured.' This is the fundamental logic of the Left. And 'If you use a man, don't suspect him; if you suspect him, don't use him' is also the Left's logic. The Left has no earning ability, but their ability to spend money is biggest.

They eat up, dissipate all, grab all, and cheat all of the state-owned enterprises.

Why is the corruption in China rampant? It just originated from 'You work, I rest assured.'

'You work, I rest assured' is coming from the theory of original goodness of human nature. So it can't be wrong to say that the corruption in China is caused by the Left.

243

82. The violence by Yang Jia proves the evil nature of the right wing

About 2007

The story of Yang Jia is actually very simple:

Yang Jia went to travel in Shanghai; he rented a bike that was actually a stolen one and was confiscated by police, and he was in the Public Security Bureau as a thief and suffered a little bit. After he went out, he thought himself wronged and asked for compensation but failed. He behaved in a vicious and unrestrained way and became so frenzied that he killed six policemen to revenge on society. Ultimately he was sentenced to death and immediate execution.

On the Internet, the right wing expresses their sympathies to Yang Jia and accuses the public security organisation of infringing upon the human rights of Yang Jia, which resulted in losing control of his emotions, to kill six policemen. They deserve their fate, for Yang Jia deserves the right to revenge on society and policemen infringe the human rights at first.

My comments on this are as follows:

There is no bike-renting business in Shanghai at all, so it is very suspicious where Yang Jia rented the bike, for it would not be rented from formal shops; but rather, it was rented from the black market, which is an illegal behaviour that the law doesn't protect. So it is perfectly reasonable to be decided by the public security organisation as stealing bike or disposal of stolen goods. For the sake of protecting the public security of the whole society, the public security organisation strikes against crimes and theft and disposal of stolen goods, which is a perfectly reasonable and lawful and righteous behaviour.

The bike that Yang Jia got in an illegal way is cooperative crime behaviour by itself, and he was caught by the public security organisation to be punished severely is a sure thing. If spending money to buy the stolen bike and renting the stolen bike are not decided as crime, then our society will become the crime haven. Goods stolen by thieves will change hands; there's no such a thing that after thieves steal bikes, they ride them in the street.

Fighting against harbouring stolen goods and disposal of stolen goods by the public security organisation is just to protect people's interests.

For this kind of getting something for nothing by thieves: As to the rats running across the street, it should have cracked down and specially harmed the neighbourhood. As to myself, two of my electric motorbikes were stolen.

My feeling then was they should be executed immediately when they were caught. For when these dregs of society and scum of a community are alive, they are just wasting social resources rather than dying clean.

Maybe when the public security organisation was handling the thieves, they didn't mention the human rights of the thieves; they infringed the rights of the rats running across the street, stimulating the mentality of the undesirables who were contaminated by the right wing. Under the glorious guidance of the right wing, these rats running across the street veritably become democratic fighters and freedom soldiers, forgetting their scoundrel identity, and they are the accomplices of thieves.

The evidence of the evilness of the right wing 1—rat running across the street = democratic fighter = accomplice of thieves stealing the bike.

It is a glorious mission for the public security organisation to protect the property of the people and struggle against crimes. When it is spoken from the mouths of the democratic personnel, it becomes the evil root of human rights infringement. What on earth is more worthy, the people's interests or the human rights of thieves? The human rights of the painstaking labourers or the rights of the rats who break the law and run across the street?

The evidence of the evilness of the right wing 2—protecting the property of the people = struggling against crimes = infringing human rights = deserving one's punishment = death is not to be regretted.

Yang Jia's assault on police officers can clearly show the evil nature of the right wing and its damage as well as contaminations of human nature, making people lose basic conscientiousness and the sense of justice.

83. Chinese people need human rights or interests?

About 2007

You cannot have your cake and eat it too.

Democracy and interests of people are two similar concepts but are different in nature and sometimes clash with each other. Under many circumstances, a person can only have one.

Now, Chinese people are rich enough to speculate in stocks, with which they are now familiar. If you have stocks that are worth 1 million RMB, does it mean that you really have 1 million RMB in your pocket? People in the stock market know that the answer is uncertain. You may become richer after several days, or lose every dime. Only if you transfer your stocks into hard currency can you say you have 1 million RMB for sure.

Democracy is like the stocks; the future price may rise or fall. It is always uncertain and cannot be predicted. It is like fortune telling or just deceitful trickery.

Interests of people are hard currency. They are practical benefits that people can touch, feel, and use on food, housing, transportation, marriage, and other related issues.

Therefore, those who boast about human rights but remain silent on people's interests are either evil-minded frauds or manipulative schemers. They take advantage of the weakness of human nature and deceive common people to achieve their unspeakable purposes.

However, human nature is so greedy, ignorant, and complacent. The sacrifice people make only benefits others. Only those who help people gain benefits whole-heartedly, who represent and maintain people's interests, are the true hope of people.

The concept of human rights is a hollow one. Frauds who deceive people take advantage of people's imagination to achieve their purposes.

For example, they always tell some ignorant people—you give me 10,000 RMB today, you will get 20,000 RMB or more tomorrow.

That is also what democracy advocates do: you vote for me today, you will get more tomorrow. What exactly will people get tomorrow? That is just a hollow promise that will never be fulfilled. However, things done by those who mean to help people gain benefits and protect people's benefits are visible and tangible.

To cancel agricultural tax is to protect people's interests.

To ensure healthcare for everyone is to protect people's interests.

To make compulsory education free is to protect people's interests.

To use profits of state-owned enterprises on employees' social insurance is to protect people's interests.

To allocate state apparatus for assistance during disasters is to protect people's interests.

You want the uncertain stocks or hard currency? You want frauds or cash? You do the math yourselves.

84. Strongly supporting the imposition of high inheritance tax at once

About 2007

The son of the robber always robs, of the poor is always poor, and of the rich is always rich.

It is true that social resources are not distributed equally at birth. However, it is easy to solve this problem—to impose high inheritance tax like Western countries.

This argument seems to have been heard in our country, but it has never been implemented somehow, just like the disclosure of the official property.

That's because both the disclosure of the official property and the imposition of high inheritance tax will absolutely affect the fundamental interests of officials and tycoons. Perhaps the Chinese government is too rich to tax the ordinary citizens, lest it's scolded. However, it is not to tax the ordinary citizens but the rich people this time.

Usually, the social issues need to be considered when taxing the ordinary citizens, but taxing the rich people will be an exception.

A friendly reminder to 'the men on behalf the interests of the people': they should not swagger and bully the small retailers and should not always pretend to be pitiable when taxing the rich a little, according to the international practice.

I suggest that 50 per cent of inheritance tax should be imposed on the rich. These taxes will be taken as state-owned assets, which can be arbitrarily administrated by the state to solve numerous contradictions and problems in our country.

The exemption of the inheritance tax on the rich is the most serious kind of corruption for 'the man on behalf the interests of the people', which is collective corruption. The imposition of inheritance tax is to consolidate the foundation of socialism and realise communism.

There are a lot of people claiming to be Maoists or leftists on the network. I think they are just some tricksters under the name of Maoists or leftists. They have never considered the fundamental interests and the best benefits of working people. All of them play the fool or act dumb on the issues relating to the fundamental interests of the people.

It's time for you to speak out. You should strongly support the imposition of high inheritance tax at once, so as to connect with the world.

85. Chinese democracy will begin from the imposition of inheritance tax

About 2007

The gap between the rich and the poor is widening, which can be solved in an easy way by taxing the rich to help the poor.

Now the poor live under high pressures, the greatest of which will be their children's education.

Although China provides the nine-year free compulsory education, the high school and university education will also cost much. The imposition of inheritance tax on the rich, the exemption of high school and college education cost, the increase of scholarships and grants subsidies mean to subsidise tens of thousands of renminbi for the poor, to give the poor an equal access to education and to increase the social competitiveness of the poor. Thus, the wealth gap will be narrowed fundamentally.

The biggest gap between the rich and the poor is the capital disparity at birth. Some children are born with fortune and some with debt. Imposing high inheritance tax can lower the gap by a half from birth. Education subsidies can let all the people stand at the same starting line when embarking on a community.

The poor in China should know what they should strive for and fight against to safeguard their own interests. It is foolish to kill children or jump to death.

All democratic countries are imposing the inheritance tax, so China should start from the imposition of the inheritance tax to develop into a democratic country.

86. Why are there many difficulties and obstacles in taxing the rich in China?

About 2007

Only corrupt officials have hundreds of millions in family wealth, but they happen to be the makers of laws and policies. So is there any possibility for the imposition of inheritance tax?

This is a good question. It is worth discussing.

Who are the rich people in China?

Reform and opening up does make some people rich. So does MBO.

Property law protects the property of those people in the meantime. The question whether the rich should be taxed or not is the touchstone of the leftist, the rightist, the Maoists, and the pro-Americans. It will immediately show who they are paid to speak for, and whether the people raising their hands are the representatives of the rich.

Wait and see.

87. Why do some people always object to economists?

About 2007

Nowadays, some people do not understand the economy, do not study the economy, and do not know economists, but they maliciously slander economists only because economists do not support them. It is a very shameless behaviour and shall be spurned by the world.

From the objective perspective, economists are not bad kids. They are just fulfilling their responsibilities.

Many people know the story of Aladdin and his wonderful lamp. In a certain sense, economists are the djinni who can help the master of the wonderful lamp to realise his dreams.

Although 'Aladdin and His Wonderful Lamp' is not a fairy tale of China, it is a well-known story. A lot of fairy tales are rich in profound philosophy; instead of making children happy, only a few people can actually understand the oracle of the fairy tales.

The wonderful lamp is an object, while the djinn is omnipotent. However, the djinn also has no feelings. He only serves the master of the wonderful lamp, and he does not care about who is the master, it does not matter if prince or witch, just or evil.

A djinn has the following three characteristics:

1. Omnipotent

2. No feelings

3. The master's slave.

However, economists totally conform to these three characteristics. Therefore, they are djinni.

1. Economists can make money for their masters, and money answers all things.

2. Economists are non-partisan, and they only serve and work for the wonderful lamp and for the masters of the wonderful lamp. They don't care about who the master is and what the purpose of the master is. Their responsibility is to help the master of the wonderful lamp to realise his dreams—money answers all things. They can provide masters with the omnipotent money, namely, realise the dreams of the master.

251

3. Why are they called slaves? Because slaves make money relying on their masters, and slaves are faithful to their masters. Masters cannot be replaced by slaves.

What is the wonderful lamp? It is the ownership of capital.

The ownership of capital is divided into the capital of the capitalists and the public capital.

At the founding of the People's Republic of China, especially at the period of Chairman Mao cutting the tail of capitalism, the public capital basically accounted for 100 per cent while the private capital was 0.

However, Chairman Mao was not capable of operating and managing enterprises, and he could only lead the workers of state-owned enterprises to belly-worship; share bonus, houses, and benefits; discourage workers' enthusiasm; and force them to be discarded, and no one was willing to work. The public capital was insolvency, and the government was on the verge of bankruptcy. They could only throw off burden and sell the state-owned enterprises.

The founding of the People's Republic of China is said to be the period of possessing the largest state-owned capital. Chairman Mao held Aladdin and his wonderful lamp in his hands but took the economic men into a cowshed to be reformed through labour. He did not understand how to use capital, and he considered capital as an enemy; thus, the best capital operation opportunity was missed.

Nowadays, the state-owned capital is spent and wasted by the workers. The state-owned capital has to reform on the edge of bankruptcy and during the almost completely annihilated period. The capital changed from the state-owned capital to the private capital. Chairman Mao regarded the capital as an enemy and persecuted the djinn, while capitalists took him as the distinguished guest.

Economists are not serving for the capitalists, but they are serving for the capital. It is just like doctors who do not serve for the health people but only serve for the patients. It is not that doctors favour a certain patient by birth and are willing to serve for a certain patient, but their work object is a patient. Properly speaking, doctors' work object is illness. It is just like that the work object of economists is capital. Doctors serve for the people who are ill, while economists serve for the people who have capital.

It is just like the ancient allusions. The coffin shops' bosses wish somebody to die, while carriages and horses shops' bosses wish somebody to be rich.

It is not because coffin shops' bosses are vicious by birth, but their work object is the dead person. Moreover, it is not because the carriages and horses shops' bosses are benevolent by birth and wish people to be rich, but because they will have business once somebody is rich.

Economists said a lot of words that were not favoured by somebody when Chairman Mao abandoned capital and the private enterprises' bosses mastered the capital. It is not because economists want to take somebody as enemies by birth, but because Chairman Mao actively abandoned capital and abandoned the work object of economists. The public capital abandoned djinni, while the private capital accepted, respected them, and put them in the important position. It is because Aladdin and his wonderful lamp were serving for the capitalists.

In the final analysis, it is Chairman Mao who made the mistake.

Fortunately, nowadays, leaders timely stopped the last batch of the state-owned enterprises to be privatised and learned to apply and protect the public capital. It is the lucky in the unfortunates.

If economists understand the times, they shall consider how to help the country to operate the public capital, making the public capital bigger and stronger. Otherwise, economists are unappreciative and make things unclear.

And indeed, it is the fact.

88. Rule by benevolence and righteousness is nonsense but by capital is valid and proper

About 2007

The core of Chinese traditional culture is the ethics of Confucius benevolence and righteousness and rule by benevolence and righteousness.

Confucius feudal ethics is entirely for realisation of his ideal of rule by benevolence and righteousness, which promoted political stability and economic development under the condition of lagging productivity in Chinese ancient natural economy of boxing and coxing, creating the ancient civilisation.

But in the Internet era of commodity economy and socialised production today, it has become complete obstruction and rubbish, dated back to the Industrial Revolution.

In accordance with the commodity economy, Western countries invented the individual culture of democracy, freedom, and human rights, against the restraints and constraints, promoting competition of the law of the jungle and survival of the fittest. Every man is for himself and God for all.

The ethics of Confucius benevolence and righteousness are pathetic and ridiculous chains and cages before commodity economy, socialised production, and the Internet. The ethics of benevolence and righteousness are against freedom, democracy, and human rights.

Benevolence is the kindness between people.

If the capitalists are kind to the labourers, their money will go down the drain. If the labourers are kind to the capitalists, they will go to black brick kilns. If the capitalists are generous to the labourers, they will be crushed and closed down by their competitors, because of lagging competitiveness. If the labourers are generous to the capitalists, their families will split up because of smaller wages and their wives' grievances.

The dramatic success of our reform and opening up has proved that rule by capital is valid and proper.

Rule by capital is not a capitalist capitalism, but a state capitalism. State capitalism is focused on rule by capital instead of benevolence and righteousness. There is no benevolence in richness, and vice versa. Benevolence and money can't both be gained, just like the old saying: you can't burn the candle at both ends.

Rule by benevolence and righteousness and rule by capital are against each other. It doesn't mean there is no benevolence and righteousness at all in rule by capital. Just as the idea that men are superior to women doesn't mean maltreatment of all women but obedience of women to men, so rule by capital means obedience of benevolence and righteousness to capital, with benevolence and righteousness behind capital.

These two concepts are not contradictory, just like the relevance between money and relationship between fathers and sons, couples and friends, officials and civilians, enterprises and workers, country and individuals.

Everything is settled with no conflicts when relating to capital first and then relationship. If relationship is mentioned first and then capital, there will be conflicts and disputes. The relationship between workers in state-owned enterprises and the country is typical.

Workers in state-owned enterprises are only labour owners, while the country is the capital owner. It has the right to fire anyone, no matter how long you have worked here and how much contribution you have made. It is clearly divided that capital and labour are what they are.

In Chinese state-owned enterprises, workers did make it clear that country and family are different, leading to dramatic difficulty in firing a worker. What to do with that?

Where is the honour of the capital of the whole nation? And where is the interest of the whole nation?

The main purpose of the system transformation of state-owned enterprises is to fire spare workers. If it were easy to fire someone in a state-owned enterprise, it would develop well, with no need for system transformation and no loss of national capital.

Rule by benevolence and righteousness is the rule by men, while rule by capital is the rule by law.

Lord Ye once told Confucius, 'There is a righteous man in my hometown who reported that his father has stolen sheep from others.' But Confucius said, 'Righteous people in my hometown are different from that you mentioned: a father should conceal things for his son, and a son should conceal things for his father. That's where the righteousness lies.'

Confucius thinks if a father has violated the law, his son should conceal it for him, and vice versa. That's what's called righteousness. This is typical of the rule by men with no discipline and justice.

Modern Chinese are still harbouring this idea. The whole family will help to conceal corruptness of an official, taking bribes and fencing them, in faith of that success is a relative term. It brings so many relatives.

This is what Confucius called the ethics of benevolence and righteousness, which are in practice the rule by men, meaning the higher position of power over law, local protectionism, and partition of national capital, and which are the theoretical basis of officials ganging their own gait with absolute monarch.

Why are Chinese local officials trying their best to stop petitioners? In Confucius' opinion, a petition is evil for it is against the local interest and the ethics of benevolence and righteousness.

Local officials are who they are. Whether you admit it or not, at least they feel good about themselves.

A petition is to report your parent, which is against courtesy and filial piety and is the worst offense. And it should be brought to justice and punished to warn others and protect the reason.

China's disasters are rooted in Confucius. Rule by capital should clarify the ownership of capital to be strictly protected. It should be identified by law: yours is yours, mine is mine, and what belongs to the country is its property.

Rule by law means what belongs to you won't be reduced even by a penny, and what doesn't will be given. Legislation is needed first in the rule of law, which is not aimed at punishing people but clarifying the relationship of property to be strictly protected and then protecting your own interest according to the law.

You have your rights to protect, I have mine, and the country has its rights. The property law is such a law that there shall be a clarification of the relationship of property regardless of the quarrels. Everything should be settled with no mistake in what belongs to the country, capitalists, workers respectively, because quarrels are endless and useless.

Ignorant, backward, and filthy, Chinese people have wasted too much time on quarrels and spent all their thoughts on petty benefits. People are always thinking about taking what doesn't belong to them into their own pockets, such as corrupt officials, couples, parents and children, and workers in state-owned and private enterprises who can't get too much not because they don't want to.

Conflicts among people are in practical fights over capital, money, and interest.

As the old saying goes, hundreds of people chase a running rabbit while never taking a look at the rabbits on market when passing, which is not because they don't want the rabbit, but there is no room for argument in settled distribution.

Settled distribution with no room for argument can be achieved by legislation, making the society stable, active, and optimistic.

This is the main idea of the ancient legalists, which is also the basic law of modern capitalist countries: 'The wind may blow through it, the storm may enter, the rain may enter, but the king of England cannot enter.'

It is by such firm faith in protecting property that capitalists pour all their energy into producing and labouring, leading to today's advanced and modern civilisation.

So rule by capital is the rule by law, while rule by benevolence and righteousness is the rule by men. The ethics of benevolence and righteousness is rubbish in governing, only useful when in textbooks to cheat little kids. Adults are talking about rule by law.

89. What is endurance? Endurance is an evil thought

About 2007

What is endurance? Endurance is an evil thought.

There is the spirit of bushido in Japan, and ninja. Japanese ninjutsu is well known around the world. In terms of Japanese culture, Japanese practice and understanding of endurance is the best. However, it's unexpected that some Chinese organisations should take endurance as their motto.

First of all, Chinese people's understanding of endurance is superficial, nothing like the Japanese. Endurance is, psychologically, suppressing temporarily the present emotion, mostly painful, by will, waiting for later revenge.

Although there is Buddhism in Japan, the concept of endurance is definitely not orthodox Buddhism. There is no such concept as endurance in real Buddhism, sometimes only a transition in personal spiritual practice, which is only a tool for people in the early stage of spiritual practice.

For endurance is temporary—there is still revenge and payback someday. There is no clue of revenge and payback in emptiness.

Orthodox disciples of Buddhism pursue the practice of emptiness instead of endurance. And the level of seeing and reaching emptiness can't be achieved by those ordinary old men and women who have nothing to do, and it's beyond their understanding. They can only have the idea of simple practice of doing well. So in terms of Buddhism or religion, endurance is an evil thought.

Religions with endurance as their motto must be cults. It calls on people to take revenge on the society, which is typically evil.

An Internet user asked me, 'Isn't it right to endure when you see a beauty on the road? Isn't it necessary to endure?'

What is endurance under such a circumstance?

You saw a beauty you like very much, but your reason told you not to be impulsive, and you should keep propriety and observe discipline. So you temporarily suppressed your lust for the beauty and then went to looking for other ways to vent, like porn sites or other alternatives to vent your feelings for the beauty. This is what's called endurance.

But orthodox Buddhism way is emptiness.

An orthodox Buddhist disciple will tell himself when seeing a beauty he likes very much, 'Women are tigers,' thus dispelling his feeling for the beauty. There is nothing, which is called emptiness.

90. Doctor-patient relationship, petition of petitioners, public announcement of complaints, Taobao

About 2007

In the past, GDP took command and money occupied the primary position. With the development of China, the Chinese government has gradually realised standardisation and rationalisation in many aspects, which should be a good thing. However, many shortcomings and even inherent defects of our system are shown in the process of realising standardisation.

It is very simple. All reforms, specifications, and adjustments are aimed at common people. The government finds it extremely difficult to carry out system reform.

Common people are investigated when the government conducts an investigation into melamine.

Common people are investigated when the government conducts an investigation into gutter oil.

Common people are investigated when the government conducts an investigation into group-oriented leasing.

Common people are investigated when the government conducts an investigation into real estate regulation and control.

Common people are investigated when the government conducts an investigation into the unlawful charges of schools.

Cracking down on naked officials gets no result.

Disclosing the assets of officials publicly gets no result.

Inheritance tax gets no result.

Separation of ownership and management right is completed very quickly, known as aircraft carrier, which can adjust direction on a coin worth one yuan.

There is no further news about making government affairs and property transparent.

Why? It is because of money.

Through separation of ownership and management right, the Communist Party can regain economic power. Therefore, you are quick in action and response.

Through making government affairs and property transparent, common people can have the right to know and supervise. Then, you walk with difficulty and pretend to be ignorant at once.

No one should be blamed. The ugliness and incurableness of human nature are completely evident. The event of Bo Xilai better reflects the same problem.

Full of ugliness, human nature does not have the concept of equality and universal love at all. Today, you are granted privilege. You hope that your descendants can also enjoy the privilege forever.

On the Internet, people usually complain about the bullying of local officials, public hospitals taking black money, and the difficulty of complaints and petitions.

I have mentioned establishing an Internet petition complaint centre and an Internet public rating mechanism of government credit very early.

I seldom praise others. However, Taobao is what I like in today's society. In the society with insufficient credibility and ugly and incurable human nature, we can feel a little comfortable and hopeful in Taobao.

If each of us can check the record of petitions and complaints, processing results and satisfaction ratings of everyone at any time someday, common people are the real owners of the country and the government really serves the people. Any concealment and black box operation deprive and trample people's power.

Many people will laugh at what I said. They think I talk idiotic nonsense. This is exactly the sadness, stupidity, ignorance, and unconsciousness of human beings.

This problem will be solved immediately as long as most of people have the same concept and consciousness state with me.

The last government has done a lot of work, tried its best, and made great achievements. However, many problems cannot be tackled for some objective reasons.

I write and publish this article on the Internet.

Now, it seems that the new government is focusing on solving related problems.

91. Reform needs awakening and support of the people

About 2007

The prime minister said that reform needs the awakening and support of the people.

Reform of China some time ago acknowledged, protected, and mobilised the elite, privileged class of interests, contribution, and enthusiasm to achieve.

But today, the reform into the deep water area, the contributions of the elite, privileged class are obvious. However, the negative impact has become increasingly evident. Social progress and deepening of reform, which need to adjust to their interests, limit their interest right away.

This time, the elite, the privileged class has shown some annoying behaviour.

Looking for a leftist bastard came to power and once again launched a cultural revolution, which is that simple-minded, well-developed limbs have inertia of thinking.

Protecting and safeguarding the interests of the people of the bottom and adjusting the elite interests are in need of reform.

It is not anticipated that only the elite and privileged themselves can do it. People at the bottom are all simple-minded brawn, well-developed limbs. Otherwise they would not be the bottom of the social groups.

The only result is a cultural revolution if you let them move up. No other choice, because they lack knowledge. In addition to beating, smashing, looting, murder, and arson, they do nothing, know nothing.

We must mobilise and rely on people at the bottom if we want to continue to reform—genuine reform. When we launch, rely on subalterns, we need to teach them what to do and what not to do.

Now, those in power are only using state-capitalist ideology to govern the country. But they did not dare to promote state capitalism. At the same time, they dare not let state capitalism be the national religion and educate the people on what state capitalism is.

In this case, the underlying best condition is to maintain the status quo. If state capitalism is not an important cultural ideology, deeply rooted in people's minds, all made in China after decades since the revolution will later return to the origin.

If the people at the bottom do not know what state capitalism is, what a country should do, what to support, and what the opposition is, then they would not need to dominate any revolution. Because the results of their revolution are to make chaos, civilisation backward, and loss of life, which does not make any sense. A group of rogues get rid of another group of hooligans, and then they continue to be rogues.

Whether left, right, separation of powers, elections democracy thoughts to be implemented in China, they must be based on state capitalism above. Otherwise, we still continue to maintain homeostasis. Do not try anything, do nothing. No matter what they do, it will lead to chaos, loss of life and will only last for decades. If state capitalism is not an ideology and culture, a universal inherent culture, then anything is false, everything is clouds.

The left and the right, if you really understand what I say, want to do something for the people at the bottom, the only way is to educate them, to give them rights, which is the only way to solve the underlying problem of the interests but also is a prerequisite to engage in political reform in China. Otherwise, do nothing, what do not think. No matter what will cause chaos, loss of life.

92. The third plenary session

16 November 2013

Our leaders ambitiously made a lot of proposals on reform during the third plenary session, with more thorough efforts than my expectation. They had a great number of wonderful visions. However, how the visions will develop in the face of the hideous nature of humans only can be proven by time.

However, I believe the Chinese are very clever; so are our leaders. They would not have pushed ahead with the reform if they are incapable of doing it. I think they were confident to pull off the visions. However, it was sure that there would be difficulties, as humans are hideous, selfish, and dirty in nature. The people with vested interests want to maintain the interests forever. People only admit two things, say, power and money, can be the topics of their talks with others; anything else will fall on deaf ears.

I proposed to separate ownership from management many years ago, in a bid to enable the Communist Party to regain economic power. That was driven by interests. People who understood that would follow my proposal. Therefore, the aircraft carrier could adjust its direction without moving.

I really don't know what I should say till today. It's time for our leaders to say.

Sometimes, I think that only after Chairman Mao and Stalin killed many people could others understand what they were talking. Maybe that was a helpless choice. I don't want things to be like that.

I hope to turn wonderful visions into an ideological culture, promote them into everything in everyone's daily life, and this is a culture.

I hope people with comprehension can spread my article to enable your compatriots to understand what humans should do, what they shouldn't, and which kind of society and social system they should establish. Only after we overcome the dirtiness and hideousness in nature, by virtue of a reasonable social system as well as reasonable relations between different people, people and society, and people and nature, can we truly share the common prosperity amid coexistence.

I don't want to see such a sad day. If you really don't understand or don't want to understand what I am talking, I don't have anything to talk with you then. If you are unlucky to block the development of human civilisation, the society, and the earth, either with or without purpose, the outcome will be awful. People are negligible, dirty, and hideous.

93. State capitalism injects power to people, with kindness tendency and justice

25 November 2013

The saying that kindness and justice inject power to people with kindness tendency and justice has been familiar to us. In addition, it seems that the governors of all dynasties used the sentence to describe themselves. They all claimed that they were upholding the justice and they themselves represented justice.

Why did they say that? It was because their governance became legal, at least theoretically legal, only after they had said that. At least all the others believed that was right and wouldn't oppose or resist at once. It can be said that all the governors at all times in all over the world said so to maintain their leadership.

Some of them were absolutely cheating others, lying to maintain their leadership, just as Lin Biao's saying 'no great things can be done without lying' and Hitler's 'lies become truth after being repeated 10,000 times'.

Some of them intended to maintain the justice and do something good at the beginning. However, various factors changed the results, and they gradually got used to that.

I believe most of the governors belong to the latter. With good starting points, they originally intended to do something good. However, the results turned out bad somehow. A person's power is limited. Sometimes, he or she has to compromise to the evil force.

What's the reason for that? It's the Taoism and methodology proposed by Chinese philosopher Lao Tzu.

Governors without the principles of truth and right will only become fatuous rulers. People without correct means can only do poor things, regardless of their good starting points. No other choices are available.

What I have said can be found in Lao Tzu's Tao Te Ching. I repeated it again today.

Though I've said and written so much, I only want to express one thing:

Inject power to people with justice and kindness tendency through state capitalism (public ownership), enable them to do things well, enable the public to enjoy good days, and allow the country, people, and even the entire world and universe to run normally and harmoniously.

What is justice?

Justice is not fixed and unchanged. So is the governance of a country. In China, the country's policies have been adjusted since the leadership of Chairman Mao.

Not all the policies are correct or incorrect. Different things should be done at different times. That is to say, reform is endless. We should keep deepening the reform.

This is like cooking. Sometimes, we need to add salt, sometimes we need to add sugar, and sometimes we need to add water, big fire, or small fire.

What is unchanged? The Three Represents is unchanged. The party should always represent the development needs of China's advanced social productive forces, always represent the onward direction of China's advanced culture, and always represent the fundamental.

The Three Represents should not be said only. It should be put into practice. Otherwise, it will become evil instead of justice.

94. Anti-corruption, anti-porn, and economic development

27 April 2014

At present, the Chinese government is in the fight against corruption. Some of my government customers complained to me that they used to have dinner and send gifts. But they don't have any welfare this year; instead, they have to pay out of their own pockets.

Some of my other clients in catering services also said that business is not as good as before. The phenomena of doing recreational activities using public funds are gone. The consumption of ordinary people is limited.

Moreover, according to today's news, anti-pornography campaign in Dongguan gives rise to low consumption.

I'm not against pornography and not against the consumption by public funds. The prostitution in China is different from sex slaves in Eastern Europe. Sex slaves belong to gangdom behaviour that violates human rights seriously, which should be cracked down. Most of the prostitution in China is a means of making a living.

If discussing pornography, keeping a mistress is much worse. Why don't you crack down? As to those hotel prostitutes, they only make a few hundred yuan each time, which belongs to retail. On the other hand, keeping a mistress means having sex every day and the mistress can make a few hundred thousand per year, which belongs to large-scale wholesale trade. If the retail on the street is illegal, why would mistress wholesale trade be legal? How does this make sense?

The only explanation is face-saving project and image project. Street-based sex trade destroys the glorious image of the government. However, keeping a mistress belongs to backroom deals, which have no direct relationship with the government image.

It is known that prostitution spurs economic development, promotes employment, and provides some people the opportunity to make a living. But China's traditional culture makes ir impossible to have a single person raise a hand and support prostitution. People only oppose from the legal level or the surface of the officer.

I'm not against pornography and I will not support it either. From the interests of the people, it needs fair discussion and study and needs to be legalised.

Before wiping out pornography, all the mistresses and those who keep mistresses should be arrested and sentenced. Rich people can have sex every day, but those who lack money will be cracked down and sentenced for one-time sex. This is unfair. This is discrimination. This is psychologically 'hate the poor and worship the rich'. One may steal a horse, while another may not look over the hedge.

Then let's discuss paying with public funds.

According to China's traditional culture, Chinese people prefer saving rather than consumption. 'Rearing children for old age, store up grain against famine.' Ordinary people don't like spending, so only the government can pay with public funds. At least, it makes sense logically. If no one consumes, what's the point of having factories?

As China's economy is indeed deformity, our government attempts to adjust the consumption structure and make reform. The government does not want more money to flow to the real estate; instead, it should flow to the entity economy. Of course, the government has the government's plan. But I have my opinion. Maybe after the adjustment of the government, Chinese economy will be on a path to the healthy development. I hope so.

But now it really has some effect.

95. The Safety Island of Abandoned Children

7 June 2014

Recently, I have noticed that our county has taken measures to build a safety island for the government to adopt abandoned children. And most of the children they adopt suffer from severe congenital diseases.

Indeed, it's progress for the government to adopt abandoned children.

How many people die of terrorist attacks and wars in the world?

They are all able-bodied people with family affection, friendship, and love. It's hard to imagine how many people would die in wars and political movements, starvation, and killings?

Are infants with serious congenital diseases so valuable?

Perhaps someone would say that our country is peaceful; I have never encountered killings or violence, and we are not short of food.

Please remember that everyone is seen as equal before God. I can't see any difference between African refugees and American citizens because they have the same value of life.

There are no so-called nobles and there are no so-called untouchables.

On the one hand, people keep talking about human rights; on the other hand, they turn a blind eye to others' disasters and misfortunes and even make disasters and misfortunes for others. These people are talking bullshit. They are garbage in the guise of pseudo-democracy and pseudo-human rights.

There is no difference between African refugees and those abandoned infants with severe congenital diseases in value of life.

It is nonsense to talk about human rights before figuring out cardinal questions of right and wrong for big disasters in the world. That's almost a heretical idea. I believe that everyone has the right to pursue happiness.

Congenital major diseases are the fault of God rather than the fault of young married couples. Such fault should be fixed by God. Young couples have no obligation to suffer from it.

We should not allow a child with some congenital major disease destroy a family's happiness.

I personally suggest that a child with some congenital major disease should be sacrificed humanely two weeks after birth. If his or her parents insist on adopting their kid, they should pay for wasting of social resources.

The fault of God should be assumed by God. He should give a healthy kid to young couples so that they have the freedom to pursue happiness.

If the parents finally decide to abandon their kid two weeks after birth, it is feasible to take the kid to a government adoption agency, but the parents should receive proper punishment for their fault at that time.

The safety island of abandoned children represents progress, but it is just a halfway progress.

96. Hong Kong is the trash of democracy

24 August 2014

It is said that there are British spies specialising in directing Hong Kongese to go against the Communist Party, to subvert the government and launch democracy and launch democratic revolution, just like Iraq and Libya.

In my view, it is the results of the mainland government's low profile and condoning policy.

Netizens said Hong Kongese would not protest even if their fathers are killed, but someone even stirred up trouble for the death of a stray dog to ask for apology from the government. It is extremely shameless.

I strongly recommend Yulin people to hold Dog Meat Festival in Hong Kong and arrest troublemakers to reform by labour in Xinjiang and never release them unless they write the letter of repentance, make an apology to all Chinese people. If they refuse to apologise, it means they are still in need of labour reform. They can only return home by posting their letter of repentance on the Internet after the completion of labour reform.

We need to let the Hong Kongese know who is the big boss—the gangdom or the Communist Party. Make them face shame and get the point. To cause trouble, just make a big sensation, rather than the sissy small-scale campaigns.

Because of the sluggish Hong Kong economy in the past two years, the mainland government encourages people to travel in Hong Kong to boost the local economy. Even now the mainland government is still offering travel subsidies.

These travellers to Hong Kong told me that Falun Gong materials were placed and distributed everywhere in Hong Kong. In Mainland China, Falun Gong is a heavy offense, but it can be freely circulated in Hong Kong.

Holy shit!

I have never been to Hong Kong so far. This is condoning, and this is the so-called 'give you an inch and you take a mile'.

Hong Kongese need punishment.

In my opinion, those making a fuss about dogs should also make an issue of pigs. Only safeguarding the right of dogs while paying no attention to the right of pig is racial discrimination. The Chinese saying 'worse than pigs and dogs' indicates that pigs and dogs are family and are one of a kind.

This protection of the right of dogs to eat pork every day is actually racial discrimination and genocide.

The Anti-humanitarian Act

Which is cut from the same cloth as fascism.

What follow the pigs are chickens, cattle . . .

It's not difficult to make trouble and we will keep your company to the end.

This is the democracy trash.

97. Education through labour system is applicable to Hong Kong

26 August 2014

Also known as reform through labour, education through labour has been used in Mainland China for many years. It was just abolished recently.

This is because people in Mainland China have good upbringing and the sense of discipline and collectivity, without requiring such system.

However, Hong Kong people, on the other hand, still need the education through labour system for further education.

I don't know who invented it. But it did work. It was and is a good system.

Education through labour is the process in which people with minor crimes or disruption to social order are reformed through labour. Generally, they are undereducated crooks. They are inflated with selfish desires, without the sense of public interest, not to mention law-abiding. Through simple collective and forced labour, they are provided the opportunities to think about their behaviour in a closed environment. What is more important? Selfish desires or public interest? Personal rights or public rights? This is a purification process of the soul. Through this process, people can thoroughly remould themselves and enhance their own awareness. In this collective and forced practice, people can wash away the dirt in their heart and soul.

The consciousness and idea are the basic moral standards. One should admit to public interest and regard public interest as more important and glorious. At the same time, complying with the social order is also one of the basic moral standards. Some education needs to be forced by the country because of insufficient family education.

Some people also need to sort out who we should listen to, the Communist Party or the reactionist.

The reactionist represents the inflation of selfish desires, while the Communist Party represents the interests of the whole country.

How could we be assured to let them in the society if they cannot think through these basic things? I am afraid they will still endanger the society.

We can abolish education through labour system only when the Three Represents theory becomes a culture and an inherent thought, and when respecting public interest comes into the subconscious.

There are a large number of people in Hong Kong that need education through labour.

We should help and save them.

98. Hong Kong judicial power shall belong to the central government

26 August 2014

Hong Kong basic law is made by the People's Congress. In my opinion, Hong Kong should realise separation of powers, i.e. executive power, legislative power, and judicial power, among which the judicial power should belong to the central government.

In fact, the natives of Hong Kong are unable to manage its public security. Our Chinese government is in urgent need of helping them safeguard fairness and justice and improve their public security.

Hong Kong's violent criminals run amuck, which makes Hong Kong people live in misery, and complaints are heard everywhere.

Chinese government needs to help Hong Kong citizens to protect their land, get rid of the bullies, and bring peace to the good people.

In the three powers, judicial power is just a power of the execution. Independent judicial power also represents social justice.

I believe the judicial officers sent by China will manage Hong Kong's public security well immediately within Hong Kong's law. All the problems will be solved in one day, and all the rioters and separatists will disappear at once.

This is real democracy. Separation of powers should be more thorough. Everyone will be free from worry. The executive power belongs to the Hong Kong people. You can do whatever you want as long as it is within the range.

The legislative power also belongs to the Hong Kong people. You can make any laws you want as long as it is within the range.

It is better to have the Chinese government send officers to handle the troublesome case in which they may face the risks of being killed. Isn't it a good thing to have bodyguards to protect you?

This is the central government's duty and right of exercising sovereignty. The People's Liberation Army has so much equipment, so many soldiers, world-class special troops, and armed forces. They can be sent to Hong Kong whenever and wherever possible. Is there something wrong with that? Do you need to fear the violent?

Facts proved that Hong Kong people can do nothing in the management of public security, which made people complain everywhere. This needs to be improved.

The separation of powers is an advanced culture and system of capitalist system. This is capitalist culture, not communist culture. It is really a good system, which should be carried out in Hong Kong. But it still needs to discard the dross and select the essence for the benefit of the Hong Kong people.

Only achieving separation of powers, making judicial power belong to the central government, can the so-called general election without any conditions be feasible. I have no opinion even if you choose a dog as the chief executive, just like the condition in foreign counties. It is very fun. We can also do it.

But I still hope the central government can choose a chief executive who is good at making money. Our Hong Kong people will make a lot of money with their help.

Paying attention to the nomination of chief executive and ruling Hong Kong through election is a thinking pattern of the rule of man. It seems that it will handle everything if you find a mayor on your side.

The real Western democracy is that under the separation of powers. The power of chief executive and mayor is limited. What power does a mayor have if he or she hasn't judicial power and legislative power? Is it real or magical? He or she only has the power of serving people. Besides, he or she should exercise power within the bounds of the law and under the supervision of judicial departments. So the essence of real democracy is making the system manage people, not people managing the system.

Chinese government's focus on the chief executive is the thought of the rule of man. They hope to find a top leader to manage Hong Kong. In fact, in democracy, the power of a top leader is separated. They even can't be called top leader and played a little role.

We need to control Hong Kong's situation by taking back judicial power, which can be called the rule of law.

Judicial power is a real power relevant to people's daily life. It is also a basic feature of national sovereignty. In the meantime, it is power needing great power to support. If this duty can't be exercised well or is limited by economic and military input lacking in deterrence, all these will incite criminals to bring serious harm to civilians.

Officials' collusion with criminals is an obvious reflection of judicial power's intervention by various factors.

Because capitalist countries have money and the expenditure of judicial power comes from capitalists, it is bound to have limitations. Their judicial fairness is limited.

It is known that it is illegal to occupy Central, but judicial authorities didn't take any actions, because law enforcement necessarily costs a lot of human, physical, and financial resources. In addition, they have minor delinquency; they have done nothing.

However, under state capitalism, in the aspects of government's law enforcement, their human, physical, and financial resources are infinite. This can safeguard fairness and justice.

Executive power is power that governs Hong Kong's economy according to the local situations and willingness. If Hong Kong hasn't executive power, they will ascribe the bad economy to the central government's limitation, like someone said earlier. Since we have reached an agreement on 'one country, two systems', the local people should have the power to govern the local economy and develop the economy according to their own will.

It is enough for Chinese government to have judicial power. They develop economy; we guard their security. We are responsible for arresting those who break the law and judge them. This is the best combination of separation of three powers.

Taking back judicial power is protecting national sovereignty and territorial integrity, which does not contradict 'one country, two systems'.

It is 'one country, two systems' for a region that doesn't have sovereignty but has executive power. Their nature will be changed if we give them everything.

The parade that happened at three on August 17 in the afternoon in Hong Kong is actually a parade that downed the Chinese flag. They spoil and tread on the national flag wantonly, throwing it to the side and trampling it, yelling such slogans as 'making the mainlander go back to the mainland, don't let locusts come to Hong Kong'.

Treason and rebellion have occurred in Hong Kong and happen all the time.

Because Hong Kong connives with terrorists, anti-party, anti-social acts and secession offend China's sovereignty of Hong Kong.

All the declarations and laws are on the basis of the inviolability of China's sovereignty. As long as China's sovereignty is infringed, all these declarations and laws can be overturned.

All the statements and laws like Sino-British Joint Declaration and Hong

Kong Basic Law, which are on the basis of China's sovereignty on Hong Kong, are absolutely integrated and respectful.

As long as the behaviour of infringing China's sovereignty occurs, all these can be overturned. When negotiating with Britain at that time, Deng Xiaoping wanted to use Chinese time and method to take back Hong Kong by force. If he did so, Hong Kong would come back in the afternoon on that day. He didn't do that just because of his tenderness towards women.

If Deng Xiaoping knew after the return of Hong Kong, Hong Kong people would still connive with terrorists' anti-party, anti-social acts and secession, he would kick some ass.

Taking back Hong Kong's judicial power is not a punishment for Hong Kong people; instead, it is the development of system. It can make capitalist democracy and socialist social management system combine perfectly.

The defects of capitalist social management are its inherent problem and fundamental flaws. The issue of terrorists is not Hong Kong's own issue, but the inherent problem of all the capitalist countries. This is a defect of the system, defect of the top design.

Terrorist activities and the disorder of social management will send the social thought and management out of control and then the productivity will decline as well. It is hard to develop the most productivity.

I hope to take this chance to combine these two systems; in the combination of the advantages of these two systems, I expect to see whether it can develop the most productivity and advantages.

Maybe it will unprecedentedly become the best social system and management model, which can be popular all around the nation. Besides, it is also within China's sovereignty.

99. Gangdom

30 August 2014

Gangdom is a main mark of social management failure and lack of control.

Common people's life will be directly affected if the social management is aborted and out of control. The harm from the underworld to ordinary people is the most serious, much more than government corruption and the outdated social system.

The gangdom bullies specially the weak, the ordinary people at the bottom of society. So I measure whether a country and society is successful or not in management by how rampant the mob is.

Because if the government is corrupted, the worst thing to the ordinary is to abandon them to their fate, the government will not torture them; they are too poor to get anything from.

But the gangdom will adopt thousands of means to oppress the ordinary people at the bottom of society. The people without any income at the bottom of the social heap will invite you to join them instead of giving you a hand. They not only grab everything from you, but control your physical power and the souls of those at the bottom, servicing the mob, committing crime: stealing, grabbing, cheating, and killing people. I vowed to make them perish from the world. I hate them.

The society full of gangdom is the most outrageous one.

No matter how advanced and developed you are in terms of economy, it is outrageous, failing to manage society. And this society has no quality to promote anything.

China clamped down on gangdom in the past, which was thought to be neither democratic nor legal by Western society. But I think this movement is necessary.

Even the comment from the Western countries which are so-called democratic countries is kind of dirty and shameless. They harbour and pamper the evils and monsters; they ignore and disregard the people at the bottom of social heap.

The so-called civilisation they believe in is exactly backward and ignorant, dirty, and evil. It is the follower and accomplice of Satan.

Marx once said, 'When falling to the world, each pore of capitalism, from head to foot, is flowing with blood and dirty items.'

Here, Marx wanted to express that the primitive accumulation of capitalism is as dirty and bloody as gangdom. When doing primitive accumulation, it is the behaviour of the underworld, but they washed themselves with money afterwards.

So the capitalist system is a system that has opened a door for gangsterdom since the day it was built. This is what they call civilisation, human rights, democracy, and freedom; those are the amulet and protective umbrella for gangsterdom at the very start.

I am not negating capitalism totally, nor banishing it like Marx did, because capitalism is a relative progress and necessary stage of human society. The idea of human rights, democracy, and freedom is a kind of progress compared with the feudalism of the Middle East region and African areas.

Marxism is surely brutal at the very start; it took the wrong way and brought harm to human beings. But the capitalist system makes me discontented and angry for it shields and pampers gangsterdom at its original design. I hope people can improve it and step forward.

If the members of gangdom commit the crime of murder, its head and executor shall be shot. They have to pay for what they did. Like the Mexican drug dealer and IS, their organs should be cut off for money to compensate the families of the victims and the people's loss, except for a life for a life.

100. Diligence

21 October 2014

Chinese people are diligent, while people from other places are relatively fond of leisure.

The reason why God creates human beings, I think, is that he expects the human beings can change the world, while all of this needs labour or hard work.

One of my friends told me that the African who believes in Islam will pray five times per day, which can't be altered under any circumstances; therefore, they only have a low productivity. The work efficiency of two African persons is even lower than that of one Chinese, while their salaries are not so low, and their labour costs are even higher than those of the Chinese.

Besides, they are absolutely lazy and never save up. The children would rather hang a bowl on the neck to beg than attend school, even if it is free education.

However, this is absolutely inconceivable in China. Why is there such a kind of difference? Why are Chinese diligent and the foreigners in some places lazy?

In my opinion, this is related to the cultures.

Why are Chinese people diligent? China attaches importance to the traditional cultures and Confucius-Mencius culture. It will be despised to be poor, backward, ignorant, illiterate, degenerate, and lazy, by the whole society. These people will be unable to find wives and will be ostracised by the society.

Why are the foreigners in some places lazy? The foreign countries pay attention to personal cultures and Islamic culture. Traditional cultures and Confucius-Mencius culture make people diligent. Personal culture and Islamic culture cause people to be lazy. God doesn't like to see lazy human beings, because that is dirty.

I once analysed the traditional cultures and Confucius-Mencius culture, which can lead to a kind of connection and system and a kind of unwritten contract and care between people.

There is a kind of unwritten contract and care between parents and children so that the parents must manage and invest in their children from childhood. They must have a requirement for the children, conducting investment and strict management to them.

The children must support their parents when they are old, which is the present morality, while in ancient times when the law implemented it compulsorily, they would be put to death if they refused to support their parents. Therefore, the children must be well educated and invested in when they are young; thus, they will have the ability to create a good living environment and support their parents. However, this kind of early investment and management is necessary.

When the parents become old, if their children are promising, people will give the credit to their parents and think they have good methods to educate their children and have made a successful investment. Therefore, they should be respected and supported, and that's a fact. The future achievement of the children is absolutely related with their parents' disciplining when they were young; thus, the success of the children is that of the parents and they deserve to be respected and supported. Similarly, the unsuccessful parents will be laughed at and looked down upon. The old saying 'There are three forms of unfilial conducts, of which the worst is to have no descendants' narrates the same truth. Namely, if some people don't give birth to or bring up children, especially boys, there will be no person to support them when they are old, which will lead to the decline of their family, and it is the worst unfilial conduct, also the greatest misfortune.

Of course, some people will say that the social security pension system of the developed countries is now very advanced, so they don't need this kind of original social relation.

1. The undeveloped areas absolutely need this kind of relationship to play a role.

2. The old people from the developed countries also need spiritual comfort, not purely material satisfaction.

3. There is also a population decrease in the developed countries, and the civilisation needs to be continued.

A child is better unborn than untaught. When one achieves success, he also wins a noble position for his wife. When a man gets to the top, all his friends and relations get there with him.

We can say that this is a kind of transaction and constraint, while it indeed conforms to the real intention of God from the angle of the social benefit, and it makes God joyous. Therefore, human beings can do well in the compulsory education and pension insurance naturally.

Actually, that the children are educated, managed, and cared for and the old people are respected and supported marks the successful management and operation of the society. In China, from the ancient times and the era of Confucius and Mencius, there exist the compulsory education and pension insurance functions, which make the society orderly and run reasonably. God feels joyous and has the sense of achievement at the sight of it filled with vitality.

However, people from other places might be not quite satisfactory. Though the European people have advanced economy, they hanker after an easy and comfortable life and are very lazy; besides, they are unwilling to give birth to and bring up children, leading to a negative population growth in the Western countries.

Two problems will be brought by the negative population growth:

1. It will result in economic recession, population decline, aged tendency of population, and reduced social demand.

2. In order to solve the labour force and supporting problems, Europe introduces lots of Muslims, which brings serious public security and culture conflicts, making the European civilisation and democratic civilisation of the Western countries disappear gradually.

Especially at present, in poor Africa, the children prefer to hang a bowl on their necks to beg everywhere rather than attend school. In addition, they also act in collusion with Islam, being so filthy.

There is a problem from the root of the cultures.

101. A life for a life and debts should be repaid

21 November 2014

'A life for a life and debts should be repaid' is a part of the traditional Chinese culture and is also being referred to as a heavenly principle.

Heavenly principles are the principles and jurisprudence being adopted universally. I have never studied exactly how many heavenly principles in China. However, 'intolerable by the course of nature' is often mentioned by Chinese people; what can be attributed as intolerable by the course of nature, in general, is also referred to as 'a life for a life and debts should be repaid'.

There are so many principles in the world, and each of them is justifiable under certain circumstances. Cultural thoughts are various and diversified.

The course of nature comes down to eight Chinese characters only, which is 'a life for a life and debts should be repaid'. Simple and clear, but it contains the most fundamental codes of conduct for human beings.

Only the people living in the places that are protected by those eight Chinese characters are granted the most basic social environment for their survival, then it can be possible for them to discuss civilisation, culture, and thoughts.

If even those eight Chinese characters are distorted and denied, the world is doomed to be in chaos. Because human beings will not even have their most basic living environment, let alone other civilisation, all of which are talking nonsense and will turn out to be frauds.

'A life for a life' can ensure the most basic security of human beings, which is the life safety and can guarantee the most basic point, which is the respect for an individual's life. 'A life for a life' is the guarantee and respect for the lives of those people who are alive.

'A life for a life' is a scope which is used to restrain the evil and devilish behaviour and to limit the greediness of all human beings, thus to confine evil spirit and demons to a certain scope.

Evil spirit, demons, as well as greediness, are born with every person; the death instinct is included in the nature of human beings.

If the damage done to any other person can be limited within the scope of killing that person, then more or less, it is possible to relieve or compensate that damage.

Therefore, Chinese people often say, 'Life is all.' It is impossible to prevent one from fighting, plundering, damaging, or hating other people since human beings are born with greediness. In other words, dirtiness and evilness are born with all human beings as they are natural instincts or inherent qualities of the latter. To sum up, these are greediness, jealousy, and evilness.

To completely remove all the greediness, jealousy, and evilness from oneself, sometimes, I think I cannot even do so, let alone other ordinary people.

Greediness, jealousy, and evilness are part of human nature, which if completely removed, would change human beings from what they are, in the absence of complete human nature.

In this sense, our social rules should be established based on human nature; to be more specific, these are established on the greediness, jealousy, and evilness of human nature.

Therefore, I oppose the act of hatred against sex industry and corruption. Lust and greediness are all about human nature. Advertising oneself as having no lust and greediness in order to manage the society conveniently and to establish a social system and rules in the complete absence of lust and greediness is a fraud and lie without any consideration of humanity, or it is even an excuse used to cover up more evil deals. The saying 'One may steal a horse while another may not look over the hedge' just originated from this point.

According to the belief maintained by Islam, lust and greediness in humanity can be eliminated by hiding women's faces. Now people have widely realised that it is a heresy showing no sign of humanity and is a terrorist organisation causing tremendous damage and trouble to human beings.

Lust and greediness are all about human nature and can be only restricted to a certain scope but cannot be eliminated. The course of nature, a life for a life would be violated if people were killed for their lust and greediness. Because Islamic extremist groups and some other organisations have violated the course of nature, they must be destroyed.

From an economic perspective, debts should be repaid is a course of nature used to regulate human behaviour. Debts refer to the compensations made for the losses of either party in economic activities acknowledged by both parties under a contract.

Each country shall set forth the rules that are used to regulate their economic activities based on their own actual conditions.

However, if this matter is to be arbitrated by God, debts should be repaid.

102. Confiscation of property shall be applied to punish Occupy Central participants in Hong Kong as compensation for loss

15 December 2014

In a legal society, one shall be responsible for his behaviour, and a man shall be responsible.

Occupy Central has brought a loss of several hundreds of billions to legal merchants in the occupied locations, and the government is required to uphold justice and help them to get compensation.

You have to pay the bill for having entertainments, instead of walking away after what happened. The merchants want to get compensation, and the civilians need to get money, so someone must pay for this. There is no reason that the merchants shall tolerate all these. The business premises were used, someone was raped, and no one took the responsibility for this? Where is the fairness? Where is the justice? Where is legal institution? Where is the money?

The rent, employees' salaries, loss of labour expenses, business operation, garbage collection, and overtime pay—all these fees shall be paid.

The participants of Occupy Central who signed in and showed up will share the fees based on weighted average according to the days and time spent on the event. Welcome to report the name of the people who attended the event but weren't found, and such report will be rewarded with money.

The mainland governments shall uphold justice and provide remedy for those merchants to pay counsel fee or organise a legal team to help the merchants in lawsuit and assist them to get compensation through legal procedures. Let's experience the so-called justice of a democratic legislative system. We will see whether it is real justice or not then. Since it happened already, what shall we do to uphold the justice? How to compensate the loss of the merchants? All these problems shall be solved well, so the national citizens can really understand the degree of democracy, how a democratic system protects the benefits of the public and the rights of the merchants.

'A life shall be paid by a life, and money shall be paid for debt.' Money compensation shall be made for the public's loss. One shall not play the fool and walk away from his mistakes. Aren't the democrats very passionate? Dare you pay for what you did and compensate the loss of others with money?

The Occupy Central participants shall have property confiscated, bank

286

accounts frozen, and be sent to jail if they don't pay others for the loss. This is justice.

103. The loss of faith in this era

26 December 2014

I felt long before that our generation is in the confusion and grief of the era.

It was not until I noticed the reflection in literary works and the social identity recently that I had an apparently same feeling. And this is shown in love as well as in the idea of family.

There is a joke saying that the generation post-seventies in Mainland China is workaholic, often working overtime, and the post-eighties refuses to work overtime, while the post-nineties, who even refuse to go to work, are all delinquents.

The post-seventies is relatively a generation of having faith, which is decreasing generation by generation. Moreover, the gradual loss of this faith is mainly reflected in the aspects of love and career.

Compared with the Israeli-Palestinian conflict, the Syria conflict, the heresy terrorism of IS, the Ukraine conflict, and Taliban, the Chinese so-called grief is just like making a fuss about an imaginary illness, so Chinese people should be content for still living in paradise.

In spite of the fact that ordinary Chinese are lacking in faith, the Chinese government still has its faith, and they exactly know where China should be led to. As for the ordinary people's faith, they would definitely know when they are supposed to know. However, the grief caused by faith problems in other areas of the world is extremely serious, which is more supposed to be called hurt, horror, evil, and hatred.

Essentially, the grief that people in Mainland China are suffering is the same as that of the world, which is actually a loss of faith. The faith of ordinary Mainland Chinese is gradually disappearing, drifting along like an abandoned ship at sea.

As for the rest of the world, their faiths have been outdated and wrong, just like a grown-up is still wearing a pair of small shoes and small clothes; the spiritual civilisation is falling far behind the material civilisation, which has been losing control, just like one's behaviour is getting rid of the control of his ideology, like having mental disease. Moreover, the conflicts among various cultures have been interwoven with material conflicts, which has brought about an extremely complex and serious situation.

I think every one of us is actually a computer created by God, having our hardware and software, which are respectively the human body and the human ideology as well as culture.

Theoretically, we all share similar configuration in hardware, while the difference among individuals is located in their ideology, i.e. the software. And also theoretically, anyone can survive with any kind of ideology, i.e., any kind of soul.

People should have different ideologies, which also means different souls, just like some people are still using DOS, while some using Windows 95, 98, XP, 7, or 10.

This is because humans' material civilisation has come to an age when a new operating system is needed. All the previous ideologies and souls need updating, or they won't be able to support the new hardware of the new era—a new material civilisation would generate its new hardware.

And all the existing griefs of the human society, the problems of ideologies and souls, are caused by this reason. The old ideologies cannot adapt to the current productivity development, which has led to serious impediments and conflicts.

Human ideologies in the past are all defective and unsound, including the chieftaincy tribalism, feudalism, Marxism, and capitalism, while anyone with any kind of these ideologies is regarded to be paranoid and defective, which is bound to fall into conflicts against the society and the world.

If humans want development and survival, all people must improve their ideologies, as well as update their operating systems and their souls; otherwise, there would be no necessity for humans to survive but to disappear. This is a task for all the humans of this era, which has to be finished, or serious consequences would occur then. Those who are unwilling to or cannot update their souls would definitely unable to coexist and to enjoy common prosperity with the world, and they are bound to be abandoned. I do not want to see any bad result on anybody, but that day will come.

Those who are unable to coexist with others are demons and rubbish, and they need to disappear from the earth. Those who don't love this world are also demons and rubbish, and they also need to disappear from the earth.

With souls updated, humans would need new missions and new tasks, so as to enter the new civilisation. Those who are reluctant to enter the new civilisation are required to leave, and to disappear. There is no need for humans to endlessly indulge in those meaningless conflicts and fights. All of these have reached their ends.

This is our mission of the era, or grief, or glory.

104. Criminals sentenced to death should be encouraged to transplant organs

3 January 2015

It is right that organ transplantation is voluntary. The problem is that involuntary can be converted into voluntary and vice versa.

Sometimes it is difficult for people to change their wills. However, it's not always difficult as long as a proper method is adopted.

Organ transplantation is not bad but can help to love to one another. If people can come around, they will agree that it should be a good thing to be able to help other people after their deaths. It is a good deed to save other people's lives.

To be honest, it is usually a taboo for people to talk about what will happen after death. Of course, death awaits all people, but they don't know when death comes, especially people who will die accidentally and come to a bad end in their day.

For organ transplantation, a young donor is the best choice. However, young people won't think about organ transplantation at ordinary times, and it's not necessary for them to think about it. Thus, it reveals a contradiction.

However, criminals sentenced to death are different, because they have enough time to think about it. In addition, the government and other people also have enough time and reason to discuss and communicate with them on this problem.

Another issue that criminals should consider is that since they have already hurt society and people, shouldn't they consider making up for their mistakes and doing some useful things for society and other people? It's a fair deal to sell organs to other people, and the money earned can comfort their families and realise their expectations.

It is a good thing to make a deal and do something meaningful before death. The key is idea communication, and the government should provide a platform and a market for it.

I think all criminals sentenced to death should be organised to attend training and study classes and compelled to learn every day. In the meantime, I think this is a practice that can enhance their ideological levels. They had no time to study, learn, and think about it before, but now they have time, conditions, and opportunities to do those things. Therefore, they should study and learn well, to purify their souls and enhance their ideological levels. As a result, they can do something useful for society and help and comfort their families.

If a market for the organ transplantation is available, maybe they can meet the right buyer and earn a pretty penny for the family.

Hitler said, repeat a lie a thousand times and it becomes the truth. Moreover, it is not a lie, so it needs to be taught repeatedly.

After becoming convinced, people just smile indifferently though it's a big deal.

'Path is shown up only when thousands of people walk through.'

People have done many ridiculous things and continue to do them. Organ transplantation is not ridiculous but serious. It is a good deed, but no one is willing to or dares to do it.

Human beings are barbarous, benighted, dirty, and hypocritical.

Human beings flaunt their glorious images over and over again. In order to enhance their images, consolidate their positions, and maintain their interests, they ignore the interests of the state and the society as well as human beings. This is the behaviour that harms others to benefit oneself.

For some flagitious devils' punishment, they should be deprived of a voluntary right and spared education and persuasion. They should be forced to transplant organs, do good works, and atone for their crimes. There is nothing wrong. People who took part in IS and other Islamic terrorist organisations should also be forced to transplant organs, because they are devils.

105. Some low-quality Chinese shopping spree abroad

23 February 2015

Democracy is the high-end consumer goods that can only be consumed and afforded by high-quality people with a certain level of quality and civilisation. Countries such as the backward impoverished countries or the extremely violent and wicked Islamic countries will always be troubled in democracy.

Democracy requires the populace's cultivation to be at the level of appreciating Mozart or Shakespeare.

Recently, a Chinese who took a trip in Thailand kicked a celestial bell in a temple and was filmed. This is an outrageous behaviour, in need of oral criticism.

In my opinion, that guy may even pee on the head of the Statue of Liberty in USA, if no one sees him.

Rich and wilful.

I believe that the guy that kicked the celestial bell must know nothing about Mozart and Shakespeare. These Chinese upstarts are characterised by being uneducated, with no quality, no faith, and no accomplishment, including doubting about communism. Except for money, they believe in nothing at all.

Democracy is high-end consumer goods. Chinese people featuring the low-quality, high IQ, shrewd, and wickedly smart are not suitable for it.

The question is, why are those Chinese so rich? This is a problem worthy of study. There is no absolute connection between being rich and high-quality, so there is no connection between being rich and democratic either. In return, the democratic system is the most vicious poison in the low-quality countries. It will just bring about disasters, chaos, and terrors to those low-level countries.

During recent years, China has undergone internal adjustment without a focus on economic development. The China mode has been adjusted in the pilot run. This means that the shopping spree of low-quality populations, such as the Chinese, hasn't started officially. In the future, such atmosphere will just be more frequent forever.

It is tolerable that the population could be low-quality, knowing nothing and nonsense, but not the elite class of a country. They shall not lead the public to death, hardship, wars, or disasters. This is just the compulsory responsibility that shall be assumed by the social elites.

America, Freemasonry, and Western states have been outputting democracy, wars, disasters, and errors to backward countries and regions in order to seek for the interests of big capital.

It is time to end them all.

The scientific state capitalism, or the scientific communist, will be the truth and righteousness to solve all of these problems, as the love and original idea of God.

106. Go home, 2012, God comes and the destiny of Chinese is decreed

15 March 2015

I knew that Christian party in Hong Kong a long time ago but didn't watch it carefully. Today, I took some time watching the video clip and 100 per cent sure God's oracle.

It was not religious propaganda, nor was it brainwashing. That was God's arrangement. Just ordinary people didn't know it.

China's traditional culture and Western culture are different since ancient times as I addressed before, and the Chinese culture is a systematic culture, Western culture is a personal culture.

Western culture is essentially different from Chinese culture.

I think that whether Western culture or Chinese culture, it's not fictitious culture like Mexican drug trafficking culture or Korean extremism. These are a masterpiece of humanity. Frankly speaking, that's what human intelligence is.

I think that Western-style democracy, freedom, human rights, and culture are the creation of Freemasonry's boss, Satan.

The Chinese systematic culture is the prehistoric civilisation left by God during the Creation.

As I mentioned, communism and China's traditional culture have the same origin. More accurately they are the same culture. That is why communism can succeed in China but failed in other countries. Because of the difference in cultural genes, communism can only be compatible with the Chinese traditional culture and prosperous. Otherwise, it can hardly be compatible with another culture, especially with Freemasonry's democracy, freedom, human rights culture dominated by Satan.

Western countries controlled by Satan or Freemasonry try their best to destroy communism.

What seems to be a struggle between people, in fact, is the struggle between God and Satan. Much more powerful forces are leading the struggle, and we're just the actors.

Life is like a drama, so is history. Just the roles vary. Human beings are small and mercy puppets either play the clown or the hero.

Perhaps only in the constant failures and struggles can human beings lift the soul and grow. Only in that way can human life be wonderful and meaningful.

I think Freemasonry and Western countries are necessary, for when human beings suffer, they get to know God's greatness. If there is no Satan and Freemasonry, humans cannot see the ugliness of his soul.

What Mexicans said also confirmed this point. 'We are near the United States, yet so far from God.'

The United States is in dominance of Freemasonry, so they are surely far from God.

As it said in Russia, 'Where there is the US, there is misfortune', which confirmed this point.

I suggest that every American should buy a Diamond Sutra and read more spiritually to cultivate their minds.

I found that mankind can only choose, not thinking, just as a woman only has consciousness but cannot think. In facing the problem of selecting communism or democracy, people can only choose instead of thinking, no matter which they choose: left or right, democracy or communism.

I have read so many articles but never found a man saying, 'Two systems are reasonable in part and we should learn from them both to improve our own country.'

There is no constructive discussion but beating, smashing, looting, murder, and arson. Democracy is a choice for a man from Satan, while communism is from God. Human beings can only choose but not think.

The cause of this phenomenon is that the human brain is limited in computing power and the abstract idea, politics, culture, and religion are hard for them to understand, let alone master.

In my opinion, all thinkers, philosophers, religionists, politicians seem to just say one thing in his life, and they do understand nothing if unfamiliar.

Frankly, Mao did not understand capitalism, while the US president does not understand real socialism. Marx did not know capital, because he had never been a capitalist, nor had he been a worker.

The reason the gods did not tell the whole truth is that human beings can neither understand nor integrate two seemingly contradictory things into a coherent whole. So God segments the truth and lets it be spoken out by different people.

In fact, I now believe that what Satan and Freemasonry said is a kind of important truth. The key point is how we use or treat the problem.

In my opinion, all the truth, culture, politics, ideology, and philosophy are just tools, which we need for different cases. Just as we have no choice but to call out the most ferocious devil to deal with the IS devil.

When dealing with public demonstrations, we need some ideas. If only the devil is in your pocket and nothing else, things will be very difficult.

As the Chinese government in solving people's things, there are many things that can be solved by money, rather than regime or suppressive power. So many options are available, and solving by force is the last resort. That is a harmonious society under the protection of power.

Democracies' government has little money in domination but has police. In that way, the contradiction is more complex.

In fact, money is everything; the government could use money to solve a lot of problems that cannot be solved by force. And I think that democracy is a tactical behaviour, not a strategic behaviour at the national level.

Communistic countries guarantee fundamental fairness and justice, and justice is guaranteed by the part of God's wealth, the main state-owned capital without obstruction, financial constraints. In simple terms, it is guaranteed by independent finance and force.

China now is implementing God's will just as planned during the Creation. That is a systematic culture or communist culture. Establishing the kingdom of God and the results are the same, no matter if you believe it or not, be it intentional or not. So it is the same whether it was called communism or the kingdom of God. It is called 'all roads lead to Rome'. That is the destiny of Chinese.

Chinese are chosen by God to accomplish the mission and led the nation's steps into a new destiny during this period in welcoming God's coming.

What I have written is the intention of scientific communism, public ownership. That means establishing the kingdom and implementing the law of God in using his wealth, which achieves 'God loves all, both black and white, regardless of the wishes of the rich and the poor', achieves fairness and justice guaranteed by money and force, achieves scientific rationality of a prosperous and harmonious society.

Establishing the kingdom of God is not chanting in the temple as before, but as the Chinese Communist Party did, establishing a model kingdom of God and stepping into the kingdom together with friendly nations. That is what we called the Chinese model.

At that meeting, the foreign Christian missionaries, many foreign workers God OF simultaneously felt the Holy Spirit and the revelation of God's oracle that is following China, and let God's nations prosper around the world.

No war, no barriers, no hatred, no poverty, no oppression, no suffering in the kingdom of God. People go there like family members coming home. Foreign missionaries handed over the key leading to the future to China's churchmen, through a symbolic ceremony.

I guess that Chinese people do not know what to do. I think that the key should be left to the Chinese government, who may not accept it. This is a formal issue that may be resolved in the future and we need to do something practical.

Chinese churches should cooperate with the Chinese government.

No Occupy Central movement, no Hong Kong independence, no Taiwan independence, no Tibetan separatists, no cult. Improve internal stability and promote economic development. Oppose separatism and terrorism.

This is not shouting slogans; if you really feel the revelation of God, you must know that this is God's will.

It is not luck that the Communist Party rules, but God's arrangements and ordination. The Communist Party has its vital important historical mission—that is, to be a role model in leading the world, establishing the kingdom of God.

Chinese destiny is not just relying on a few Christians. As I observed that when you took that key, you might feel puzzled about what to do.

In fact, the Chinese ordained mainly relied on the Chinese Communist Party in fulfilling its mission, which has taken a long age and is almost accomplished now.

107. Student movements are absurd activities led by simple-minded students with well-developed body

5 May 2015

I have gone through and seen several student movements, for example, the riot on June 4, the turmoil in Hong Kong of occupying Central, and the student movement in Taiwan on March 18.

Thinking about us as students in school—in the history book, the Youth Movement of May 4 is flattered as a legend, and May 4 is kept as the statutory youth festival.

I have a stronger and stronger feeling that it's total nonsense.

I think the Youth Day of May 4 should be abolished, while the content concerning the Youth Movement in textbooks should be deleted.

Besides, the reason why our government praises the Youth Movement highly is that the whole nation was uncivilised at that time, and it was in the semi-colonial and semi-feudal era. Students at that time are the batch of people standing at the frontier of modern social civilisation; therefore at that time, they could represent social civilisation.

But nowadays we are not living in the semi-colonial and semi-feudal era. Generation after generation, there are batches of modern university students and social elites. Students nurtured by schools nowadays cannot represent advanced culture at all. On the contrary, they have no practical and social experience. Compared with those social elites, they are wholly trash. They are nothing but some young playboys and playgirls. They are merely some unemployed youth yearning for jobs and the employed population. Except that, they are otherwise nothing at all.

Lyrics of graduation songs such as saving the country and the people and relieving people from miseries are obsolete stories. If you are talking about these nowadays, others will suspect that you are yawning or you have taken the wrong pills. Our country has strong national defence power and scientific research groups, so it's not your turn to save the country and the people. You want to show off, make some contributions to the society first. Otherwise it's nonsense. So the labour movement is more or less reasonable, while the student movement is total nonsense.

The Communist Party of the People's Republic of China is under the leadership of the working class and based on the alliance of workers and peasants. Because it's not under the leadership of students, it has nothing to do with them. Students are merely led and administrated by others. Thus, the student movement is fiddle-faddle, absolutely ridiculous. Students are simple-minded with body well-developed.

The reason is obvious. Who is the student? Students are people living on the labour of others, quite conceited with half knowledge.

There is a common saying abroad, 'Half knowledge is worse than knowing nothing.'

A Chinese saying says, 'You can't tell the expenses of living without housekeeping.'

Those students have neither been capitalists nor workers even a single day. Everything is merely hearsay for them, so they have no practical experience at all. Besides, in their own conceit, they are coming fresh out of the ivory tower, and hence are superior to others. Frankly speaking, they are too simple-minded and absurd.

I have been a student before, but I think for all things, without one's own experience and attempt, one is not qualified to speak or even take actions.

Why have so many people sacrificed their lives in communist movements? Just because Marx had never been a capitalist or a worker even a single day. In his own conceit, he thought he could lead the world worker revolution after reading a few books.

Marx typically represents students with a smatter of knowledge. But human society cannot step forward without blood. That's the destiny of human beings. So sacrificing man's life in revolutions guided by Marx is also a necessary stage to get through. Without sacrifice of predecessors, China cannot make such achievements now. The achievements in China summarise the historical experience of mankind.

Foreigners said, 'Making the same mistake twice, one deserves to be ruined.' Those ridiculous students with a smattering of knowledge kidnapping society are just like Marx leading worker revolutions. They are of the same nature.

The riot on June 4, the turmoil in Hong Kong of occupying Central, and the student movement in Taiwan on March 18 led by students are the same as Marx's pat on the head, which resulted in the same disastrous failure.

Business leaders have different opinions from students in the movement. They thought the government should pass through political reform. That's a practical action and a choice facing the reality. That's the thought of mature entrepreneurs.

But those students are merely hatchet men hired by conspirators. They are wholly terrorists hired by politicians, and wholly trash. They are absolutely delinquent juveniles disturbing public order, the undesirable people in the society.

The existing caning in Singapore is completely and perfectly applicable for these delinquent juveniles, undesirable people in society, and disobedient students as well. And we shall execute caning in front of their classmates.

108. Psychoanalysis of the troublemaking from some people wearing masks in the streets in Hong Kong

13 May 2015

Making trouble in the streets aims to draw the attention of others. However, some people in Hong Kong wore masks in order not to be recognised themselves.

When the people in IS make trouble, they also wear masks. However, it is impossible for some people in Hong Kong to be incomparable to those in IS. There is the essential difference between them in terms of psychoanalysis.

It should be the national culture to wear masks in IS. They also wear masks while they are in peace. So there is no necessary connection between wearing masks and making trouble.

However, some Hong Kong people usually do not wear masks. Only when they make trouble do they wear masks. We need to employ Freudian psychoanalysis to scientifically analyse the psychological motivations of the Hong Kong people with masks.

According to Freudian psychoanalytic theory, there are motivations hiding behind all the behaviour of human beings, which provides the power for human behaviour. The appearance of this type of motivation is caused by the basic reason that the sexual life is not satisfying. This is Freudian pansexualism.

A lot of people are not likely to accept pansexualism because it is a subconscious issue of humans. The subconscious is the consciousness that humans cannot perceive. However, it influences human behaviour all the time. Therefore, numerous non-professionals find it impossible to comprehend the subconscious; neither can they even comprehend pansexualism. But still I think pansexualism is perfectly suited to certain Hong Kong citizens, which also covers certain Taiwanese students.

According to the psychoanalysis, some Hong Kong people made trouble in the streets because they have not achieved sexual satisfaction at home for a long time and needed to seek some other ways to satisfy themselves. The best way to vent their feelings is to make trouble in the streets and the sexual venting is a kind of relatively private affair. Therefore, they could not let their sexual venting be exposed to acquaintances and needed to wear masks to conduct venting. This is the psychoanalysis and the psychological motivation of the bottom of the inner heart for the troublemakers in the streets of Hong Kong.

The most reasonable way to solve this issue is they ought to be whipped and to use Viagra. Whipping is also a proper way for them to receive sexual satisfaction. You can find they are sold in the sex shops in all our streets, which indicates that this product is now in great demand.

Hong Kong Special Administrative Region government should meet the reasonable requirements of those troublemakers and whip them without mercy. Then, it should hand out a certain amount of Viagra to everyone according to the budget and ask their families to take them home and to conduct the instruction for them well. It is estimated that this issue can be successfully resolved and their sickness can be thoroughly cured.

109. The Kuomintang should promote a referendum on reconciliation

5 August 2015

I think some of the Taiwan Kuomintang's ideas are correct, but its practices need to be improved.

Now I see that the Democratic Progressive Party mainly attacks the Kuomintang for its black-box operation in that Kuomintang hopes a lot of affairs can be carried out by the administrative means of the ruling party.

For example, if the Service Trade Agreement had been carried out by means of a democratic referendum,

> 1. the Kuomintang would have had no responsibility for its failure

> 2. people would have been roused by a feeling that they were not circumvented, and thus the Kuomintang would not have been caught tripping

> 3. politicians should play their role in clearly analysing the pros and cons of things and telling people about the interests and benefits of things. Thus, the party can get more support and more political propaganda. In this way, its influence is expanded

> 4. through a referendum on specific events, a party can know the people's ideological trends and their responses to some things. The party can adjust its practices and deploy the next focus of work, rather than just do some reflection after the election results come out, which will make no sense at all.

Many things in the West are handled by means of a referendum. Before a referendum, the politicians make a lot of speeches, stating clearly their position, just like the Greek referendum.

The referendum rarely occurs in Taiwan, only demonstrations and the impact of government agencies, which shows that Taiwan's democracy is not mature.

Democratic politics is that politicians are responsible for stating things clearly, and people are responsible for making decisions, especially for significant decisions.

The political ideas of the Kuomintang are basically right, but are not practiced in the right approach. The party needs to make good use of democracy to provide help and political support for themselves.

In particular, in terms of such a big event like reconciliation, politicians in their statements should say, 'Promote cross-strait referendum on reconciliation' rather than say, 'Promote cross-strait reconciliation'.

'Promote cross-strait referendum on reconciliation' means the initiative at the mercy of people, and thus no one will oppose it. If one referendum does not achieve success, another one could be held again next time.

'Promote cross-strait reconciliation' will give people a sense of being manipulated and betrayed, which will bring trouble to the party itself.

110. The cross-strait status quo is maintained on the basis of reconciliation

6 August 2015

Taiwan has maintained the status quo in recent years because the people of Taiwan ousted Chen Shui-bian and proposed reconciliation that very year. Of course, Mainland China needed to give both sides time to heal the rift and repair the relationship.

However, the pro-independence forces in Taiwan have increased in recent years and it seems that they don't want reconciliation at all. The Kuomintang Party releases the goodwill to repair the relationship, while the pro-independence forces in Taiwan undermine reconciliation in all aspects and adhere to the Taiwan independence.

In my opinion, only the reconciliation faction is in power, and it will be necessary to maintain the status quo.

If the Taiwan independence faction comes to power, it is absolutely impossible for us to maintain the status quo. We should accuse those pro-independence forces of supporting Taiwan independence, carry out military exercises around the island of Taiwan every day, always get ready for a war, and be ready to solve the Taiwan issue by force, thereby forcing the Taiwan independence faction to make a choice between peace and war immediately.

The pro-independence forces in Taiwan would rather surrender to Japan and admit the words as follows than accept reconciliation with Mainland China: 'Taiwan signed an agreement with Japan that very year and was active and willing to provide comfort women for Japan.' Where is the dignity of Chinese people if we do not start a war?

Taiwan should take a good direction for the sake of a good result.

However, if Taiwan wants to throw the handle after the blade and is not willing to seek a good result, Mainland China will keep it company and fight to the finish.

China has developed so many high-tech weapons, and it also should look for a target to give them a try; otherwise, nobody knows whether those weapons are useful or useless.

Taiwan is nothing but a rascal, and it refuses to be convinced until it is faced with grim reality. Talking at random is just for the sake of time-wasting. Mainland China needed some time to enhance its economic and military strength at that time, but now, I think Mainland China has the ability to solve the Taiwan issue by force. After all, to solve the issue relies on force ultimately, and there is no use in discussing.

The entire world is anti-fascist, and Japan is asked to face up to history and offer an apology. In order to become royal subjects of the Japanese emperor, the pro-independence forces in Taiwan unexpectedly agitated students to cry out loud in front of the Ministry of Education, which has made me furious. The ugly and dirty human nature of those forces and students has been revealed, but I feel people cannot be shameless to this point. China should start a war to kill them if these forces and students do not commit suicide for an apology immediately.

Both anti-course outline and sunflower are small movements. The pro-independence forces in Taiwan and those anti-course outline students should die on the battlefield if they do not die at home because they are devils and should die, in short.

Chinese people are most particular about trying peaceful means before resorting to force. After saying something nice and reasoning things out, it is time for China to meet them on the battlefield and solve the issue by force.

Do not always let others have the misconception 'Chinese leaders dare not start a war'; otherwise, it is not good that someone thinks they can do whatever they want. Therefore, it is necessary to start a war at an appropriate time.

111. The Taiwan issue must be solved

7 August 2015

That year, the people of Taiwan ousted Chen Shui-bian from office and helped the Kuomintang come to power. They just hoped that the Kuomintang would have a solution on the cross-strait problem.

When the Kuomintang first came to power, the people had great hopes that it should be the best time to sign a reconciliation agreement on both sides, but ten years later, the people's hope gradually turned into disappointment. Because everything is still the same.

Instead, the pro-independence become much more irritating. On one hand, the people are very disappointed with the Kuomintang. On the other hand, the Taiwan independence party seems to know exactly the pulse of the continent, so they only hope that Taiwan will take the initiative to surrender and compromise with China, then leave the risk of the war and the responsibility to the next generation.

Bluntly the independence party has calculated the mainland government's motion that they only hope for peace and dare not fight against Taiwan.

This is the so-called appeasement, and giving face for shame.

Ten years ago, talking about the solution to the Taiwan issue was premature, and lacked preparation for the mainland, because China's economic, military power, and international environment was a bit harder for a military solution to Taiwan.

But now you can think about this question.

I think that it is much more appropriate for the mainland to put forward the conciliation problem, as Taiwan always takes herself as a big beauty, so she doesn't like to marry the man from the mainland.

Actually they have already admitted defeat as they take themselves as a big beauty. They know they can't do it, but they still don't want to give in so easily. However, the people of Israel have never thought of themselves as women; they want to be conquerors, and they want to conquer the Palestinians.

To the Taiwanese, no matter who mentions it, the settlement problem will be thought to mean selling themselves, black-box operation, etc.

This kind of thing must be the man. And you must give the Taiwanese a reason that they can't refuse. Then they will submit.

I think that when China can use force smoothly to solve the Taiwan issue, they should make a more appropriate settlement or negotiate a settlement for the Taiwan. Let the people of Taiwan have a referendum. If it fails, then we can let the defence department make a plan for an attack by using force to solve the Taiwan issue.

1. From the recent sunflower movement, and the curriculum, the idea of the Taiwanese people in the development is towards the vicious but not to the direction of a settlement. The longer the time, the higher the cost to the next generation on the solution to the Taiwan issue. So the Taiwan question must be resolved as soon as possible.

2. If the settlement of referendum can't pass, it also illustrates the deterioration of the Taiwan people. When the forces of evil are more and more powerful, then our dream for the settlement will be in tatters. The longer the time, the higher the difficulty of the solution to the Taiwan issue for posterity will be. As long as the referendum is not through, we should immediately open the war and use the military force to solve the problem.

3. We should let the Taiwan people clearly know the Chinese government's determination and not let the Taiwan independence party take any chances, fantasise. What's more, we should let them know that the longer the time, the more people will die in these things. No matter how many people die, the things must be solved.

4. If someday the Chinese government needs to use force to solve the Taiwan issue, a person like Lee Teng-hui, who expressed traitorous, pro-independence remarks, must be treasonous, all of them to be shot and never be forgiven. Now you can say anything, and we just take it as a joke, but when the time comes, the old account and the new account will be dealt with together, so you need to merit doing good.

I think the solution to the Taiwan issue is to set up two new departments.

1. The cross-strait reconciliation leading group, who can organise and lead on both sides of the settlement negotiations

2. The combat command, who can regularly issue Taiwan's military and deployment.

If the two departments operate reasonably, no matter the spirit or the material of Taiwan defence will soon collapse. As long as the brand is hanged out, Taiwan will be messy, and we can accomplish this task.

112. Taiwan's democracy is the world's dirtiest democracy

10 August 2015

Today I see a piece of news saying Taiwan's democracy is the world's dirtiest one. It seems that the author is an American who regards it as the dirtiest and worst democracy in the world.

As I said before, Hong Kong's democracy is like trash, while that of Taiwan is a barrel filled with poison, which is more evil and poisonous than the former.

I also said that Chinese are of high IQ and everyone is extremely shrewd and bad, so they are not entitled to democracy, which is seemingly recognised and confirmed by the whole world.

Those good things that work well in Western countries will soon lose their origin and even become something like a cult when adopted in China.

Just look at multilevel marketing. When Amway was first introduced to China, I went to its classes. Amway has witnessed a rapid development in Western countries, with good products and efficient marketing means. There is nothing wrong about it.

However, the current multilevel marketing in China works just like cults, using means of illegal detention, beating, stalking, intimidation, and murdering. It takes armed police and military army to crack it down, with malefactors of every arrest reaching several thousand. How could this happen?

Chinese people's IQs are so high that they can do anything as bad as possible. The goods sold by Amway are special products with good quality and adopt a marketing method of word of mouth. But the multilevel marketing businesses in China often sell fake goods, which are commonly sold to their own relatives and friends. Their intention is to cheat and harm their relatives and friends.

Taiwan's democracy is a cult, just the same as multilevel marketing.

Although there are many flaws in Western democracy, it has advantages too, with social negotiation and compromise as well as the balance of powers.

But Taiwan's democracy is a cult. They organise minor students to attack the governments, commit suicide, slander their opponents unconstructively, and disrupt public order.

As a loophole, Taiwan's democracy becomes a tool, of which politicians

309

take advantage to seek personal gains without talking social negotiation and compromise. Therefore, the government in the mainland needs to immediately liberate Taiwan, saving Taiwan people from the barrel of poison.

113. Chinese government should make clear the attitude to dogs

8 September 2015

Today, there is news about dogs in China again.

A peasant woman from Xi'an was intercepted by a dog-loving mob on her way to a dog shipment. At last, the woman stabbed herself in her protest of social injustice.

The attitude of Chinese government towards dogs has been always ambiguous.

As to Yulin Dog-eating Festival, Chinese government asked restaurants that sell dog meat not to hang their brands and not to kill dogs in the street.

People can eat dog meat as usual. However, it is just not allowed to kill them in the street (quietly kill them in the backyard). No restaurant is allowed to hang brands about dog meat, but one can give dog meat order with code, just like formal underground activists before.

What is it? This is called Western hypocrisy by the Israelis. I don't know whether Chinese have learnt other things, but I am sure Chinese have mastered Western hypocrisy.

That the peasant woman stabs herself today has direct relation to the ambiguity, injustice of government.

That the peasant woman stabs herself is a kind of protest with Chinese characteristics.

When encountering this kind of injustice, people should not stab themselves, but fight against the dog-loving mob with musket and stagger.

The activities of the dog-loving mob are illegal infringement of citizens' legitimate rights and interests. Citizens shall exercise their legal right of self-defence to protect their own interests with appropriate weapons.

Average people can be shameless, rogue, or ignorant.

Law enforcers or the authorities should not pretend to be blind towards this, or even good men.

Black is black and white is white. Right is right, wrong is wrong. Government needs to have a clear attitude and clear statement about what it shall do and shall not do.

A series of these incidents about people and dogs have occurred many times.

1. If the government wants to please the dog-loving mob, it's okay, but it needs legislation. National People's Congress should vote on this issue that it's banned to eat dog meat in China. It is understandable and applicable with this proposal.

2. If the legislation fails to pass, then eating dog meat is legal. The government needs to crack down on the dog-loving mob's illegal activities, which seriously disrupt social order to protect the legal rights and interests of citizens.

3. The law should be enforced by law enforcement agencies, and the dog-loving mob has no legal enforcement right. Intercepting dog shipments will seriously disrupt social order. The government needs to severely punish these mobs according to law as a warning to others.

To do nothing or to be a good man is to avoid conflicts. This is a kind of malfeasance, a kind of inaction and corruption.

When such security problems happen, the police shall arrive on the spot within five minutes to solve the problem in accordance with the law. Don't let the disadvantaged groups be threatened and harassed for nine hours by rogue mob, and at last commit self-stabbing.

The final result is that the dogs were snatched and taken by the dog-loving mob.

This is purely a kind of government-assisted robbery of private property. If government thinks the dogs fail to meet standard of health and epidemic prevention and pose a threat to the society, government should seize these dogs and burn them with fire and bury them there. Or throw them in a cremator for humane destruction like the Western practice. No matter how to deal with these dogs, these dogs should not be controlled by the dog-loving mob.

This has encouraged the thugs' arrogance and spiritual motivation to continue to harm and harass people next time.

114. The government shall audit the authenticity of P2P project

4 February 2016

P2P and P2B started to overflow in China since 2013,

Since it is a newly sprouted thing, the government did not supervise.

This created a readily exploitable loophole for the swindle criminals of Ponzi scheme;

Now, the problem exposed is that Ezubao is a pure fraud.

In my opinion, government supervision shall start with the authenticity of supervision project. All financial projects must audit the authenticity in private organisation, fact-finding organ, or government. As a result, the false project financing is illegal fraud in financing, where the business personnel and relevant staff will be sentenced.

Because it is simple to audit project authenticity, it is available for us to judge the operation condition of units through the tax amount of financing unit. The reference is that the tax amount is in proportion to financing amount means authenticity, but the enterprises without tax payment indicate fraud if asking for financing in tens of millions.

The operations of P2P and P2B are different in various enterprises because their investment directions are distinct. Thus, it is difficult to formulate game rules for them; instead of supervising until all rules are implemented properly, government shall start with simple things, with expelling swindlers such as Ezubao from the market. Such enterprises are so many that they occupy about 20 to 50 per cent; some projects are just talking nonsense upon hearing about them.

It is normal and understandable that some enterprises encountered some problems and are in bad management while the projects exist. For the projects in legal operation, the losses can always be redeemed and compensated when encountering difficulties.

Governmental task firstly is to separate the swindle enterprises from those in normal operation. There could be some dirty tricks if government failed to achieve it.

115. In economic crimes, if the victim commits suicide, the main mastermind should be executed

3 April 2016

China recently is in the financial reform period, and there is much economic crime and fraud rampant.

Previously, such economic crimes were executed as illegal fundraising frauds, which some later thought were inhumane and needed integration with the West. So economic criminals are not sentenced to death.

Of course, this is justified, because the definition of economic crime is relatively vague. It is difficult to strictly distinguish the difference between investment failure and pure fraud. The recent death penalty for several economic crimes is more controversial.

Normally, if the money was raised to the actual investment behaviour, it is investment failure, and if with no investment behaviour, it is purely a fraud.

Of course, there are some loopholes, such as a small part of the money is invested in some unreliable projects, but a lot of money is transferred. It is difficult to define by using whether there is an investment.

Fraudulent acts can be criminalised in two ways.

1. The authenticity of investment behaviour. It requires professional professionals to evaluate the truth of the investment and whether the investment was worth so much money at the time, or a false project to concoct various pretexts and transfer assets. If the vast majority of money was used to invest in physical projects, the criminal can be considered to be investment failure, and avoid death.

If the investment project doesn't exist at all or it is assessed as a purely bogus investment project by industry insiders to transfer a lot of property, it can be characterised as malicious fraud and the criminal can be executed.

If the criminal invests in fake projects or projects without worth at all, in order to defraud money, we should sentence by standards for the consequences of it.

If the victim, because of a large amount of money loss, with mental breakdown, commits suicide by jumping, poisoning, hanging, drowning, or other, the mastermind is the murderer in the crime, and should be executed.

If the victim is emotionally stable, no one has committed suicide, the

314

criminal can avoid death.

On the one hand, the punishment conviction is based on subjective investment behaviour. On the other hand, sentencing is based on the consequences, which is more appropriate.

On the one hand, we should protect the legitimate investment behaviour; on the other hand, we should punish the acts of malicious fraud.

You can't let the bad guys go by in order to protect the good guys.

You can't hurt a good man in order to fight bad people.

Business is complicated and I see a lot of that.

There are many bosses who work hard every day but fail to invest. They are heroes, and they should be protected.

There are a lot of people who are pure swindlers, have no bottom line, and have no humanity. This kind of person should be executed.

The two types of people are almost identical in appearance, and it is hard to distinguish them from outsiders.

But if we condemn at will, it will cause injustice. And we will destroy the economic development of the society and become the accomplices of demons.

We can collect money to invest, but we should explain the use of the money and it can be confirmed. If it is not clear, it will be a fraud and the criminal can be executed.

116. There should be legislation on compensation of dogs hurting people

7 April 2016

Today there is news a woman was bitten by a cur, while the owner fled with the dog. While walking, the owner said, 'If you catch up with me, I will give you compensation.'

There is no wonder that the man who owns a dog should practice running every day, for they can flee on time if their dogs hurt someone someday, so they can escape the responsibility and compensation. Buddha said, 'Everything happens for a reason.' He is so clever and reasonable.

I think there should be legislation on dogs hurting people. What's more, the legislation should be strictly enforced.

There is management of dogs in China, but it's futile and it can't protect people.

I think if dogs hurt people, the owner should:

1. Compensate the victim ten times the amount of the local minimum wage as the compensation for loss of work and mental damage. 2. Compensate the victim twenty times the amount of necessary hospitalisation costs as the hospitalisation costs and follow-up nutrition subsidies.

3. The dogs hurting people should be sentenced to death.

The dog owners should pay a certain amount of third party liability insurance premium when they buy a license for their dogs, just as people should annually inspect the car and buy compulsory insurance for traffic accident of motor-driven vehicle when they buy a car. If you want to keep a dog, you should buy a compulsory canine insurance for it. If there is an accident, some compensation is paid by the dog owner and the other parts are paid by the government from the compulsory canine insurance.

If the stray dogs hurt people, the government should be responsible for all the compensation. The government doesn't do a good job in security, so they should compensate the victims according to the above standards.

Only in this way can the dog owners supervise their dogs and the stray dogs are killed on time. And there will be no accidents of dogs hurting people. People's rights can be truly ensured.

Of course you can show love to dogs, but you must have a sense of social responsibility. When you show love to dogs, you can't do harm to a third party, or you are not showing love to dogs.

If you show love to dogs but hurt and threaten other people, this is not love and it is heresy. The demon has totally controlled the souls of people who love dogs, and they should be strictly punished and relentlessly stroke.

117. Taiwan has sent one hundred thousand spies to destroy the economy of Chinese mainland; this is a war

14 April 2016

There always are phone frauds on the Chinese mainland. What's more, it is said that 90 per cent of the frauds are from Taiwan and are in an organised way.

Fraudulent groups conduct fraud in an organised way and systematically. Some people specially collect the bank information of the victims, some people specially make calls to defraud, some people specially provide political protection for the fraud and extradite the swindler back to Taiwan, acquitting them.

It is evident that these are acts of war of the secret service of Taiwan, who attempt to overthrow the regime of the Chinese mainland, destroy the socialist economic construction, and break the economic construction of the Chinese mainland seriously.

So the Chinese mainland should solve the problems of Taiwan by force, protecting people from the destruction of the enemies and spies. This is not a crime but a war.

The multiform frauds on the Chinese mainland can even be called wild.

I myself receive a fraud from phone, message, or Internet every three days. At first, I called the police. The police thanked me for my trust to the public security organisation and then the fraud continued, even more than before.

In my opinion, the Chinese People's Liberation Army but not the public security organisation can solve the problem. It is beyond the purview of authority of the public security organisation, and it is a war.

I command that Taiwan authorities bring the one hundred thousand spies to justice. Hand the spies to the Chinese mainland and let them be judged by the Chinese mainland, sentence them, and let them return the money. Or the Chinese People's Liberation Army would be sent to attack Taiwan, catch the criminals personally, and protect the rights of people.

The Chinese mainland once chased after the democratic society and thought it was paradise. Now the democratic society has descended to fraud and prostitution and drug trafficking. What's more, harbouring fraud, conniving fraud, and fraud in an organised way are included in the democratic society. The counties and districts that are swindled are mainly those which are thought poorer than Taiwan.

Democracy is done, so is Taiwan. The suffering people of Taiwan need to be liberated by the Chinese People's Liberation Army.

Today, Malaysia ignored the demand of China, sending twenty swindlers back to Taiwan and acquitting them.

The government of China should send war craft and aircraft carrier to intercept the Malaysian airliner on the high seas, return the airliner with swindlers to the Chinese mainland, arrest the swindlers, and then send back the plane.

There are criminals who will jeopardise national security on the plane and the Chinese People's Liberation Army should take necessary actions to protect security interests of the motherland.

The government should make an announcement than any airliner with swindlers is not allowed to fly to Taiwan or it will be shot down.

The swindlers who are remanded to the Chinese mainland should hand over the money immediately and return the money to the victims, or they will be sentenced to life imprisonment. Even if they are beaten to death, sick to death, or old and dying, they are not allowed to be freed.

Those who hand over the money can go home after an appropriate punishment, while those who are unwilling to hand over the money can never be released from the prison.

118. Taiwan issue and South China Sea dispute

19 April 2016

In my opinion, the Taiwan issue and the South China Sea dispute are the same problem, and both relate to Chinese territory.

It seems that the Taiwan issue can be solved only through the use of force, because the Taiwan issue has been increasingly complicated in recent years.

This is reflected by the common aspiration of Taiwanese people.

That Taiwan becomes independent someday is what Taiwanese people want. Those who are under the illusion that Taiwan will actively come over to China Mainland are deceiving themselves as well as others.

Those viewpoints that insist the Taiwan issue cannot be solved through the use of force but the South China Sea dispute can are illogical.

From the aspects of firepower coverage and force projection, it is much easier to solve the Taiwan issue than solve the South China Sea dispute through the use of force. If we cannot beat Taiwan, we cannot win in the South China Sea dispute definitely.

If the Taiwan Issue can be solved through the use of force, the South China Sea dispute can be solved inevitably. Those countries against China on the South China Sea dispute will button their lip.

Taiwan is internationally recognised as a part of the People's Republic of China, while the South China Sea belongs to China under dispute.

If we cannot recover the internationally recognised territory but want to recover the territory under dispute, those countries against China on the South China Sea dispute will be unwilling to submit.

According to the art of war, befriending a distant state while attacking a neighbour is common sense.

We can build up some islands around the South China Sea and suspend the dispute. The issue and the dispute can be solved only by attacking Taiwan.

119. Arresting prostitutes indicates that the social system is in favour of the rich and against the poor

13 May 2016

I talked about this issue before.

It is tolerable that the rich keep one and even more mistresses by paying them luxury car, mansion, and big money in China.

A few days ago, a friend pointed at an upscale residential area and told me, 'Look, that residential area is for mistresses. You cannot see anybody go out in the morning, but see beauties drive in and out in the afternoon. We call it mistress residential area.'

If prostitution is defined as the business or practice of engaging in sexual activity in exchange for payment, other than marital sexual activity, then keeping one or more mistresses should be regarded as subscribing to a package service of prostitution, of which the sum of business transactions is huge, and the nature is bad. Girls kept by others as mistress and those keeping a mistress should be accused of engaging in prostitution for a long time. Their behaviour is absolutely lawless. According to the measurement of penalty for prostitution, they should be sentenced to at least eight to ten years' imprisonment and fined hundreds of thousands of yuan or even millions of yuan. Their luxury cars and mansions are essentially payment for prostitution, which should be confiscated.

I am confused why some leading authorities of law don't voice any viewpoint on the measurement of penalty for keeping mistress, but have concern about street prostitution.

I am confused why police don't investigate and arrest those committing prostitution by keeping mistress or being kept as mistress, but concentrate on street prostitution.

Such actions are absolutely in favour of the rich, but against the poor.

120. Fighting-to-death lawyers are cults

6 June 2016

Recently there was a case in China which causes fierce arguments. There is a question of factual justice and procedural justice in it. It indicates that fighting-to-death lawyers and the procedural justice completely violate the facts and the factual justice, which belongs to the behaviour of cults.

The most basic principle of judging any event and case is the fact, the truth of the matter. Just like Detective Conan said, 'There is only one truth.' If the truth of the matter is ignored, concealed, intentionally overturned, and rejected, then it is deliberately distorting and fabricating the facts, knowing the truth but not admitting it. This is a cult's and demon's act. They are the demon's disciples, who need to be exterminated. They need to be sent to another world, to reunite with the demon.

The fact is already very clear after online discussion as well as the evidence provided by the police and website users. The course of the incident is very simple, which however becomes a shaky case after the promotion and hype by the fighting-to-death lawyers.

According to some evidence, somebody is a highly educated young man, just being father, with a history of heart disease. He is also a skilled whoremonger who often went to erotic places though serving as a deputy level of government official. In accordance with the current Chinese law, government officials who prostitute are to be removed from office. That day, when somebody was going to the erotic place, he was reported by someone to the police who conducted the arrest in plainclothes. Afraid of losing the position, ashamed of his family, somebody strongly resisted the arrest, and ran away two times. He kicked the driver, bit the police, and tried to forcibly jump out of the car. Finally he was attacked by some disease and died on the way to hospital.

However, the fighting-to-death lawyers believed that plainclothes police in law enforcement did not wear police uniforms and record instrument of law enforcement; hence, there was a problem in the process of the police's law enforcement. Therefore, prostitution testimony provided by the police shall not be accepted. They insisted that the court should only consider the police violence, law enforcement killing an early father and gifted youth. The police shall be called to account the liability of killing the good citizen.

This is a typical example of cults. The fighting-to-death lawyers are the followers of the demon who are against God.

The basic logic of the fighting-to-death lawyers is the procedural justice that the West praises highly, and as long as any negligence is found in the procedure, all the evidence will be overturned. Finally, there is only the case of the police killing the good citizen.

This is a case where procedural justice completely overthrows the facts justice, as well as a case of the West and the world being controlled by the demon. They are completely finding the excuse to overthrow the facts, to help those criminals and the demon get rid of the crime. They are helping the evil and the demon to escape the righteous punishment of God. They are the tool of the demon against justice and God.

Black is black, white is white, right is right, wrong is wrong. The truth is the truth. There is only one truth.

The only basis for judging a case is the fact. Even the truth can be deliberately overturned, arbitrarily fabricated, not to mention justice and God. There is only the demon's grin.

The most important job of investigators is to restore the facts. As to how to get the truth, it does not matter whether God told them in a dream, or they went to hell to find the ghost. The case only requires the fact.

And the fact can be verified by verified by multi-angle and multipart. Because it is the truth, it can be verified.

As for the investigators exacting confession by torture, resulting in injury or injustice wrong case, this is another problem of the law and discipline. The punishment shall not cause the interrogator serious injury or excessive injury, within the limits of the range that the interrogator can afford. It is more worthy of praise when the evidence is obtained with no harm.

The West is called 'the great whore riding a beast' by God in the Revelation of the Bible. The fighting-to-death lawyers, incited by the West, regard the procedural justice as an excuse. Helping the demon get rid of the punishment is also a major sign of the great whore. They make peace with the demon, prostitute with the demon against justice, against God, and need to be exterminated.

People need truth, people need justice, people need God.

121. Marriage for the purpose of beauty is a kind of whoring, while marriage aimed at benefit is like prostitution and financial fraud

18 August 2016

The liveliest topic these days is a divorce case.

Both the husband and the wife rebuke each other for extramarital affairs and provide evidence.

Netizens stand on the contrary, cheering for the side that they support and joining in the fun.

But in my perspective, both the two sides are not good eggs and are troublesome.

It's purely a typical affair about prostitution, whoring, and financial fraud in Chinese style.

The man obviously married for the purpose of beauty, while the woman for money.

Their initial purpose is wicked. So how could they get a good result? That's daydreaming.

What annoys people most is that monks also join in this debate. The mortal may not see through the emptiness of the material world. But what about the monks? Why do they enter into religion if they cannot outguess this swindle? It's ridiculous.

It is true that all the religious magic disappeared in 2012.

Prostitution and financial fraud in marital form aimed at beauty or benefit is widespread in China.

I estimated then that the proportion of P2P fake investment is about 20–50 per cent.

The proportion of prostitution and financial fraud in marital form is higher than P2P fake investments in China. It is around 80–95 per cent.

There are marriages with the purpose of love as well in China. But the proportion is extremely low. Those people are rare.

Of course, it's normal that people take beauty and benefit into account in marriages. However, what occupy most of the proportion should be moral, ideal pursuit and values. If the proportion of beauty and interest is too large, the marriage will become an act of prostitution and whoring.

I think actual behaviour of prostitution and whoring is purer than this kind of marriage. After all, prostitutes mark the prices clearly and never deceive people, no matter young or old.

Why does the Chinese government prohibit pure act of street prostitution, but support vigorously dirty prostitution and financial fraud in marital form?

I hold the belief that it's a combination of Chinese traditional culture and Occidental liberal human rights culture. It is a consequence due to the fact that people combine the filthiest things in the two kinds of culture, according to hideous human nature.

Chinese people discard advantages in the two cultures and utilise the shortcomings that are favourable to themselves to bring about nefarious, Chinese-style prostitution and financial fraud in marital form. And the government shares the spoils as well.

According to Chinese traditional culture, the men should earn money to provide for women and should let the women be in charge of money, while the women must be attached to the men. The men can divorce their wives and be in polygynous marriages. Furthermore, Chinese traditional culture came from the feudal system of landholding. The greatest property in a family was land and house property. Those couldn't be transformed to cash, renamed, and transferred to foreign countries like the market economy now. They were fixed assets, which can only be inherited instead of being sold for cash. Even if the treasure was in the charge of women, women had only the right to operate instead of ownership. Men possessed eventually the right to handle the fortune. They were masters of their houses.

When it comes to the Occidental human rights culture, the property of both men and women is completely divided. The distribution of prenuptial properties and postnuptial properties is clear. Men and women only have to be on their own behalf. Women have title property and can convert their property into cash or transfer it.

The situation of marriage in China at present is: men earn money to provide for women and they let women be in charge of money, but the distribution and transfer of property are based on Occidental human rights culture. It is considered to be a merit in China that men have no rights in financial affairs. According to the man in this event, his wife diddled his 100 million yuan and fled to the United States. All of that is because of his lust for women. He even has no money to go to court. All of the relationships between men and women in China can be described as metamorphic psychosis and false pretences.

325

If an Occidental man wants to marry a Chinese woman, they have to make sure of this relationship. Otherwise, they may suffer losses and trouble somehow.

On the basis of Chinese traditional view of marriage, women think that they are entrusted to men for life when they get married. So they require the men to give them the right of being in charge of property. Therefore, they must sign an agreement that has legal effect before they get married.

> 1. If the woman put forward the idea of divorce, then all of the property will belong to the man. The woman will leave without getting anything.

> 2. If the woman has extramarital affairs, the man will have the right of divorce and possess all of the property. The woman will leave without getting anything.

> 3. If the woman is infertile or refuses to procreate, the man will have the right of a polygynous marriage.

This is the real 'commit one's lifetime to someone' in Chinese traditional view of marriage. Otherwise, it's completely a flimflam and deceit and a kind of financial fraud in the name of marriage.

According to Occidental view of marriage and human rights, men and women have Dutch treat from beginning to end. They protect their own rights of economy and personal liberty. The prenuptial property belongs to themselves, while the common property in marriage will be divided according to the law. And each of them undertake half of the marriage expenses.

Two views have their cause and effect, as well as their own logic, which cannot be confused. Otherwise, it is behaviour of grift. And such behaviour will destroy social order and tarnish social morality. It likes that all kinds of evil spirits dance in riotous revelry and the evildoers appear everywhere.

The situation of marriage in China at present is: women think that they are entrusted to men for life and sacrifice their youth, so they ask men to put their property under the name of woman. Then women divorce their husbands for various reasons after a short time of marriage. And they require a large amount of property that should belong to men. It is shameless financial fraud.

Furthermore, there is a luxurious custom in wedding. The effect of this custom is letting their family members and friends know their wedding and letting men sink deeper in the swindle. The costs of wedding and house

326

have risen up to hundreds of thousands, even more than a million. And the money is supplied by men. If they divorce, men have to seek another mate, which means that men are likely to suffer a similar loss once again.

In this economic activity, men may suffer great loss financially. In a word, men are in a disadvantageous situation. They may sink deeper in a financial fraud. And once they reach the end of their forbearance, they will make difficult decisions and start over.

The phenomenon that men are blackmailed by bad assets lies in another aspect: women refuse to sleep together.

Men have been locked up by bad assets at the start of the marriage, and they are blackmailed by the woman during their marriages. And women's main method is refusing to sleep together with men.

Women will ask their husbands for all sorts of unreasonable and shameless demands during their marriages. They want to control all the money and family affairs. Provided that their requests are not satisfied, they will refuse to sleep together. It is not a lie. We can find such plots in all Chinese movies, TV programs, dramas, and so forth. It is a prevalent phenomenon. Chinese men are blackmailed by the women without shame. They even think it is a sort of glorious mission.

So the humanness of Chinese people has already distorted and become abnormal. They have no self-esteem, either self-determination. All of them are eunuchs and swindlers.

The reason why telecommunication fraud is so rampant in China right now lies in this situation. Everyone grows up in deception and cheating. They grow up in a distorted and abnormal environment. So this sort of thing has a mass base.

Occidental view of marriage of democracy, freedom and human rights, is certainly purer by comparison. The intelligence of Chinese people is so high, and sometimes they are too shameless.

122. If telecommunication frauds make victims commit suicide, swindlers should be executed.

7 September 2016

Everything has its vanquisher in the world, and one thing would be overcome by another once it exceeds the scope.

Telecommunication frauds become more and more violent in China, like frauds committed by Taiwanese and frauds cheating university students out of their tuition.

Why it would become unscrupulous? It is mainly caused by the free-death theory developed from the Western human rights theory.

Seen from the behaviour, swindlers just tell a lie, since people won't be executed for telling lies, and telling lies is nearly irrelevant to the execution.

If swindlers are executed just for telling lies, Westerners would argue that it violates human rights, especially the right of personal liberty and democratic rights.

This is another case demonstrating that Westerners collude with demons to betray God.

Similarly, the conviction of swindlers should not merely be based on behaviour, while the results and essence are also equally important.

Killing for money is offensive to God, and it should be sentenced to death. This is a traditional Chinese culture, as well as the will of God for the Chinese.

If telecommunication frauds result in death, it is completely in conformity with all elements of killing for money, including money and lives killed. Therefore, swindlers (including the chief plotter or the one making phone calls), either mainlanders or Taiwanese, must be executed if victims suicided. But a rope can be provided for them to suicide, and it would save troubles for all of us.

123. Nail households should be settled by demolition

7 September 2016

Nail households refer to the phenomenon in which some people are unwilling to remove their houses for some engineering projects related to the land, building or road construction, resulting in the sharp turn, or the shabbiest small house among some modern building projects, which is unwilling to relocate.

It is a common phenomenon in capitalist country, due to the private ownership of land.

In China, where public ownership of land they are, it is ridiculous to see such a phenomenon.

Because hundreds of houses would be removed, rather than one or two, for a project. Others would be able to reach agreements with the demolition group, but one or two would refuse and become nail households, suggesting that the compensation would satisfy most people. Only a few fail to reach agreements, showing that they ask for too much, even things that are not supposed to be achieved by them.

Therefore, nail households are unreasonable and should be settled by demolition, to uphold justice.

Nail households actually damage the state interest with their individual actions. Especially, a nail house in the middle of the road might do harm to others' lives; thus, it should be demolished immediately.

The land is created by God and belongs to God. Public ownership is just government's execution of ownership on behalf of God. Besides, the government is entitled to change the use right of land, to make new plans for the use of land. It is a basic right of titleholders.

It is unreasonable for some people to refuse relocation once the government changes the use right of land. If some interests are harmed by the change of the use right of land, it is a problem concerning the compensation for interests, while disputes incurred by the compensation of interests shall be economic disputes, which shall be investigated, mediated, and judged by the court. It is not the relocation-or-not problem, since these are two different concepts.

Once the government changes the use right of land, local residents must relocate, court decision can be cited for those who are not satisfied with the compensation conditions, and the court decision must be executed.

Other protests, like murder, arson, assault, etc. fall into the category of criminal offence.

But suicide belongs to the basic human rights, and people have the right to commit suicide.

124. It is mandatory for pet keepers to pay to charitable foundations

29 December 2016

I have visited some relatively underdeveloped areas of China, where I have seen some emaciated old people were begging. In a sense, begging differs between poverty-stricken areas and developed cities.

In developed countries, beggars are mostly professional and don't deserve sympathy, because some of them even earn much more than workers. Furthermore, some people specially cripple orphans, force them to beg, and then exploit them. All of these constitute occupational crimes, so they are worth less sympathy. They will hurt more orphans if they are given money.

However, old men who beg in poverty-stricken areas are really poor and pathetic.

I even saw one who was still making crafts and arranging flowers for money and living in spite of no fingers. Besides, it was extremely cold and close to 0° there.

I really felt that they were worth sympathy and rather pathetic, but I didn't give him the money, because it was your business instead of mine. I would like to tell you who are supposed to pay to them—namely those who raise dogs and other pets. It is they that have to pay to those who need help.

People who don't raise dogs or pets need to supervise and force pet keepers to pay to wretched and needy people, which is not only generally acknowledged, but also justice.

They raise pets, which indicates that they are kind-hearted and have idle money. However, they don't love human beings, but animals. They raise animals, whereas they don't support people who need their favour. This is a distorted cult behaviour that shall and must be corrected.

It is right to be kind-hearted, which is necessary for all people. Nevertheless, people shall be firstly warm-hearted to human beings, or else it is impossible for them to love animals and beasts.

It is only in line with God's will and human interests when people give priority to love towards mankind before they treat animals nicely.

Some people don't love human beings but animals, and their love for animals outperforms their love for human beings, which implies that they are just demons with human skin and simply demon heretics.

I have only heard that some people fight for dogs, but have been never told that any people quarrel for giving money to beggars, which suggests that people who raise dogs love dogs more than human beings. All of them are cultists and demons.

To prevent pet keepers from being led astray by dogs and becoming demons, people like us who don't raise dogs have to help them.

Anyone who keeps pets must donate to charitable foundations at 1/1 and based on general costs for raising pets. How much they pay for buying pets and how much they roughly spend monthly may be calculated. They are required to donate to the poor based on the costs, and these donations shall be received by governments on behalf of the poor.

At first, they must express their love to the poor. Only in this way are they qualified for loving animals, or else they are just cultists.

They must firstly donate to charitable organisations at 1/1 at least. If not, they are disqualified for keeping pets.

Those who are stubborn are apostles of demons, who shall be sent to another world to unite with demons.

I don't need much money, but I think that some people who raise dogs also have to give generously to the poor.

They shall give the poor as much as they spend on dogs. I have downgraded the poor to a level comparable to dogs, in an attempt to ask you for money. Do you think this is too demanding or necessary? Isn't this a generally acknowledged truth, a justice, and the minimum requirement?

Furthermore, dogs shall be sentenced to death if they bite people. Meanwhile, ten times the costs shall be paid to the injured as medical expenses and nourishment subsidies, while twenty times the costs shall be compensated as subsidies for lost work and mental compensation.

Provided that people are bitten by ownerless dogs, local governments shall compensate the victims based on above standards, because the injuries shall be attributable to their inappropriate control over strays and unreasonable protection of people's interests.

Moreover, such compensations shall be shared among the poor at the equal amount, because they are just the costs for raising dogs. Meanwhile, money shall be also donated to the poor at 1/1.

To be sure, working dogs shall be differentiated from those for fun. Work is assigned to guide dogs, police dogs, shepherd dogs, and explosive detection dogs. Rural people who raise dogs for meat are not required to donate. Instead, urban residents who raise dogs for entertainment and fun shall donate money to poor people.

125. Citizen information should be publicised in default, and the fraud should be heavily convict

1 January 2017

I have been engaged in sales, which is the most difficult job in sales—promotion.

Product sales are related to the business survival and death, and the number of customers has the most direct effect on the promotion. Where are the unfamiliar customers? It's the customer information. It's the name of a strange customer, telephone, address, mailbox, QQ, cell phone, SMS . . .

The specific products require specific information. The information of the parents just giving birth to a baby can sell a lot of products. Children's insurance, baby supplies, milk powder, diapers, parent-child activities, early childhood education . . . anyway, you need to buy these things from this store or another one. Sometimes young parents also do not know where to buy, and they need to inquire around for advice.

It's good to collect some marketing information appropriately for your own choice.

The Western countries proposed to protect citizens' privacy. I think the purpose of Western countries is not to protect the good guys, but to protect the bad guys.

There's fraud, murder, violence, drug trafficking in Western countries that are commonplace. Criminals that killed dozens of persons are not sentenced to the death penalty, but they are just enjoying themselves very much in prison. Those criminals even seem to be more chic than the outside world.

Fraud is nothing.

So they want to protect the privacy of citizens, fraudsters cannot find information, so they have to do other illegal things. This is to remove trouble for everyone; it's not to protect the good guys, but to protect the bad guys. They have insufficient policemen in order to deal with few troubles. The criminals won't be punished; there are bad guys everywhere. There are won't too many troubles for customers. The bad guys cannot find more customer information, so they do fewer illegal things. However, it also undermines economic growth.

At the early stage of China's reform and opening up, China developed itself by feeling the stones across the river, and it could do anything. There's no citizen information protection. So the economy grew rapidly in double digits.

Later, everything is standardised, and nothing can be done randomly; it's difficult to sell out the product. Economic growth rate has declined.

The problem lies not in the publicised citizen information, but what people want to do with such information.

If there's any person killed by a criminal with a knife, then all the shops are not allowed to sell the kitchen knife.

If there's any person killed on the road by a car, then all the cars are not allowed to be driven on the roads.

If there's a terrorist hijacking a plane, all the planes are not allowed to take off.

It's the safest to walk on the road. No one can complain in case of any troubles, it's your own business if you fall down on the road.

The problem is not that the properly publicised citizen information is an issue, but the bad guys are problems.

If it's the problem of the bad guys, then it's necessary to solve the problem of the bad guys. This has nothing to do with other things.

It is not because of bad guys that we do not develop our economy, and the enterprises do not survive, the people do not work, and there's no tax of the state. This is ridiculous.

It's essential to heavily convict the fraud, and the fraudster should be put in prison for ten years, eight years, until they get old. They ruin our market, and I want to ruin their life. Those ones leading to the death of the victim must be executed. Their heads must be cut; only in this way will no one else dare to commit a fraud.

The loss caused by those criminals is not the money, but they destroy our market and economic development.

The fraud turmoil in China started from the death immunity for economic crimes. This is really a calamity with serious harm.

Some people must put to death. You can let them commit suicide, or hang themselves; anyway, they must be cleared out of this world.

In short, fraud that does not lead to any death can be immune from death; otherwise, the fraudster must be sentenced to death.

Now there are a lot of people stealing the user's bank account and password

335

through a variety of channels, and someone withdraws the money in the bank card through a one-stop service.

This does not belong to the behaviour of stealing customer information, neither does it belong to normal business behaviour, but it's robbery, high-tech means of crime.

It's only to disturb the customers by getting the name, phone, and address of a customer. It is harmless. However, the access to the customer's bank card information does not disturb the customer, and it is part of the robbery. Both seem to belong to getting the customer's information, but the nature is completely different. It's necessary to treat this completely differently.

P2P false investment is a fraud, and the actual investment belongs to the commercial business; both belong to completely different behaviour. Both will be with completely different responsibilities.

For the behaviour of stealing the information of customer's bank card, such criminal must be executed. Because this is part of the robbery with huge amount, thus there must be the execution.

Other behaviour of obtaining the general information of the customers belongs to the normal business practices, and such behaviour should be protected and encouraged.

Robbery and commercial behaviour are not the same behaviour, so the treatment and punishment should also be different.

I think that the current government is very backward and slow towards the conviction and sentencing of the new criminal acts. The government cannot keep up with the situation, and it hits the good guys. However, this is a connivance of the bad guys and the demon.

126. Housing price in China is higher than that in America, is determined by Chinese culture

8 January 2017

Pursuant to Chinese traditional culture and Confucius-Mencius culture, there is a saying 'bring up sons to support parents in their old age, store up grain against death for a bad year'.

Actually, the culture is quite advanced. The sayings like 'bring up sons to support parents in their old age' and 'the son's errors should be blamed on his father's failure to teach' reflect that in ancient times in China, the traditional culture had the function of endowment insurance and compulsory education. Because of such functions, Chinese civilisation is able to have a sustainable development.

Being affected by traditional culture like 'store up grain against death for a bad year', Chinese people have held the ideology 'save money and accumulate wealth'.

Actually, the aforementioned Chinese culture is totally different from Western culture—democracy, freedom and human rights.

For the Western culture, democracy, freedom and human rights, the highest pursuit is that at the moment when he dies, he just runs out of all the money he made in the lifetime. That is, he does not waste any that he made and he does not leave any to others.

For individuals, such a culture can maximise his interest, while for a nation and a society, this is really bad or even the worst. If one runs out of all the money, he does not make any contribution to wealth accumulation of his family, the country, the nation, and the society.

Is wealth accumulation is necessary to the family, the country, the nation and the society? What role can the wealth accumulation play?

If one is born in a rich family, he will lead a happier and cosier life than the one who is born in a poor family; apart from the happiness and cosiness, the value that he can make and the way he makes value will be different.

If one is born in a rich family, what he needs to do is to increase the wealth, from million to billion or even more. Therefore, the value he made is the gap between the value he made and the value he inherited.

If one is born in a poor family, it is quite difficult for one to make millions in wealth.

This example reflects what Chinese people are widely talking about—different starting line. Actually, starting line is also the impact on individual value by family wealth.

Similarly, the more wealth one can inherit from one's ancestors, the more benefits will be provided for the country, the nation, the society, and the government.

For a government, how to govern the rich and how to govern the poor will be different; the tax income from the rich and the poor will be different too. Of course, the social management will be different.

Why there are so many differences? Because capital varies. Actually, the wealth given by the ancestors to the younger generations is a kind of capital. Normally, increasing the value of the capital is a kind of wealth accumulation, which is also a way to make money. In fact, this is an important way to make money.

Therefore, we can say that for an individual, the country and the family, accumulating wealth and continuing the wealth will play a great role, which is also meaningful and beneficial.

In China, some economists said that the phenomenon that the housing price in large cities in China is higher than that in America is quite abnormal. This is an economic bubble and the bubble needs to be removed. I think they are wrong.

Why do I think so? Because the value of a house has different meanings for Chinese and Americans, the social demands in China and America are also different. This is a result of the different cultures in China and Western countries. For Westerners, they do not need to 'store up grain against death for a bad year', so it is not necessary for them to accumulate wealth. For Chinese, it is necessary for them to accumulate wealth and continue the wealth.

A house can have its value preserved or increased. So buying a house is being used by Chinese people as a tool to manage money and save money.

For example, if one spends several hundred thousand yuan buying a car. Some years later, the car is damaged and broken, thus its value will be zero.

If one spends several hundred thousand yuan buying a house. After dozens of years or even hundreds of years, it can still have the use value and economic value. What's more, there is a great possibility to have its value increased.

In my opinion, if China is able to make its population increase stably, a couple can have two or three children, the value of house will be always there.

However, if the fertility is low and the aging is getting serious, there will be fewer people needing to buy a house for marriage. If so, the housing price definitely suffers economic bubbles.

For Chinese people who are used to 'store up grain against death for a bad year' and wealth accumulation, buying a house can play such a role.

But for the Westerners who hope they can run out of all the money when they die, a house cannot play such a role. Instead, a house will be a kind of burden for them.

This is just like that in China. One crab, which costs 5–10 yuan, is a luxury and delicious. But in some Western countries, crabs are considered to be toxic, no one wants to eat them, and no one buys it. For Westerners, crabs are valueless.

So the value of a crab is different for Chinese and Westerners, while the value of a house is also different for Chinese and Westerners.

Therefore, we cannot say that the phenomenon that housing price in some cities in China is higher than that in America means an economic bubble.

Normally, different cultures will lead to different social demands. Therefore, the value will be different.

Of course, drawing up policies to control and stop the house hype is a good measure. In first-tier cities where the housing price is too high, it is mandatory to control the house hype in order to avoid some risks. However, in the second-tier cities, third-tier cities, and fourth-tier cities, house hype shall be allowed in order to make people able to manage their money by buying house, as well as to inherit the wealth.

127. Criminals disfiguring a woman tourist in Lijiang need to be beheaded

26 January 2017

These days, an event is heatedly debated on the network; that is, a gang of rogues beat a female tourist in a restaurant brutally, cut her face with a piece of glass bottle, and shot it into a video for memorial.

I have just been to Lijiang, a place inhabited mostly by ethnic minority, and Han people there just accounted for a small portion.

Close to the southwest edge of China's railway line, Lijiang is an mountainous area with less developed economy and large population of ethnic minority.

In general, China's ethnic minorities are scattered on the border areas of China, so transportation there is inconvenient and the economy less developed than that in other areas.

For some reason, the police did not disclose the identity of the assailants. I estimate that they belong to the minority nationality.

China has a large number of minority autonomous regions, not including Lijiang, but it is surrounded by several minority autonomous regions.

Only ethnic minority in China dare to run amuck at society so fearlessly. They receive ultra national treatment in China, and their punishment for beating, killing, and doing bad things is different from people in big cities.

That is called ethnic minority policy in China, whose sympathy to and harbouring, connivance, and forgiveness of minority criminals can be seen from ways of police investigation.

The perpetrators said it was clear: They are not afraid of the police as they are with the police.

Such a thing may be very normal in the United States but a big event in China because in China it is a rare case that criminals call themselves as family of police, beat a woman, disfigure her, and shoot video in the scenic area, of course, except for Islamic terrorists.

From the analysis of the most primitive psychological motive, the event is all out of the supernational treatment of ethnic minority. They assume that the Han people have occupied their land and have a request from them, so what do Han people dare to do with them? 'Han people, do you accept it? If don't, tomorrow I will declare independence.'

Although no one speaks openly, that is what they believe. If you dare not speak, let me help you. Let me express what is in your mind.

Why did God give the Arabs the Koran? It is because they live in harsh desert area lacking living materials.

With the Koran, Arabs' population grows.

So the Koran is specifically applied to people living in poor areas, while the democratic system and the concept of human rights suits only capitalist countries with highly developed economy.

The idea of democracy is completely inapplicable to such a poor area as Lijiang, the result of which is the disfigured woman, who is able to directly shoot horror film without make-up.

Lijiang, a poor area, is fully applicable to the Koran, and according to the law of Saudi Arabia, those rogues shall be beheaded.

Without severe law like Koran, it is impossible to regulate rogue behaviour in Lijiang.

The poorer the place, the more applicable the Koran is, which represents justice.

We should treat people in people's way, while the demon in demon's way, defined in the Koran.

This event is not an isolated case in Lijiang, as a few years ago there were tour guides abusing visitors, which was shot by a video spreading on network.

In fact, it all boils down to remoteness and poverty of minority areas. Seeing crowds of wealthy tourists in their hometown, they are distorted in mind with serious jealousy and hatred to the rich. Abusing, beating, and disfiguring tourists are venting such abnormal psychology.

Ideology, culture and social rules of the rich are completely inapplicable to poor areas, as the poor have a set of logic, ways of thinking, and codes of conduct of their own. The reason of local police and government being considered a family is that they have a common living environment, culture, ideology, and logical thinking.

In the eyes of the locals, the disfigurement is called minor injuries, a matter of a few hundred yuan for medical expenses. While for the disfigured women, it is a serious injury that hundreds of thousands or even millions of yuan cannot cure. This is the difference between the poor and the rich in culture, ideology, and values.

Treating the poor with the law of the rich will provide rogues with surviving space and political protection.

This is why the revolution of Arab Spring does not work in the Middle East.

God tells the people through the Koran: In economically underdeveloped areas, need to be more brutal to deal with brutality, need to be more cruel to deal with cruelty, need to be more irrational to treat irrationality, need to use more bloody to treat bloody.

Humans' language is used when talking with human beings, while demon's language must be adopted talking with demon. The language that the demon understands are savage, cruelty irrationality, and blood. Only in this way can those who convert to God be protected, and the demon can be driven away.

There are no prices for the majority of goods and restaurants in Lijiang and Dali's tourist attractions. Goods and food there will be tagged with names but no price. Once I went to a roadside booth, for two steamed buns. I think the cheapest are several times more expensive than those in the big cities. In large cities, standardised market environment, such conduct is purely a commercial fraud.

I am willing to buy things with price tag even it is expensive. Without price and selling expensively, it is a commercial fraud.

Do they really not know that pricing goods is the most basic rule of doing business, or do they believe that they needn't put a price tag because of their hospitality?

Or do they think that the rich are granted to be swindled?

Or does the local government not regulate the market, and the Trade and Industry Bureau does not investigate such a fraud?

Or are the local government and the lawbreakers simply working together?

Because they have a common living environment, culture, ideology, and logical thinking, they are essentially a family.

The steamed bun reflects the attitude of the locals, and it is not difficult to understand the psychological motives of disfiguring the woman tourist— the rich hatred. Hating and bullying the rich are the psychological distortions in all the ethnic minority areas from top to bottom.

Gentlemen love fortune in a proper way. The poor area needs prosperity, but should in proper and appropriate ways rather than through the rich hating and bullying. The rich do not owe you anything. Tourism of the rich to the poor places is a way to help the locals get rich as well.

Dealing with the rich in such mentalities and ways is what a demon does.

128. The have-nots are not afraid of the haves

27 January 2017

'The have-nots are not afraid of the haves' is a proverb in Chinese language, which is not collected in the classical literary works or school textbooks. However, it is a social culture and social logic that exists concretely. In addition, since ancient times, it has been in existence, and it has guided people's behaviour. It is a social guideline that runs in parallel with all the classical cultures.

The classical culture and the culture learned from school textbooks are the cultures of the wealthy and the logic of wealth, and those poor people and the civil society have folk cultures and the logic of the poor. Without a comprehension of the cultures and logical thoughts of the poor, it would be impossible to administer the poor.

A very simple truth is that the social impacts and harms exerted by the drug use by the wealthy and the poor are not the same.

The aftermath of drug use by the wealthy is bankruptcy. They would deteriorate from the haves to have-nots and have to live on the street.

In contrast, when the poor use drugs, in order to raise money, they can do any evil things, such as robberies and murders, thus severely harming others: black society, blackmailing, drug making and drug trafficking, counterfeit currencies, robbing banks, illegal trade of guns, forcing women into prostitution, etc., which are all evils committed by the members of gangdom.

During the early establishment of the new People's Republic of China, almost all people were proletariats; with the implementations of reform and open-up, a great number of people have become proprietarians. Almost all the current urban dwellers are proprietarians. No matter how poor a person may be, their apartment is worth hundreds of thousands of yuan; these are the assets. Of course, for various reasons, a small number of people have no apartments, no bank deposits and are the have-nots.

In China's remote mountainous regions and countryside, their real estate are not the commercial apartments and cannot be traded on the market in case they have no money. They are the have-nots in the true sense, They are the poor people.

The logical thoughts of the haves and have-nots are totally different.

For the haves, since they have money and assets, first of all, they hope to protect their existing properties and create more opportunities for earning more money and lead a better life. Since they have assets, they are very afraid of losing their assets. They intend to lead a better life, and of course, they are more afraid of death.

The wealthy are fearful of running into troubles and are afraid to get involved in fighting, and they are afraid of being penalised. This is because in the capitalist nations, most people are wealthy and are proprietarians; therefore, their social culture and social logic are established on the basis of the wealthy.

Democratic culture, abolishment of capital punishment, compensation for spiritual damages, equality between males and females, human rights and liberty, etc.—all these things are sheer nonsense if they are taken in front of the have-nots.

This is because the have-nots and the proletariats have their own logic, and what they are most concerned about is not democratic culture, abolishment of death penalty, compensation for spiritual losses, equality between males and females, human rights, liberty, and philanthropy.

When the poor are together with the wealthy, what they feel first of all is a kind of psychological gap, self-abasement, fury, jealousy, and hatred. The reason why the democratic nations have been advocating philanthropy and equal rights is that they want the poor to listen to these so that they will not become hateful and will not hate the wealthy and the proprietarians. In the advanced Western nations, in contrast to the impoverished, most people are proprietarians and they are all wealthy people. They need to encourage the small number of impoverished not to have hatred and grudging against the wealth. They need to reach the level of the wealth through their own efforts.

While the wealthy have such thoughts, the poor have their own logic, i.e. the have-nots are not afraid of the haves. Since I am poor, I can do anything—for the poor have nothing to lose. When the poor make efforts, they could get the whole world. Therefore, the poor can commit robberies, severely harm others, be members of the underworld, commit blackmailing and kidnapping, make and traffic illegal drugs, make counterfeit currencies, commit bank robberies, sell illegal weapons, force women into prostitution, etc.

This is because the logic of the poor is different from that of the wealthy. For the haves and have-nots, the administrations of the poor and the wealthy should also be different.

The effective administration of the wealthy is such things as the current legislative system fines, imprisonments.

For the impoverished, the most effective administrative system is strict laws execution and vigorous behavioural norms, which is management like the Koran-type management in Islamism. If the poor commit robberies, severely harm others, are members of the underworld, commit blackmailing and kidnapping, make and traffic illegal drugs, make counterfeit currencies, commit bank robberies, sell illegal weapons, force women into prostitution, etc., all these are the social trash and tumours and all of them should be executed immediately.

The wealthy have different logic from the poor, and they have different starting points for the thinking about some issues. Therefore, the laws there lenient to the wealthy are not applicable for the poor, and the poor need strict laws. In order to make the laws executable, no matter they are the wealthy or the poor, when measuring the sentences, it is possible to make the litigant compensate in money. For those who can afford to pay or have assets, their penalties can be lightened. For those poor people, when they have committed crimes, they should be executed.

Just like the suspect who ruined the facial appearance of a woman, firstly, he was requested to compensate 2 million yuan; when he failed to do so, he was executed. Those people who have a worth of 2 million yuan would never have done something like that. In my opinion, since it was not affordable and he risked everything, he should have been executed.

For those wealthy people, their severe harms to others might have been caused by impulsions and they can be compensated with money.

For those poor people who have harmed others, they committed despising of God and should be executed.

However, regardless whichever people, whether they are the rich or the poor, intentional murders of people should be compensated by the death penalties. This is the law of God, and is also the most fundamental fairness and justice.

In China, social security is guaranteed by the government with God's wealth, and the government uses God's wealth for conducting scientific administration, and employments, training, education, urban development, and social security are all operating normally. Therefore, it is necessary to take effective measures on those who damage the order.

In a democratic society, regarding personal safety, it is partially provided by the nation, while the individual has to safeguard the other part. The nation is unable to provide complete safety assurance and effective and scientific management of the society; therefore, regarding the penalties for crimes, they can only resolve the contradiction. It is impossible to realise fairness and justice.

Since a nation has no obligations for individuals, you have no rights.

In democratic nations, it is necessary to collect God's wealth to the nation; only when the scientific administration of the society is realised will it be possible to completely apply the crimes and penalties for fairness and justice.

129. Game regulation shall be required in usury; those going beyond the limit shall be executed

30 March 2017

When we watch the ref film during childhood, the usurious loan is deemed as the unscrupulous approach for the landlords to ride roughshod over the poor. Yang Bailao fails to repay the usurious loan. Hence the landlords ask Yang to pay the debt with her daughter. Yang's daughter escapes to the remote mountain and gets her hair white. Later on, the Communist Party carried out the revolution, and the landlords are killed. Hence, the white-haired woman wins a new lease of life.

The story of White Hair Woman was the model opera that everybody from our ages is familiar with.

Unfortunately the landlord staged a comeback, whereas times have passed and circumstances have changed. Currently the Communist Party no longer tries to suppress the landlord. These groups are requiring human rights and legal protection from the party.

In today's news, a male sophomore is required to repay 1 million yuan as he borrowed 40 thousand yuan half a year ago. Hence he is forced to drop out of the school, and all his family are avoiding the creditor.

Another piece of news several days ago is that a woman is required to repay 1.5 million yuan after borrowing 40 thousand yuan. The old couple lose their only daughter and are forced to repay the debt. Unfortunately the company of usury wins the lawsuit.

Why shall the borrower repay 1 million or over 1.5 million yuan after borrowing 40 thousand yuan half a year ago? During this term, plenty of means for fraud and coercion have been adopted. The borrower is induced or coerced to write the receipt for loan. The lender shall firstly remit the money to the victim's bank account, secondly induce or coerce the victim to counterfeit the money-borrowing evidence through drawing the money from the bank and returning to the lender.

The court shall require the victim to return the huge money amount of 1 million yuan merely in accordance with the evidence acquired by creditor through coercion and fraud. As a matter of fact, the additional 960 thousand yuan does not even exist.

Accordingly the civilian is jointly oppressed by the government and the criminal usurious loan. The usurious loan is perceived as financial fraud, and the government is deemed the accomplice.

In accordance with the current laws of China, for the loan with the rate four times larger than the interest rate of banks, the exceeding part shall not be protected by the government.

If the creditor requires the borrower to repay the interest with the interest rate four times larger than that of banks, the victim, namely the borrower, is able to refuse the repayment. If the usurious loan company adopts the oppression and fraud methods, it shall be recognised as a criminal offence and financial fraud. The public security organisation shall promptly file the case and carry out the investigation.

The government capital is the treasure created by God. The civil servant raised by the government capital shall maintain people's interests, rather than be the accomplice of the landlord, or requiring the innocent people to repay the borrowed money that doesn't even exist.

Such usurious loan company shall specially ride roughed over the students without he social experience. They require college girls to take a naked photo to mortgage the usurious loan. Students are praised as the future of our country. They are oppressed by the gangdom before they can graduate. What shall they hold their view on the society and country? Is there anybody to still love our country? Is there anybody to safeguard our country?

In my point of view, the one issuing the usurious loan towards the students with the interest rate surmounting the legal scope and adopting the oppression and coercion, with the loaned money over 100 thousand, shall be executed at the gate of the school.

The usurious loan companies with the interest rate surmount the legally regulated interest rate are basically operated by the criminal syndicate. Such organised crime is notorious for beating, blackmailing, coercing, and even killing people.

Once in China, a man was sentenced to the fixed-term imprisonment for eighteen years for stealing somebody's hat. Accordingly, one who illegally acquired 1 million yuan through fraud, blackmail, and robbery shall be executed over 100 times.

The Koran invented by the God is to regulate the savage. For this reason, the Koran is suitable to regulate the criminal syndicate. The Koran shall be adopted to resolve the problem of criminal syndicate, in other words, the criminal syndicate shall be executed.

130. If financial fraud involves a whole family, all members should all be executed

22 April 2017

Yesterday I went to a party where a couple of customers tearfully complained to me that their money has been conned by P2P boss, and they wanted me to help them figure something out.

There are more than 1,000 customers, and one of them lost 800,000 yuan. Approximately 2 billion was taken.

Although the man behind this has been caught, he is acting dumb, claiming that he knows nothing about it. They only managed to retrieve some cars and salesman's commission, with a total amount of 50 million.

The boss has been caught, yet he dares to deny everything. It is clear that he is relying on the Western human rights system and is convinced that he can act provocatively without punishment.

It is right to talk about human rights, but ordinary people need money; they want their money back.

You give back our money, and you can talk about any right you want. Anything you say we will believe, you can literally talk about anything.

But without the money, it is all just bullshit and total nonsense. The whole system is plundering the wealth from people with the help of criminals; the system is the accomplice of demon and a part of demon. The whole system is demonic.

Human rights are suitable for the people who speak for humans and do the right thing for humans. This is understandable.

But that the P2P boss defrauded ordinary people's money is not what humans will do. He is an out-and-out demon. Since the P2P boss is a demon, we should treat him in demons' language and demons' way of doing things.

The first thing we need to do is to arrest all the family members of the P2P boss and then take out all the ancient instruments of torture, try them one by one, and let them be tortured. The money will go back by a miracle.

Even a fool knows that the money does not vanish into thin air. It was just transferred by the P2P boss.

As far as I know, some victims of this case, mostly old men and women, have committed suicide.

So the P2P boss has reached the threshold of exterminating every one of the family.

All the money has been transferred by his family, so they are all accomplices. All the family members get the benefit and kill others for money.

Once he gives the money back, the family can be saved from the execution.

Applying tools of torture before the decapitation in order to cut people's loss is reasonable and lawful. It is called waste utilisation.

As long as the money is back, everybody will be saved.

131. Westerners Ought to Help Persecuted Old People in China to Safeguard Rights and Interests

9 July 2017

Some people in the West-like to criticize China and seek the dark side of China to help some democrats, democratic lawyers, and priests-defend rights.

You were running wild before, and now there's a big chance to behave yourself. Don't let the people and the democrats down.

I went to the park and saw a lot of old people organizing the revolution the other day. Their rights have been badly hurt, and even many people have committed suicide. They have no way to safeguard their rights and interests, so they hope that the Western democratic countries give them some help.

According to what they said, the number of victims reached to two hundred million, and the amount of fraud was two hundred trillion, and they are the victims of financial fraud by P2P companies in recent years with most of the elderly. Due to the savings cheated, many victims choose suicide in despair.

Although I am not the staff of the Bureau of Statistics and do not know where these figures come from, I estimate that the data should be very close to truthful data.

According to those people, Chinese government officials colluded with the P2P bosses to cheat their money and then refused to recover the stolen money, even indulge the P2P boss. If someone calls for rights protection, he will be threatened and asked to shut up.

Westerners should send reporters to investigate because of too much of these case, evidence and witnesses are easily collected. They are worried about the lack of attention to them and you're just in time to help them. They need revolution, and you ought to help them protect their rights.

Trump always said that you make fake news, but this time you don't need to fake anything because it is genuine sensational news. People are expecting your real news.

132. The Phenomenon That Mainland Tourists Are Seized for Extortion often Happens in Hong Kong. The Chinese Government Should protect People's Interests.

23 July 2017

Today's news is about the event that mainland tourists are kidnapped and forced again to consume in Hong Kong. Such event is commonly seen and has existed for about a decade. A tourist has been beaten to death. The manner that the Chinese government has taken is to reduce major issues to minor ones, and then minor issues to naught. It's called as "harmonious society."

"Harmonious society" can't be interpreted in this way that "harmonious society" will not let offenders well alone or take an ostrich policy.

"Harmonious society" needs fairness and justice firstly and then "harmony."

People's life is threatened, and money swindled. The government must get their money back, and the offenders deserve punishment, which is fairness and justice.

The Chinese government can't implement sovereignty abroad and thus can only pursue and capture the escaped criminals if the victims' money is swindled.

But Hong Kong is a part of China and within the sovereignty scope of the Chinese government.

The Chinese government must protect the interests of Chinese people and uphold fairness and justice within its sovereignty scope.

It has constituted the crime of kidnapping for ransom and has completely been criminal act to force the tourists to go shopping or let them suffer personal abuse and menace if they refuse to do so in a shopping tour. The government should redress the injustice and uphold justice for people, bring lawbreakers to justice, and get illicit money back.

Tanks will enter into Hong Kong for military control if you don't hand the offenders over the mainland immediately for punishment and get money back to people.

The Hong Kong Special Administrative Region Government is unable to control crime so the mainland government should take over the public security of Hong Kong.

The reason why some Hong Kong people hate mainlander is that a large number of Hong Kong people used to be dissidents in mainland who escaped to and settled down in Hong Kong. They have deep-rooted hatred against mainland. It's these people who took the mainland tourists into custody and conducted illegal robbery and still got shielded and connived by the Hong Kong Government.

There are a large number of dissidents in the Hong Kong Government who extremely turn against and bear a deep malice toward the mainland government.

They are unable to figure out the situation and need to see the situation clearly with the help of tank, prison, and indoctrination through labor.

133. Some of China's Pyramid Selling Organizations Are Evil Organizations, and the Chief Criminal Should Be Beheaded.

5 August 2017

About pyramid selling, Amway should be the earliest pyramid selling that I have ever contacted with since China's reform and opening up. I once attended their activities several times. They have their own unique products, which are marketed through the way that the upper line extracts profit of the down line.

I have also participated in the pyramid selling activities of some health products, which claimed that their health care products imitate the natural environment of the longevity village and can produce miraculous health care effects.

Of course, their products cannot be explained by western scalpel and microscope, so they cannot be referred to as clinical medicine. Not only their products but also the phenomenon of longevity villages can't be explained by scalpel or microscope. They can't be marketed through the propaganda of medical institutions. Hence, they can only be marketed in the form of pyramid schemes.

I didn't try their products and I am not sure about the effect. I only know that many people claim the magical effects of the products. Of course, I can't tell if they're sheer fraud. They only promote their products by means of pyramid selling. No accidents like detention, violence or murder has been heard.

Another type of pyramid scheme in China has been more outrageous. Recent news reported that some university students in Shandong province had been cheated into a pyramid scheme and then they were died of starvation and beatings. Bodies were found in puddles.

The multi-level marketing organizations with Chinese characteristics first introduce the victims to the pyramid selling dens in the name of recruitment, work, parties, and other reasons, and then illegally detain them, brainwash, and publicize heresies. They force the victims to join the MLM with money. Then let the victim deceive other relatives and friends to come to the dens and join them to continue the activities: illegal detention, brainwash, and heresies propaganda. Let the second generation of victims join the pyramid scheme and then the third generation, the fourth generation.

The recently reported victim was brutally murdered and tortured to death because he refused to cooperate with the pyramid organization. This so-

355

called pyramid organization is not a commercial marketing activity, nor is it a marketing organization, but an evil organization, an underworld organization, or a criminal organization.

I have only heard of the violence of the heresy and underworld pyramid organization, but I have never seen it myself because I live in a big city. If there is violence, we can call the police. In a few minutes, police will be there to deal with the situation. How can there be mass violent detention behavior?

They tend to be in remote rural areas with low population quality and poor policing. The place will be convenient for them to carry out their activities.

When dealing with this kind of matters, I think, we should first separate the commercial pyramid selling with the underworld and heresy-like pyramid selling because their properties are different.

The commercial pyramid selling is commercial activities, while the underworld and the heresy-like pyramid selling is in the business form but actually a kind of underworld and heresy-like activity. Therefore, their properties are different. The mushrooms look like the same, but some are home cooking, and some mushrooms are poisonous. People will die immediately after eating them. It is not right to forbid all mushrooms because some are poisonous. It is not right to prohibit all P2P because some P2P are fraud. It only demonstrates that the ruler is simple and rough, with simple mind and well-developed limbs.

I think the boss of the P2P purely in the purpose of fraud should be decapitated immediately. I think that a pyramid selling organizer with the nature of the underworld and heresy should also be decapitated immediately. They are neither pyramid organizations nor business organizations. They are heresy and underworld organizations clothed in pyramid selling.

P2P companies in the purpose of fraud are not P2P companies. They are pure financial fraud companies that wear P2P clothing. Business organizations are built on the voluntary basis. Illegal detentions, threats of violence, beatings, maltreatment, and murders are completely out of the realm of voluntary trade but underworld and heresy-like behaviors in essence and their organizers should be decapitated immediately.

As for P2P financial fraud, cut off the heads of several fraudsters, and other fraudsters will hand over the money they swindle from ordinary people, and such behavior will not happen anymore.

The same is true for the underworld and the heresy nature pyramid selling.

If some organizers have been cut off heads, the other group would break up, and that will be the end of such behaviors.

134. The Girl Who Was Dropped from the Building Has Sexual Blackmail Behavior

24 August 2017

The hot news of today is a girl who was thrown down by her boyfriend from 19th floor. The parents of this girl required ten million compensation which ignite the argument of Chinese netizens.

It is normal girls killed due to passion, but this incident highlights a problem in Chinese society—that is sexual blackmail.

In ancient China, the requirement for male and female is forbidding the non-couples to have excessive contact. And Islam require women to cover their face to prevent other men from seeing any part of the woman's body. All these are for the prevention of sexual blackmail. While the combination of China's democratic freedom thoughts and ancient traditional culture has produced unique sexual blackmail culture in China.

First, women receive various gifts in relationship, and receive great number of bride price, besides, they all want to charge all the income of the family or they refuse to have sex with their husband. These are all sexual blackmail.

And the man in this case can't endure the nine-year sexual blackmail (give gifts to the girl in the long-term but receive nothing) and loses his sanity. He dropped the sexual blackmailer from the 19th floor due to the break out of psychosis. This behavior is wrong, but people who suffered from it all can understand. People who suffer from long-term sexual blackmail need resistance, or they will lose their dignity, especially the man's dignity.

In consequence of the girl's intended blackmail behavior, I think the male perpetrator needs to sentence to ten years imprisonment, which can serve to warn others against following a bad example.

All the compensation requirements of the girl's parents are unreasonable; it is a further sexual blackmail behavior, which can be done either by living people or the dead. Both parties should take the case as a warning. This is a punishment for wrongdoers, and for other sexual blackmailers, warning still be needed.

135. Game Industry Should Be Limited in Development

1 October 2017

We have already discussed many topics about war and death but the Middle East War is about to come to an end, so from my perspective, we shall discuss the problems of game. Originally, I am a senior game player. My skills in games are not rated as "supreme," but at least above middle level. The game industry in China which has started from scratch is a hot industry now; I have witnessed its growth. The harms brought by games are less serious than that of gambling, drugs, gangland, terrorism, cults, and demons.

If we solve the problems of "gambling, drugs, gangland, terrorism, cults, and demons," we are supposed to turn to games.

The sentence in Chinese textbook of middle school "it takes a teacher to transmit wisdom, impart knowledge, and resolve doubts." Means that people are required to explore the truth and learn the great truth in this regard.

I think all the countries in the world are facing serious problems, since people all over the world are giving up pursuing "the great truth."

What people have learned in schools is just the production skills used in laboring process, while not "the great truth."

So what is the great truth? All that God has imparted to human beings is "the great truth" including: Tao Te Ching, the Buddhist Scriptures, Bible, the Koran, Huang di's Canon of Medicine, Science of Chinese Materia Medica, Yin-yang Philosophy, capitalism, communism, and so on. These are all included in the great truth. However, if they are not understood and integrated by people, the world will be in severe conflicts.

Since the great truth is imparted by God for human beings to use as tools, they will definitely solve one aspect of problem existing in human society. Only all the tools are used flexibly and all the problems be solved finally. That is the conflict and truth in the world. People are more willing to spend all the money on enhancing their ability of earning money and vying with each other in this way while no one actually learns the great truth imparted by God.

The parliament members of Hong Kong who have insulted China, as well as those leaders in student movement are obviously the student representatives who are ignorant and benighted. They never know what is called "the great truth."

We may wonder why they are ignorant and benighted because they, as the young generation, are intoxicated by games.

Beside learning the skills to survive, they always spend their spare time playing games, what is worse, there is no time for them to learn great truth at all.

In my childhood, I also play "games" every day, such as searching bird's nests in trees, finding out the "booty" and killing them for feeding chicken, doing some farming work as feeding chicken, sheep, rabbits, and pigs or just playing some games for children, which is so interesting at that time.

Then, I come to the big city, everything in my childhood has gone away. All the activities and sports I take part in cost money, except for running, but I hate it.

From my perspective, it is for someone whose energy is excessive, so they would choose such activity to run out of it, otherwise they would get sick in spare time. Playing computer games is the best tool for people in the city to kill the time.

In rural areas, playing games can exercise our body, enhance our physical quality, flexibility, strengths, and body coordination. When playing with peers, children may enhance their social, organizational, communicating skills, and so on.

Computer games can never provide all the above functions. Except for no any benefits, they bring some negative reactions to the body, at least, there are people who have died in front of computers of Internet bar. Computer games are something like drugs which will control the thoughts of men for a long time. Before being bored to games, they occupy a majority of the thought of people, even all the thought in some situation.

When they do not finish the task in games, people seem to be lost in something they have not completed and keep thinking on how to finish it. The harms of games are known to people all over the world, otherwise the governments will not restrict teenagers and children to enter game room and Internet bar.

Now, game room and Internet bar are outdated; what is popular is mobile game. The game not only brings harm to the teenagers and children but also intoxicates the adults.

In spare time, people are just thinking about how to play games while not the great truth. It is not to say that some ignorant people are selected as the parliament members in Hong Kong, we just need to select some people with great wisdom and knowledge. But all the people are the ignorant ones, include those who insult China.

I have researched on the great truth, then in spare time, I have studied on games. But you are ignorant and keeping studying on the useless thing, which is the fundamental reason for the chaos of the world. No one study on the great truth, the simple and basic principles for running of the world.

I think playing games should be limited to one hour.

When one has played game for one hour, he should be forced to leave and play again after twenty-three hours, in this way, the control and interference of games will be relived and addiction in games is also prevented.

Children in rural areas are always able to find various activities and games, such as farming work and feeding livestock. You may regard it as production activity, but it is actually the entertainment. There are rare entertainment activities for people and children in cities and communities, since there are no sites and facilities for such activities at all.

Currently, there are exercise facilities for old people in communities, but no facilities and sites for adults and children at all.

In commodity economy, every piece of land is valuable, so there are many commercial facilities for adults and children, but you must pay for them according to market value. It seems that the population density is considerable in cities, actually, people and children are isolated to their peers, with no connections at all. It is not reasonable and deformed. I think the facilities in communities should be provided for free compulsorily and the site area should be calculated and determined according to the residential area within the community such as the indoor and outdoor table tennis.

According to the construction area of the community, the free site and facilities should be provided accordingly to residents living in it. They are as necessary as supporting facilities of water supply, power, and coal.

Communication of children and teenagers with their peers, as well as the activities they are engaged in will help to enhance their physical quality, mental health, and the communicating and organizational ability. It is very important. They should be kept away from games and take part in more beneficial activities and exercise.

Another problem is that most of the hot games, provide platforms for players to communicate, so players are free to send information to each other. Because the group game requires cooperation, organized offence, changing strategies, and attacking highlights of different players if they want to win the game, the players with lower level and more failures will be a burden to the whole group and make the game more difficult. It is originally a kind of game tool. However, in practice, it becomes a platform for players to abuse each other. The players who are willing to spend money buying equipment and time studying on how to play are accustomed to insulting those players with less experience by using insulting and intimidating languages.

Moreover, the game operators are not only encouraging such behavior, but also engaged in the insulting those players with lower level of skills in order to encourage more players to buy equipment.

One hot game in China also provides the so-called report platform. The game operator will send information with insulting intention to players, intimidate, and abuse them so as to warn the players with lower level of skills. Additionally, they also limit the behavior of those players.

In this way, they are trying every possible means to encourage "those players who are willing to spend money buying equipment and time studying on how to play."

I think the reason why the game can become hot is greatly related to the so-called report system. It is able to encourage players to buy more equipment, spend more money on games, and waste more time while insulting and attacking those players who are not willing to buy equipment and spend time on games.

Such game does no good to players themselves, but brings harm to their body health, decreases moral cultivation, and destroys the social harmony.

Games are based on corrupting the society, destroying social harmony and morality except for those behaviors to make money.

136. It Is a Ridiculous Thing to Punish Someone That Stop Another One Smoking in the Elevator

9 November 2017

Recently, a sentence arouses heated discussion on the network. An old man smokes in the elevator and another passenger tries to prohibit such action. During their quarrel, the old man dies of sudden heart attack. Family members of the deceased gather together to beat up the passenger and lodge a lawsuit against the passenger for claim. The court judges the passenger to pay fifteen thousand RMB to the family members of the smoker. This is a typical case in China. Old people often blackmail others. Once old people fall down to the ground, family members would solicit huge compensation from another party involved in the conflict.

Many old people who fall down the ground by themselves would in turn incriminate other rescuers or passengers as the wrecker and accordingly solicit compensation from them. However, the court supports the request of old people and their family members in most cases and the so-called wrecker, needs to pay the expensive medical fee.

a) In above case, the passenger who prohibits the smoking action of the old man is the innocent party who should be encouraged. While the old man who dies of sudden heart attack actually dies of natural death causes and the old man himself is the guilty party. The passenger should not assume any responsibility. Moreover, the government shall take it as a typical case and award the passenger five hundred RMB.

b) Family members of the deceased who gather together to beat up the passenger shall pay medical fee and cost of lost labor according to the state of injury.

c) Family members of the deceased who gather together to beat up the passenger shall be detained for fifteen days.

137. HIV-infected Patients Who Deliberately Contact with and Infect Others Should Be Executed

9 November 2017

There takes place a fantastic event in China recently. A man knows that his wife is an HIV-infected patient after getting married and having children. In addition, in the premarital medical examination, the hospital does not inform him about the disease of his wife. When the party involved files the hospital to the court and asks for compensation, the court refutes his lawsuit on the pretext of protecting HIV-infected patients. This is another case about the collusion between the government and the demon to do harm to the ordinary people. This event should be viewed from two aspects.

1.Judicial injustice of the court

Obviously, premarital physical examination institution fails to detect the severe venereal disease of the object. This should be attributable to work fault or malicious shielding. The institution should assume responsibility for this. It is a totally reasonable minimum requirement for the party involved to ask for compensation from the premarital physical examination institution. However, the court's sentence for the non-fault of the premarital physical examination institution actually belongs to malicious shielding and malpractice and impairs the fundamental interests of the public.

2. Defects in the legal protection for HIV-infected patients in China

HIV is a kind of infectious disease. Although HIV is not infected via spray and air like flu, it also belongs to a malicious epidemic with extremely high death rate. The Chinese government does not control malicious epidemic but approves its free diffusion. This proves the severe defects of law and lawmakers.

In order to defend their own great, glorious, and righteous image, lawmakers take all means to misuse their power rather than to defend the rights and interests of the ordinary people and defend justice and fairness. This is the most serious problem.

Few years ago, some HIV-infected patients once stored their blood in the needle tubing and randomly plunged into passengers on the street. However, it is impossible to verify whether it is a rumor or fact. I believe that even this is a fact, it would be still concealed by someone as a rumor.

However, in this case, the HIV-infected patient deliberately conceals her illness and even gets married to bear children with the victim. The victim is not being informed of the fact until there is no retreat.

In addition, the government maliciously indulges HIV-infected patients with their random diffusion of disease and maliciously helps such patients conceal the fact from the victim. That's the way it is.

In my opinion, the correct practice is to (i) isolate HIV-infected patients from ordinary people, (ii) demand HIV-infected patients to wear obvious marks clear to others if they live together with ordinary people, (iii) instantly execute HIV-infected patients or other patients with malicious epidemic who deliberately contact with and infect others.

As the old saying goes in China, "Do as you would be done by."

I suggest supporting all lawmakers in favor of HIV-infected patients to live with HIV-infected patients and have sexual relation with them for several times before their vote. This is the most reasonable solution. It is nonsense for those lawmakers who eat special supply food and have security guard to enact such law when they simply shake hands with HIV-infected patients.

As commented by some netizens, many black people who steal into Guangzhou are HIV-infected patients. It is well-known that Africa is the high incidence area of HIV. Black people who infect Chinese people via sexual relation must be instantly executed too. Moreover, all black people in China should receive the compulsory physical examination, or otherwise, illegal immigrants should be repatriated.

138. The Central Bank and China UnionPay Should Form the Government's Mobile Network Payment Platforms

26 November 2017

Now non-cash payment has become a new wave. It seems to be the mainstream and a new trend. However, the current payment platforms are all run by private enterprises. Moreover, they are controlled by foreign bosses. This poses a potential threat to our national security. There will be a problem if the government's role is absent from the main financial payment channel.

The development of Alipay certainly has its value, which adapts to the needs of social development. Internet transactions require online payment platforms. Initially, Alipay only served as a credit guarantee for online transactions. It used to be the temporary prepayment pool before the customer received the goods. Its role was to meet the requirements of almost all customers across the country and served as all the banks to pay and temporarily deposit payment for goods.

Later, after the fund pool of temporary deposits had financial management function, the funds in the pool can not only be withdrawn at any time, but also bring about the interests of fixed time deposits.

Driven by the interests, people deposit all their working capital into Alipay to obtain certain interests and are able to withdraw their capital at any time. The functions of smart phones are becoming more and more powerful with their popularity. Among the functions are fingerprint recognition, face recognition, QR code recognition, positioning, and high-speed data processing. In addition to supporting online transactions, new functions of Alipay have been developed, namely instant spot transaction, instant payment, and QR payment.

Many people now go out with their mobile phones instead of cash. Technology is developing so fast, Alipay is leading and has been leading the trend of the times. This is of course the value of its existence. Private enterprises are creating wealth for sure. It is right to create wealth. If enterprises do not make money or do not develop, it is just like soldiers do not fight or flee.

In contrast, our banking system seems to be working for Alipay. In fact, it does. Because all traditional banking belongs to bureaucratic system, they are afraid of risks. Although I have heard that some banks are also engaged in mobile payment but they have no methods to promote it. I don't think this is what a bank can do. But what the Central Bank or UnionPay should perform.

Since mobile payment has become the mainstream of the society, the government cannot be absent, or it is ineffective governance.

1. In the financial sector, people believe in the government-owned institutions but not in private enterprises. The state needs to be responsible for the security of all funds entering and leaving the state-owned payment platforms, while the responsibilities of private enterprises are limited.

2. Moreover, the formation of a payment platform is simple; it's all about establishing a website, finding some technical staff, and downloading an app. There's not much technical difficulty involved.

3. The state-owned payment platforms need to provide services to all e-commerce providers, rather than being monopolized by a few companies, which is conducive to fair competition between e-commerce enterprises.

139.Crime of Disobedience

9 December 2017

In ancient China, the crime of disobedience was the crime of seriously infringing upon the rights and interests of parents and causing serious harm to parents. If found guilty, the one shall be beheaded and executed immediately. I said before that "filial piety" has the functions of old-age insurance and compulsory education, which can make the population increase and parents have the will to have more children in the age of filial piety. Because you don't know which child you gave birth to may become a helpful figure in the future, a president, a prime minister, or a rich person, and bring prosperity to the family. Those who have committed the crime of disobedience are not filial to their parents, instead, they do serious harm to their parents.

In China and today's world, this kind of behavior is considered as a common crime of injury or fighting. In China, I have seen a news report that a rebellious son often raped his mother in addition to beating his parents. His father was so unbearable that he killed the rebellious son. However, the court found his father guilty of intentional homicide. This case shows that the current legal system is not doing justice but making accomplices to the devil. The court made the above judgment according to the existing law. The framers of the existing law were largely influenced by the western human rights culture. They also want to play with human rights and claim to be a human rights democracy. It should also be in line with the West.

Western countries place too much emphasis on individual rights and interests and completely ignore social management and social order. They are already tasting the consequences. All western countries and democratic Russia have suffered severe population decline.

Chinese tourists traveling to Japan met an eighty-year-old man driving a taxi because they did not have enough pension. They can't retire. At the age of eighty, they still need to work to support their family.

Europe has a shortage of population, an aging population and a large shortage of young people. To solve the problem of pension for the elderly, Europe actually introduced Muslims to pay for their pension on the grounds of accepting refugees. This has caused serious dissatisfaction among the local whites and has seriously infringed upon the interests of the local whites.

The problem of European whites giving birth to their own children cannot be solved, and they introduce demons to support them, which is evil in itself. This clearly shows that western culture has serious problems. The solution to this problem is filial piety and disobedience.

Both Europe and China must promote "filial piety" and setup crime of "disobedience."

Giving all parents a guarantee and a power, a contract will surely make them confident and bold to have children.

If you can't bear your children any longer, you can tell God to take them away.

What we need to do is to make laws to send those who have committed serious disobedience to God, letting them negotiate with God in person and letting God decide whether they should be left in heaven or sent to hell.

Of course, the death penalty should be carried out in a civilized manner, so that they can choose a way to see God at a specified time and place. Everyone needs to have a bottom line in their behavior, including their attitude toward their parents. Of course, we advocate filial piety, which is not mandatory and absolute. You may not like your parents, or you may stay away from them but you can't seriously hurt them and seriously infringe on their interests. This is the bottom line as a human being. Otherwise, you need to go to God to make your words clear. This is called warning to others. After killing a few typical ones and a few leaders, the folkway will naturally be right, hence the problem of population reduction is solved naturally.

140. If Juveniles Deliberately Injure Others at School, Which Cause Other People's Death or Suicide, They Should Be Executed.

28 December 2017

Today, I read the news telling that Chinese government issues document dealing with the bullies in school, and the response is to send them to the reformatory school. In my perspective, for the ones with minor circumstances, they can be educated in the reformatory school. But for the ones with wicked circumstances who have caused other people's death or suicide, they should be executed.

The current Chinese law give juveniles and mental patients who have committed crimes with light sentences or exemption for the punishment. If juveniles and mental patients commit serious crimes, except for endangering the whole society, they are also people who are useless to the society compared with other people, thus they should receive harsher punishment.

For the juveniles who have committed serious crimes, they are just like the subquality products, which should be returned to the factory for reproduction. After executed, their living space should be left to the physically and mentally healthy people. Being lenient to the juveniles and mental patients is the evil law made by devils. Specially to protect the devils, generate devils in rebellion of the God and undermine fairness and justice. The best education approach for the juveniles is to execute one as a warning to others. The best teaching material is to use some people's death and blood to teach the next generation how to be an educated person, and whether to be a good man or a bad man. This is the effect of examples.

If there is a typical and educational case, the criminal should be executed at the school gate. Life for life is the doctrine of God. For the ones who deliberately injure others or bully others causing other people's death and suicide, they should be executed life for life, which is the will of God.

The mental health of juveniles is not fully developed, they are easy to be impulsive when encountering difficulties in life and commit suicide. Therefore, the juvenile bullies should think clearly. For the ones who bully others causing other people's death and suicide, they should be executed life for life. This is the best protection for the juveniles.

141. Good People and Bad People

8 January 2018

I grow up with my grandparents, although I only live with my grandfather for a few years before he passed away. They have always been telling me to be a good people. The distinction between good people and bad people is quite blurred.

Now, let me define good people and bad people in my own viewpoint. I am not a big fan of my grandfather, who is an alcoholic and gambles a lot. However, he is an intellectual and speaks English very well. He used to do business with foreigners before China's liberation.

However, whenever he is drunk, he will tell the story of "biting mother's nipples." I have listened for dozens of time and this makes me disgusted. However, the story tells profound truth. Modern people are anomic.

I think my grandfather should come back to life and tell the story of "biting mother's nipples" to all the Chinese parents and foreigners repeatedly. Everyone should listen to it for dozens of times, and the parents should then tell it to their children. This is the basic education and the good and the evil.

The story of biting mother's nipples:

There is a robber who has done a lot of bad things and finally got caught. Before being executed, the judge asked him if he had any requirement. The robber said that he wanted to be breastfed again by his mother. The judge satisfied him and brought his mother to him.

When the robber saw his mother, he bit his mother's nipple off. Her mother asked the robber why he did this. The robber said that when I did bad things when I was young, my mother never told me that this was wrong. Instead, she spoiled me, which made me do more wrong things with more serious consequences until now, I was executed. My mother was the one who I hate most.

In the past, the robber does highjack, now it is the financial fraud.

In my perspective, the definition of good people and bad people are like this. Whoever can create wealth through labor and serve others so that people can benefit from him or her, those are the good people. Good people create wealth through making contributions to others and the society. Whoever harm others and the society or country to become rich are bad people. No matter if his behavior is rightful or not, it can be measured through the two standards. Because the law can be taken advantage of, some people are too powerful to believe that they make the laws. Therefore, it is not absolutely right to distinguish good people and bad people from whether their behaviors are legal or not. However, it is absolute right to measure from the perspective of whether they have brought damages to other people, the society, and the nation.

This is especially true to our times when the new things keep emerging and the development of law always behind, just like P2P and payday loan. When the robbers are robbing through P2P and payday loan, they are totally legitimate, however, they should be executed considering the consequences they have brought about.

I distinguish the good people and bad people through this standard in the conditions of P2P and payday loan.

If the companies and management are benefiting the country and people, I will follow them to help them and bless them.

If I determine that they are scamming, I will figure out how to destroy them and get them out of the market. I am the most familiar with the insurance company, there are good people and bad people within the insurance company. There are good companies and bad companies, good management and bad management.

Some say that insurance companies are deceiving people, this is not correct. Because the pricing, protection provided to the customers and services of the insurance products are following certain rules and scientific truths. Therefore, anyone who have bought the insurance product cannot be described as being cheated. Every product has its own value. Therefore, you cannot say that the insurance salesmen are deceiving people when they are selling the products. In fact, they are doting the good things, at least not bad ones. However, some of them are doing evil things and being the bad guy.

For example, a product needs to be paid for five years, but the salesman informs the client that only one year payment is needed, which causes great financial loss for the client. This is the evil thing.Also, in order to earn commission, the salesman will sign some invalid contracts and make the clients cancel the insurance in the next year, which brings huge losses for the nation and the company.

There are more than one thousand people who are doing this in my former company, this is coming across the bad people, bad bosses, bad teams, and bad companies.

Are they legitimate? Of course, they are, their bosses make them do this, which makes it legal.

Are they robbers? Of course, they are. If our nation and society do not execute them, there will be a lot of people protect them. Not only a lot of people are protecting them, there are also the white-left wing in the western countries, the great whore, and devils.

Compared with the real immoral people, big liars and robbers, the bad people in my former company sound like nothing because there are too many people who are worse than them in this world. Too many people are harming other people. What we need are not laws and regulations, but also faith. The faith to goodness and evil. No matter you are legitimate or not, we will fight with the bad people to the end. Until we destroy them all.

We can analyze some typical cases and events.

1. Selling crutch

Selling crutch, the short sketch of Zhao Benshan, is widely known in China. Although this is an artist work rather than a typical case, the assessment and evaluation of the artist work is of great realistic significance.

Some people think that it is illegal to sell crutch, which should not be advocated and should be fought again. I don't think so.

Selling crutch to the not lame people is like selling insurance to the people who do not understand it. What we should care is not about bragging, but about the nature of the incident.

Now let's go deep into the nature of the phenomenon.

a. There is the part of deceiving and bragging in the transaction.

b. The transaction is based on real substance, which is the production cost and certain reasonable profit. Selling crutch and insurance is to sell the intrinsic value and reasonable value to the buyers through bragging. Although this is not right, but it is within the acceptable tolerance scope.

To lie a little bit so that the product with value can be sold to others is not a big mistake. Especially when people are in great poverty and need money, it is not making a little lie to sell a valuable product. Whether it is wrong, it is not determined by the fact of if one lies, but by whether the product is valuable or not, and by if you have sold the forged and faked products, toxic

373

products or unreal products others in high prices.

To sell valuable products to other people is not making mistakes. However, if you have sold the forged and faked products, toxic products or unreal products others in high prices, this is something wrong and should be fought against and the criminals should be executed.

We are criticizing selling crutches verbally and flaunting about ourselves. However, to the people who have cheated others for millions of moneys, we ignore then and tolerant them, this is the real evil and behaviors of devil.

Recently I read a news telling that the staff of Agricultural Bank of China transfers billions of moneys from the clients in the name of deposit, and the bank claims that this is the employee's personal behavior and the bank is not responsible for it. This is the real robber and real devil.

Who is qualified to criticize the selling of crutch? If the real bad people and robbers are executed, then you are qualified to judge whether it is fraudulent behavior in people's defective behaviors of normal transactions. This is the nature of the incident, that is whether you are selling valuable products, or it is pure fraud. To play dumb and make profit in the pure fraud. But being critical about ordinary transactions, this is showing off, not upholding justice.

2. Selling Health Care Products

Some health care products have real values, but some are purely cheating the consumers. For example, I believe the products of Amway are of their own value. However, some products are just starch, which is to fool the consumers. I think it is robbing people when you make the consumers to buy products with prices much higher than the real value through cheating.

When they are making money, they are not making contribution to the society and other people.

3. Transacting Poisonous and Harmful Food

There is distinction of levels in regard to the poisonous and harmful food.

  a. Expired food

  b. Moldy contaminated food, such as meat of dead sick pigs, edible oil recovered from garbage

  c. Harmful foods, such as nuclear radiation foods, cadmium

exceeding rice, melamine milk powder, plasticizer cream, Sudan Red and other dyed food, industrial additive foods.

d. Chemical raw materials, synthetic food, fake eggs, fake noodles. These are not real food but pseudo food.

The bad people and robbers are also classified into different levels according to the harms brought to the society and other people.

142. The Wealth of the Condemned Should Be Used as Compensation for Victim

23 January 2018

Today, I saw a hot news on the Internet. Recently, a Chinese killer raped two underage feminines, causing one dead and another one serious injured. In consequence of nine hundred thousand RMB compensation from the perpetrator, the court decided to free him from death sentence. Because of the verdict, netizens believe that if one can free from death as long as he has money, then it is an action of selling righteousness and making deal with devil.

Why is the court made such judgment? Because of the request made by the family of the victim. Because the victim's family is very poor, they can't afford the medical expenses, thus the killer's family proposed this deal, that is saving the killer from death sentence with nine hundred thousand RMB.

It is said that China's has hidden rules—if the killer pays for money, he can free from death sentence. While if the killer is sentenced to death, then the family of the killer doesn't need to pay money for the victim's family.

I don't know where these hidden rules come from, which law they are based on. Because in according to normal logic, people should take responsibility with their own actions. The killer must be responsible for their own behavior. There's no need to kill all the perpetrator's family. People who commit crime or kill people have nothing to do with their family, the family needn't assume joint responsibility. It's okay. But it is a common sense that the killer should assume responsibility for their act of murder.

The responsibilities of the murderer, in addition to their own life, need to be compensated by the property bearing their own name. Therefore, wealthy people who commit crime should pay money and their life for the murder. These are two completely non-conflicting things. The court should compensate the victim by the property bearing their own name, and the rest wealth is legacy, which should be inherited by the murderer's family.

Once the murderer commit crime, the court should seal all the wealth of the murderer immediately, and allocate it after the end of the case, the money that used for compensation should give to the victim, while the money that belong to murderer's family should inherited by his family. Because the criminal need to assume the responsibility for their own behavior, it is not only the need to pay their life for the murder, but also the wealth of the criminal belongs to the subjects that need the court to judge, sentence, divide, and settle.

Because in the relationship between criminal and victim, the victim is entitled to require compensation for the loss that caused by the criminal's behavior. Therefore, the victim's family has the right to the property of the criminal. It is justice and righteousness. But it is necessary for the court to decide how much should be compensated for the economic joint liability other than the death penalty, and how much should be inherited by the family.

Given the criminal's age is about fifty years in this case, he must have respectable property, and it should more than nine hundred thousand RMB. The property that bear his name shall be sealed by the court, and shall be judged after trail, other than employed by the criminal's family to negotiate with the victim. This is ridiculous. Unless some destitute criminals, they don't have property, but some people are willing to pay for his life, this is negotiable.

143. Medical Trouble Profiteer (MDP) Who Cause Severe Injury to Doctor Shall Be Killed at Site

16 February 2018

Medical trouble has always been in China. In a recent news, an MDP caused four times comminuted facial fracture to the doctor with a hammer. In other words, the MDP used at least a big hammer and hit the doctor's face four times.

In my view, the criminal shall be killed at the door of the hospital according to his behavior. On the basis of current judicial system, medical troubles belong to fighting and brawling due to economic dispute. Economic dispute, emotional outburst, and the amount of involved money is huge, so it looks like the dispute is reasonable, so death sentence is unnecessary in normal condition.

Some netizens believed that the hospital just earn blood money and want to strip every penny of the patient family. So the doctor deserve it, and the dispute is reasonable.

I think this is because the judicial system protects the devil. Because they are not sentenced to death, so they harass with unreasonable demands and breach the order intentionally. They should be killed at site as a warning to others.

Let's analyze this case. First, whether the disputes are reasonable or not. As for the netizens and medical trouble profiteers accuse the hospital earn blood money and strip the money of the patients' family, I admit that they are right.

For me, I will ask clearly about what I had done with my money, what effect it will cause and what I can gain when I spent every penny. Whether it is used to buy some things or cure sickness of my family. Even cure the sickness of the people I love most; my interest shall not be damaged. For this reason, I was called ruthless by my family. I know normal people can't be ruthless like me. But for living people, this is the most sensible choice. I think the reason that cause the conflict between doctor and patient is the doctor gave wrong guide and bad advice to the patient's family

Some diseases can't be cured at all, so it is useless to spend money on it. But as the family members, they don't know, don't want to admit or don't want to think in this way, but as medical organization, they should give reasonable advice to the family members.

When cure the patients to certain degree and the patient's family spend enough money, from the reasonable perspective, the medical organization should suggest the family members to treat conservatively or given up treatment, don't spend more money on it.

The patient may have a high probability cannot be cured, but the living person needs to keep money to live well. And if the family needs to continue treatment, they must sign, and admitted to voluntarily pay the money on treatment under the condition that the hospital explicitly recommends giving up treatment.

Family members are often irrational when treating their loved ones. But the doctor knows very well that the patient is cannot be cured. Even spend more money, the doctor can only prolong a few months for the patients.

So I think the family members should get rational advice. And authoritative doctors should tell them to stop spending money and stop useless investment. From the perspective of the hospital, this is impeding them to earn money. But this is morality.

When medical troubles happened, majority netizens commiserate the criminals; the fundamental reason is the doctor has no morality, they didn't give rational advice to the patient for the benefit of patient's family. Not only will they not give rational advice to their families, but they will also receive red packets and kickbacks.

Second, from another perspective, medical trouble profiteer should be killed at site if they cause severe injury to medical personnel. I think maybe some medical troubles are to let off the dissatisfaction for the system. I suggest those people whose dissatisfaction with medical system to perish together with doctors with explosive and commit suicide bombing like Huang Jiguang (revolutionary hero) Dong Cunrui (revolutionary hero) and extremist of Islamic state.

People who commit suicide bombing are all fight for their belief. No matter they believe in God or devil, it is all beliefs. Although I want to eradicate Islamic state, but I think they are all real fighters, while the medical trouble profiteers are not.

If medical trouble profiteers want to become a real fighter, if they really fight for belief, fight for truth, then they should commit suicide bombing like Islamic state to attack doctors and hospital.

If some medical trouble profiteers carry on bomber to kill doctors and hospitals with an explosion. I think only when they swear to dead with black heart doctor can our society realize problems in the medical system, then our country will change the medical system.

Those hit the doctor's face with hammer thought that economic dispute cannot be sentenced to death. Is this a warrior? Is this fighting for the truth? This is the devil who utilize the bug of regime and judicial system, they utilize the collusion between the judicial system and the devil to extort and conduct hooliganism. Therefore, medical trouble profiteer who cause severe injury or death shall be killed at site to safeguard the order of the society. If suicide bomb which aroused by medical troubles, changes shall be done at medical system.

144. The Problem of Multi-level Marketing Can Only Be Eradicated by Sentencing the Leaders to Death.

9 April 2018

I happened to meet a group of multi-leveled marketing personnel in my travel the other day. This group of people, guided by several leaders, was brainwashing some college students on the train. They were so rampant that they even didn't care about the passengers around, including me.

I knew something about normal multi-level marketing in large cities before. The multi-level marketing comes into being because of the specificity in products. Mouth-from-mouth selling is needed in promotion and marketing.

In normal multi-level marketing, the product is introduced in the meeting or marketing. New members are attracted to promote the product into market in view of the advantages and benefiting effects in the product.

Differently, the multi-level marketing that I came across on the train had nothing to do with material products. It was absolutely fraud. I think this kind of multi-level marketing belongs to the illegal pyramid selling scheme identified by the Chinese government, which is nothing but getting something for nothing, mind control and fraud. It should be deemed as heresy and crime.

I think this kind of selling belongs to the illegal pyramid selling scheme identified by the Chinese government, which is nothing but getting something for nothing, mind control and fraud. It should be deemed as heresy and crime.

In my opinion, the leaders of pyramid selling shall be executed by shooting, instead of being imprisoned. They are devils and disasters to the society.

A strong hand is the only effective way when faced with devils. They should pay with their blood. It is also true of those who possess nuclear weapon and the suicide attackers.

Preach makes no sense and is in vain for the devils. The one and only way in dealing with evil is iron hand and blood repaying. Only the pictures of shooting execution of those leaders can stop innocent college students and teenagers from going astray. Any preach is a waste of time.

In my view, the pyramid selling that is similar to a cult and product-based multi-level marketing should be treated separately. The difference is in the product. We should confirm whether mouth-from-mouth selling is needed for the product; whether the product is good for human and the society; and whether the product is truly worthy.

It is fraud if the members just get some useless and shoddy things that can be made in a workshop after giving in a large amount of money. This kind of selling should be defined as the pyramid selling that is similar to a cult, whose leaders should be sentenced to death. However, we should protect normal product-based multi-level marketing, in which the product is in fine quality with good feedback and reasonable price.

145. The Petition of Victims of Shan Lin Financial Fraud (Shanghai) to the Central Inspection Team

15 May 2018

The financial fraud cases in Shanghai happen frequently, but all of them are sentenced very lightly, I think this is problematic and unfair, and this is the root cause of the problem.

I was the former sales manager of Xinhua Insurance Company and worked for this company from the salesman to the excellent team leader for eight years from 2007 to 2015. So I am very familiar with the financial industry in Shanghai.

From the beginning of financial fraud up to now, I become a victim. I am a witness.

I think all the frauds are purely the collaboration of fraudsters and corrupt officials who take advantage of loopholes in financial reform and fraudulently engage in activities of financial fraud. Moreover, this is a premeditated and well-planned fraud.

The financial reform initiated by Premier Li Keqiang around 2013 aims to encourage the financial industry to serve small and medium-sized enterprises and private economy, invigorate private capital, and promote inclusive finance.

Its starting point is good, and some P2P, P2B, Internet platforms are indeed serving small and micro enterprises and the real economy.

But at the same time, there are a lot of so-called financial management companies, P2P, P2B, funds, online, offline, which use various names and flags, they don't do any physical investment, and don't serve any physical economy.

They fabricate false objects and contracts, engage in Ponzi schemes, and ravage the people's lifeblood for asset transfers and profligacy. I think the government has played a very bad role in this fraud campaign. Not only they did not protect the people, recover stolen money and crack down on fraudsters, but they also pass the buck to the victims, accuse them of coveting small profits, and ask them to bear the losses.

a. I think the financial fraud is claimed by the government as illegally absorbing public deposits or illegally raising funds. It is a conspiracy of some officials and fraudsters in the government.

As for the nature of the case, is it illegal absorption of public deposits, or illegal fund-raising, or financial fraud? It is understandable that common people do not know the difference among them. But the economic investigation departments that deals with economic crimes all day long are also confusing right and wrong, which is seriously doubtful.

Shanghai's judicial system and fraudsters are premeditated to setup a trap to plunder the people's lifeblood.

In fact, the difference among them is very simple, all those moneys collected by investment companies from customers are doing physical investment in according to the projects agreed in the contract, this is the behavior of private lending. It is in accordance with the policy of inclusive finance.

Those who fabricate false contracts and fabricate false projects are financial frauds. People do not understand, but the economic investigation department that deals with economic crimes every day are impossible not to understand. But almost all of malignant financial fraud cases in Shanghai from reporting to court trial, there is no word of "fraud" from beginning to end.

What does this mean? Does this mean that the whole judicial system in Shanghai has been bought off by fraudsters and is deliberately sheltering fraudsters? Are they helping fraudsters get rid of crimes? Besides, what else does it mean?

What is fraud? What is deposit? What is fund-raising? These simple nouns can be made clear by consulting the Xinhua Dictionary and by asking a Chinese teacher of primary school. And those economic investigation departments and judicial personnel that deals with economic crimes all day long are confusing right and wrong. They deliberately fabricate charges for we, victims of financial fraud, describe us as participants in illicit fund-raising, as the people who go for wool and come home shorn and need accept experience and lessons.

So I believe that there is a suspicion of corruption in Shanghai's judicial system. They collude with the fraudsters and maliciously setup traps to defraud us innocent people's lifetime savings, pension money, and life-saving money.

They conspire to treat us victims as Tang Monk's meat, lambs to be slaughtered, and feasts, everyone wants to have a piece of meat.

b. I think another proof that some people in the government conspire with fraudsters is the Disposal of Illegal Fund-raising Ordinance, which clearly states in Article 4 that "participants in illegal fund-raising shall bear the loss of their own participation in illegal fund-raising."

The government takes taxpayer's money, they do not recover the stolen money, they do not protect the people. Instead, they let the victims themselves bear responsibility.

It's like the villain rapes the beautiful woman, but the government accuses the beautiful woman of wearing too revealing, deliberately seduces the bad person. The government lets the bad person go, and letting the beautiful women go home and take the responsibility for self reflection. The government cannot be irresponsible like this. Are there any heavenly principles? Is there justice? Are you still communist?

It goes out to see that the streets are full of socialist core values, "Prosperity, democracy, civilization, harmony, freedom, equality, justice, nomocracy, patriotism, dedication, integrity, friendliness." Of course, people need faith. That's right. But our real society is that the common people are being maliciously defrauded of finance, there are thousands of cases of big size and small size. The amount of money from tens of thousands to tens of millions basically like a stone dropped into the sea to this day.

The Chinese government does not help the people return to the lost money but requires the people themselves to bear the losses of financial fraud.

Hundreds of millions of victims and families, what do they think of this twenty-four words on the street? Do they have faith? Do they make people around them have faith? I can say that only when they take back their money, will they have faith.

c. In 2013, I felt that there were great intrigues and risks in it.

When I was the manager of an insurance company in 2013, many colleagues of my team switched to financial management companies. I also interviewed and inspected many financial management companies. Because I was a group leader of the insurance company, they took a fancy to my client resources. Many financial management companies tried their best to get me.

Some financial management companies told me directly, "You can pull in the money from the customers. If something goes wrong, it has nothing to do with you. Don't be afraid." From the beginning, they thought about how to cheat customers' money and how to retreat. This is purely a malicious financial fraud. All the financial fraud companies are conspiracy, they designed how to cheat money, how to retreat five years ago. The junior salesman was unaware because their grades were not high enough. Senior business executives must know the inside story.

I have seen too much. These are all a series of well-planned malignant fraud cases. Instead of fund-raising case and savings case. In summary, I ask:

a. Any case that fails to carry out physical investment in accordance with the project of contract and causes losses to the victim. They should be convicted as crime of financial fraud, and they should be heavier, faster, and more severely punished. Fraudsters with more than one hundred million fraudulent amounts who are unable to recover their clients' losses should be executed.

b. The regulations on illegal fund-raising should be abolished immediately. It is a political conspiracy that the government shirk responsibility, and a few conspirators blame the innocent people for the responsibility of financial fraud. The people firmly oppose the implement of such policies and regulations.

c. We call for the characterization of Shan Lin Financial cases as financial fraud.

d. If the boss of Shan Lin doesn't bring our money back, we strongly demand that Zhou Boyun be sentenced to death. China used to execute all these financial fraudsters. So at that time, the social order was good and there was no malicious financial fraud at all. In recent years, financial fraud has been exempted from death penalty in our country. That's why financial fraud has erupted frequently. And those fraudsters actually cheat in the name of the Great hall of the people and the state. If this can be endured, what else cannot be?

Our country must take action to resolutely curb the rampant and unscrupulous situation of financial fraudsters for giving people justice.

If the state does not kill them, this is not enough to calm the people. If the state does not kill them, this is not enough to uphold justice. If the state does not kill them, there is no heavenly principles. If the state does not kill them, it will not maintain normal social order.

However, our intention is not killing, we want to retrieve our losses. If Zhou Boyun and his colleagues can retrieve most of our losses, they can be exempted from death penalty. Never forget what happened before. Finally, the victims of Shan Lin Financial ask the government to protect the people and bring justice to us.

146. Issue of Sex Trade Legality

24 May 2018

I have talked about it for many times before. A recent case happened in China makes people discuss this issue again.

An airline stewardess was raped and killed by an online car-hailing driver. And then this driver committed suicide by jumping into a river. Some people discuss the issue of sex trade legality. They think it's time to make sex trade realize disclosure and legalization, so as to reduce these malignant sexual assault cases.

In fact, if this taxi driver can satisfy their sexual desire in the sex trade market, why did he rape and kill her and kill himself to perish together with the so-called beauty?

If sex trade is legal, we can find out more beautiful beauties in the sex trade places, which have low costs and various types. Therefore, it has no need to rape and kill someone, let alone perish together with the beauty and head toward disaster for satisfying sexual desire for once.

It is really unworthy for this driver. And it makes people feel bored for ugliness and hypocrisy of the society. This is the law formulated by some so-called noble people in high position. To some extent, the old-fashioned law is the demon. The old-fashioned law can't regulate the social relationship between people but creates conflicts and tragedies artificially. This is an evil behavior.

Desire for the opposite sex and sexual behavior are neither criminal nor unforgivable. This is the inherent procedure of people. Without desire, mankind can't be called as the human anymore.

People formulate various laws and morality for realizing social management, maintaining social order and completing social governance. Instead, it is not the tool for people in high position to maintain their status and satisfy their vanity. To some extent, I think they are the demons in a sense. I have repeatedly emphasized that our social reality is that sexual behavior of non-marriage has become the social mainstream and consensus. However, fair sexual behavior of non-marriage in buying and selling is defined as an illegal behavior by some people in high position, so as to create tragedies and conflicts constantly.

Marriage in transaction and sexual blackmail have become the mainstream of China. Moreover, through the propagation of news media and cultural performance, the financial swindling in extremely ugly marriage form is being the mainstream culture of Chinese society.

Of course, sexual slaves become tools to persecute people in some western countries because many sexual workers can't be protected by law, so they become objects to be abused cruelly and crazily by ganglands and become their money-making tools.

It doesn't mean that I advocate sexual behavior of non-marriage, while this phenomenon exactly becomes the social mainstream. This is the objective existence and we must confront with it. Any person who denies the established fact and objective existence, they are the demons of heresies.

The fact is the fact. No matter what it is, we must confront with it and must admit it. It doesn't mean admitting this fact will affect reputation of politicians and their political career, so these politicians just don't admit it. This is the heresy, and this is shameless.

Why can this phenomenon become the mainstream?

Social development, development of human rights, and economic development greatly increase economic rights and other rights of women, which are almost equal with men.

In addition, those social regulations and cultures that restrained power and conditions of women previous are gradually disappearing. Previous cultures and social regulations can't adapt to the social reality anymore. Many people think that the Bible and the Koran greatly oppose to prostitutes. That is right. In fact, God not only opposes to prostitutes, but also refuses the sexual behavior of non-marriage.

Nevertheless, if God denies that the sexual behavior of non-marriage is the social mainstream, no one believes in God, the Bible and the Koran.

Words that God said several thousand years ago, the Bible, and the Koran can't provide guide and help for the current society. The issue is that after women have more rights, they refuse fertility and marriage for enjoyment. Meanwhile, they engage in the sexual behavior of non-marriage. Because marriage affects their quality of life, they make a higher price for marriage.

Therefore, the subsequent social phenomenon is the reduction of populations and reduction of total social demands. In addition, reduction of populations also lowers the speed of economic development. Meanwhile, western countries introduce Muslims and Africans or other low-quality populations, resulting in the serious national issue, failure of social management, and sharp social contradictions.

388

In China, marriage in transaction causes deterioration of social morality, reduces the overall moral character of the society, and forms the sharp social contradictions. Also, China has the trends and risks in aging of populations and reduction of populations.

About how to solve this problem, the practice in ancient times, the Bible and the Koran was to constrain and oppress women. Now, we should solve this problem on the basis of protecting women's human rights. We can't solve it by oppressing women.

I think that we need polygamy, transaction of babies or production of babies in factories, and legalization of sex trade. All of these can simply solve this problem.

147. China's Stability Maintenance

16 June 2018

I am fortunate enough to declare that I am a victim of Shan Lin financial fraud. I was defrauded of RMB fifty thousand yuan by Shan Lin Financial and I am actively participating in the so-called maintenance of legal rights.

It is just fifty thousand yuan for me but the biggest financial fraud case in history for Chinese people. I have analyzed much about the case.

Financial reform in China started around 2013, during which private capital was required to serve for small and micro enterprises and entity economy. There emerged thousands of financial management companies in China overnight that absorbed deposits with the interest rate five times higher than that of banks for the following P2P investment.

There were exactly some financial management companies serving for entity economy but the majority of them were making false investment escaping with your money under various names

Under my appeal, Chinese government cracked down on false investment three years ago but there were still some financial management companies with support having escaped the crackdown, such as Shan Lin Financial.

Under my appeal, Chinese government also combated and attempted to ban the usury last year. It is said that Shan Lin Financial made money by usury. When the government started to crackdown on the usury, Shan Lin Financial lost its profitability so it prepared to escape with money.

There are about 170,000 victims and 20 billion yuan failed cash of Shan Lin Financial. I do not know how Chinese government handled with this case. What I know only is how Chinese government prohibited the victims from protecting their own rights and interests.

1. According to the previous case law, Chinese government has identified all the financial fraud cases as illegal fund-raising and illegal absorption of public deposits. Furthermore, Chinese government has also formulated regulations on treatment of illegal fund-raising that requires victims to shoulder the losses and responsibility by themselves. Chinese government has identified their behaviors illegal, so they shall not be protected by laws.

When the government promotes financial reform, each major media, official media, various conferences, and officials also help to promote the reform. However, after financial fraud cases, the government identifies the behavior illegal and requires victims to shoulder the losses and responsibility by themselves. Thus, I am fully convinced that it is a trap. We do not know who set the trap, but we were definitely cheated by money, or even the country.

2. The special stability maintenance system of China. There have been tens of thousands of financial fraud cases in China and some even took place five years ago. However, as I know, there has been no one getting a penny back.

The investigation toward fraudsters of Chinese government is completely useless without any achievement. As far as I am concerned, the police said that there were thousands of fraud cases in Shanghai every year while there were only five hundred cops in charge of economic cases. Therefore, there cannot be anyone recovering for the money cheated. It completely owes to the insufficient police forces and the imbalance between the police force and the number of cases. Nevertheless, Chinese police have achieved greatly in controlling, suppressing, and intimidating victims.

> a. Firstly, the police forces of each place have arrested all the salesmen of Shan Lin Financial regardless of the business volume. In order to cut off the connection between salesmen and customers and prohibit the salesmen from organizing customers for right maintenance, a large number of salesmen were arrested and the salesmen who were not under arrest yet were intimidated or threatened by the police. They were required not to contact any customer. Because the customers do not know each other, they cannot mutually contact. Only the salesmen know the contact information of customers. Chinese government has numerous police forces with extremely high efficiency for arresting salesmen and stability maintenance instead of any time or police forces for catching the fraudsters.

> b. Chinese government has assigned a large number of Internet agents to monitor and scout the speeches and behaviors of victims. As victims, we often get together for meals and information exchange. During meals, most victims received phone calls from the police to be required to report where they were.

> Now, network real-name system is required in China. If the police attempt to investigate any speech online, they can obtain all the information of the spokesmen, such as phone number, name, and address, at any time. The police have arranged agents in the group chat of each victim to monitor the speeches and behaviors of victims at any time.

c. Chinese government suppresses the petitioners. In a petitioning activity yesterday, some victims entrusted a representative to Shanghai Public Security Bureau to know about the case progress. Because the economic investigators failed to provide the victims with any case progress after two months, the victims were eager to know how much Zhou Boyun could compensate for them. They were so eager to know how much they could recover because some money comes from their parents' lifelong deposits or the young's years of struggle while some money is for patients' lives or children's education.

Thus, they assigned some representatives to know about the situations in Shanghai. There were about seventy representatives in total in each province. However, since the day before yesterday, there was news that all the representatives had received phone calls from the police that they were not allowed to go to Shanghai for inquiries.

Yesterday, some representatives were intercepted by the police halfway while some representatives were arrested by the police in disguise when getting off the train.

There were seventeen representatives being arrested by policemen one to one when they were having meals in a Shanghai restaurant. It is said that the police have known from technical and agent measures that they have discussed the petitioning in Wechat so they must be arrested and repatriated home.

There was even one representative repatriated home calling me to ask if I could help them to prosecute that Shanghai police intercepted their petitioning at a Shanghai people's court. I was too busy to accept the appeal.

According to what I know, there was one representative reached Police Station of Pudong District to inquire after overcoming numerous difficulties and obstacles but failed to get any useful information.

Chinese government is the richest government in the world because it masters a large number of large monopolistic state-owned enterprises apart from taxation. However, it only arranges five hundred cops for tens of thousands of economic crime cases in Shanghai. For lack of money for hiring cops? Definitely not. The government owns numerous money.

It can be indicated how much the government has spent through the efficient suppression and arrest of salesmen, the efficient monitoring of victims' Wechat records and efficient arrest of petitioners.

However, for the past five years, in the numerous financial fraud cases, the criminals were only sentenced for about five-year imprisonment while there was not even one victim recovering a penny. Furthermore, the government has even formulated Regulations on Treatment of Illegal Fund-raising to legally require the victims to shoulder the responsibility and losses by themselves.

Apparently, state machinery is serving for the fraudsters, for the corrupted officials. The officials are colluding with the banditry to persecute the citizens.

In view of this issue, state machinery becomes the tool that helps the monsters and persecutes the citizens instead of serving for the citizens.

In my opinion, there shall be police forces of corresponding quantity for cases. It is a must for them to recover the money of citizens and catch the fraudsters. If the fraudsters refuse to return the money, they shall be sentenced to death. The citizens will always support the government no matter how much recovery of cheated money costs. Otherwise, it is the collusion between officials and the banditry. Don't talk nonsense.

According to the latest information, there have been more than twelve petitioners among the non-local petitioners who went to Shanghai to inquire about the situations these days losing contact with their family. They might be arrested by the police. Since it has been several days, they even did not inform their family within twenty-four hours.

There may be more people losing contact. This is the current known number of people losing contact.

148. China's Harmonious Society, Fairness, and Justice

9 August 2018

Since 2013, there have been countless Internet financial fraud case where fraudsters have swept away the hard-earned money of countless innocent people. Instead of helping victims recover their money, the government slandered victims, "The sufferings were caused by their own actions with vicious expansion in their greed and blind pursuit for trifling advantages. They've lost their own money. It was just penny-wise and pound foolish."

They misjudged their crimes or even released crooks and refused to recover the money for victims. What's worse, they even formulated Regulation on Disposal of Illegally Raised Funds, based on which victims should take their own responsibilities and undertake their own losses in a legal sense.

"Public service advertisements" of Shanghai Municipal People's Government are released in subways in Shanghai every day, which say, "Any participant in raising funds illegally is people's enemy. They are negative examples for sacrificing their money on trifling advantages. Those involved in illegal fund raising deserve bad luck. They need to undertake their own losses and take their own responsibilities."

After the victims of Internet financial fraud have been cheated out of all their property by the government in partnership with the fraudsters countless times, and after they have failed to defend their rights and lost their money countless times, finally they figured it out and decided to unite to safeguard rights.

The first thing they did was to defend their rights together in Beijing on August 6th. But what is the final result? The victims suffered Chinese governments' "Harmony."

What is Chinese governments' Harmony? It means strictly monitoring the words and deeds of all victims, using the resources of all countries to undermine the victims' rights protection actions.

Because the action on August 6 was an online call and organized for a long time, everyone knows about it. Of course, the Chinese government, which has mastered the world's most advanced monitoring technology and has the world's largest number of banknotes, is fully aware of it. They issued documents, demanding all local governments and departments to adopt different methods to prevent victims from raising complaints in Beijing. They knew who would protest in Beijing from surveillance on social media and communication tools like QQ, Wechat, Micro-blogs, and mobile phones. They put everyone who ever bought wealth management products and suffered losses into a blacklist.

Then,

1. Put some people's ID information into a blacklist for traffic control so that they were not allowed to buy any trip tickets which required for real-name certification like train tickets and air tickets.

2. Required all local police stations to warn all potential petitioners, who were demanded to write guarantee letters for no more petitions.

3. Sent policemen on trains to arrest people who bought P2P and train tickets to Beijing.

4. Grounded or deliberately delayed some train schedules and flights to Beijing.

5. Policemen arrested people in hotels based on blacklist in Beijing. Sometimes they just broke in.

6. Blocked people on blacklist by establishing checkpoints on roads to Beijing.

7. Chinese governments sent out policemen to examine everybody's ID cards on roads to Beijing. Anyone who was listed into blacklist would be arrested immediately. Chinese governments were said to have arrested several thousand people on the day of August 6th, most of which would be forced to send back home while a few organizers and activists would be sent into prison.

8. A large number of buses and policemen stood by on roads near some petition officers in Beijing. The policemen would load those people who reached petition destinations after barriers one after another into buses, which would be locked up in temporary detention locations and sent back home or sent into prison.

It was said that Chinese governments had accomplished their task for harmony once again. And China was in harmony again with nationwide celebrations for peace, prosperity and praises for merits and virtues.

The following are some representative online comments from netizens or participants in petition in Beijing.

1. The most classic sentence today, "No one ever hopes for utter chaos, and everyone knows how important social stability is. But such social stability

395

must be established based on universal respect and promises for social fairness and justice, instead of keeping us silent in the face of your corruption through misuse of laws or blackmails. So damn well said! (Reprinted)."

2. "I do not know what on earth is going wrong! I went to Beijing because I felt so dark in Hangzhou; I thought that it would be brighter in Beijing!"

"At the beginning, I always could not figure out why we were so afraid to be known by Chinese governments. Wasn't it the exact intention to let them know to go to Beijing? I ever thought that so many people's joint strength would surely arouse their attention and that Central Government would issue a highest order to maintain social stability by speeding up cracking criminal cases in Hangzhou.

Unexpectedly, the highest order that we received was to block traffic at home, forcefully detain us, arrest people in public on trains, delay or even cancel flights!

I always thought that my enemy was fraudster. What the fuck! Suddenly I realized that I was a wanted man and that I was an enemy of the state! Right, policemen in Beijing said today that they would arrest anyone who ever bought P2P. Goodbye, Beijing! I ever thought I only hated Hangzhou!"

3. Thanks, my dear comrades. Thanks, everyone, and thanks, my dear comrades. Thanks for being around with me from the very beginning. If I were alone, I would surely be driven crazy, or even scared the hell out of my soul!

I ever thought that I was looking for a light, but I realized that bright roads were filled with absolute darkness! I ever thought that people's interests were above everything else, but people turned out to be nothing.

It looked like that today's campaign had failed. Layers of siege interceptions separated all of us. But actually, today's campaign did not fail at all. For these financial refugees, they have doubled, tripled, even quadrupled police presence. Because they were scared!

Meanwhile, today's spontaneous campaign presented us with strong awareness on truth, firm wills and clear directions.

Dear, comrades, we must live well. Let's see what's going to happen to these claw-baring demons!"

A harmonious society should be realized only after social internal conflicts are truly settled and social fairness and justice are truly protected.

But not that when people suffer injustice, persecution, fraud, blackmail or serious injuries, governments do not stand up for people's rights and benefits, maintain social justice, wipe out the evil or save people from sufferings while making people undertake their own losses, admit their own misfortune, swallow up their grievances and accept persecution, fraud, fraud, extortion as well as serious injuries.

It is not a harmonious society. It is heresy.

149. The Chinese Government Protects Deadbeats

16 August 2018

I used to publish an article to call for crackdown on usury. The Chinese government did act positively and cancelled the usury. However, I participated in a client meeting of a financial management company today. The boss told us that the state prohibited violent collection when cancelling the usury and said that it was underworld behavior. This generates a problem that is to protect deadbeats.

In this society, a large number of clients of debt companies maliciously don't repay. The company I invest in now also has the problem. The arrival rate of the accounts receivable greatly declines. It poses a serious threat to the financial security of the clients.

Surely it is contradictive. Usury must inevitably require violent collection. Without violent collection, there would be no usury. But dealing with deadbeats also requires violent collection, and without violent collection, it will inevitably support deadbeats.

Does the usury need to be hit? Of course, it needs to be hit. Does a deadbeat need to be hit? Of course, it also needs to be hit. So is there a need for violent collection? I think that violent collection is required for deadbeats, but there must be no violent collection for usury. And it is necessary to ban the usury. I think that it is most reasonable to go to the county magistrate to sue in ancient times, and deadbeats not caused by usury must be beaten with a board. They must repay.

In the event of arrears caused by usury, the debt should be declared invalid. There is no need to pay back. Loaners of usury should be beaten with a board. And the debtor-creditor relationship caused by usury should be announced to be invalid. Loaners of usury should be beheaded when a person dies because of it. But in modern society, why do police only enforce the law like a robot? The superior said that allowing usury is turning a blind eye to violent collection. The superior said that cracking down usury and cracking down violent collection are protecting deadbeats and supporting deadbeats. This is because the police cannot properly handle things and do not know what to do? Or are the police in the policy taking advantage of the policy, deliberately picking a fight?

CPSIA information can be obtained
at www.ICGtesting.com
Printed in the USA
BVHW071330190819
556217BV00001B/67/P